The Wicked Wine of Democracy

THE WICKED WINE OF DEMOCRACY

a memoir of a political junkie, 1948–1995

Joseph S. Miller

UNIVERSITY OF WASHINGTON PRESS

Seattle & London

© 2008 by the University of Washington Press
Printed in the United States of America
12 11 10 09 08   5 4 3 2 1

Design by Thomas Eykemans

All rights reserved. No part of this publication may be reproduced or transmitted in any
form or by any means, electronic or mechani-
cal, including photocopy, recording, or any
information storage or retrieval system, without
permission in writing from the publisher.

UNIVERSITY OF WASHINGTON PRESS
PO Box 50096, Seattle, WA 98145 USA
www.washington.edu/uwpress

LIBRARY OF CONGRESS
CATALOGING-IN-PUBLICATION DATA

Miller, Joseph S. (Joseph Spencer), 1922–
The wicked wine of democracy : a memoir of a
political junkie, 1948–1995 / Joseph S. Miller.
p. cm.
Includes bibliographical references and index.
ISBN 978-0-295-98801-6 (hardcover : alk. paper)
1. Miller, Joseph S. (Joseph Spencer), 1922–
2. Political consultants—United States—
Biography.   3. Lobbyists—United States—
Biography.   4. Political campaigns—United
States—History—20th century.   5. United
States—Politics and government—1945–1989.
6. United States—Politics and government—
1989–   I. Title.
E840.8.M528A3   2008
320.092—dc22   2008006193

The paper used in this publication is acid-free
and 90 percent recycled from at least 50 percent
post-consumer waste. It meets the minimum
requirements of American National Standard
for Information Sciences—Permanence of
Paper for Printed Library Materials, ANSI
Z39.48-1984.

To my beloved wife, Erna Wahl Miller,

whose support was invaluable to me

throughout our forty-one years of marriage.

CONTENTS

FOREWORD

Shelby Scates

JOSEPH SPENCER MILLER—OR, BETTER, JUST PLAIN JOE—PRECEDED me at the Seattle *Post-Intelligencer*, Northwest outpost of W. R. Hearst, by a dozen years and damned near as many titles. I worked politics. Joe handled music, drama, literature (book reviews), labor, sports, and politics. Those were the days in Hearst journalism that had this maxim: if you can write sports, you can write anything. Joe was an exemplar.

From Seattle and Hearst, Joe moved to Washington, D.C., and to the other side of political life, from observer to player, first as a campaign strategist and then as a lobbyist, an engineer of political consent—the same fun, he might say, at triple the pay but four times the risk. So doing, he collected the raw material refined into this memoir, which may be the most revealing look at American politics in the last half of the twentieth century that you will ever read. Journalists glimpse in from the outside. If they work hard and care, they may tell a great deal, but never so much as those working the system from the inside—assuming they care and aim to remain honest. Thus, honest Joe.

This is no place for a full roll call of the politicians Miller helped make famous, or at least hold high office. A few familiars: Henry Jackson, Warren Magnuson, Gene McCarthy, Morris and Stewart Udall, William Proxmire, Wayne Morse, Frank Church, Richard Neuberger, Ed Muskie, Phil Hart, Robert Byrd ("Byrd by name/Bird by nature/Let's send Bob Byrd to the legislature" is the way the future Senate leader pitched it in his first run for the

West Virginia legislature. Ugh.), Jack Kennedy ("I remember him with ach-ing fondness—lighthearted, irreverent, endlessly curious." So do I.), "Max-imum Leader" Lyndon Johnson, as described by Miller, an imperious populist (forget the contradiction), and Estes Kefauver. Miller might have been labeled a name-dropper, but now we know he has only named those with whom he was up close and personal.

Growing up in West Tennessee, Senator Kefauver was my political hero, a Southern liberal in the strictly segregated South. Teddy White, the great presidential chronicler, would later call Kefauver "the best President we never had." In 1960, Miller had the challenge of getting Estes re-elected in the state's Democratic primary against a much-favored, fire-breathing segrega-tionist, Tip Taylor. Tennessee seemed tired of its liberal anomaly, Senator Kefauver. A John Kraft poll showed Taylor dead even and coming on strong. Miller killed a bottle of whiskey with Judge Frank Gray, Kefauver's life long friend, and was cheered when Gray said: "Ol' Estes hasn't made his move yet." "When he does, ain't no sonofabitch going to beat him."

Estes won almost every county in the state—even my home county, Obion, where it was said by members of the gentry that Kefauver might be lynched should he venture to wage his campaign among Obion's rednecks. I mention this episode because Miller didn't, in a book replete with enough other political stories to keep you survivors of the twentieth century awake all night.

Miller came west from New York—the passage by hitchhiking—after his family went from riches to rags early in the Great Depression. Before the crash, his maternal grandfather was a vice-president of the U.S. Rubber Company (remember Keds, kids?); his paternal grandfather Martin was a Civil War veteran (Yankee, dammit) of the battles of Prairie Grove and Vicksburg. Joe's father was an actor, lawyer, and lecturer; his mother, a school teacher.

A good athlete, only a busted knee ended Miller's football career at the University of Oregon; a few semi-professional prizefights taught him the effects of brain concussions that leave a fighter brain damaged or, as they kiss it off in the sports world, "punch drunk." "Thank heaven for sports," Joe once exulted. "The language of youth that teaches thinking and discipline are essential tools for success."

Having failed in a tryout with my beloved St. Louis Cardinals ("Good field, no hit"), like Miller, I found American journalism as the next best thing.

Where else would one get paid for doing what's fun, meeting interesting people from all walks of life—criminal to saintly—with lots of free drinks, occasional adrenalin, and admiring women? Well, who needed sports? Journalism is the most comfortable place for failed jocks at ease with words.

Jonathan Miller, my friend and classmate at the University of Washington in the early 1950s, told me of his older brother Joe, now gone from Seattle and newspapering to run political election campaigns, initially with home-state heroes Jackson and Magnuson.

"Money," writes Miller, "is the wicked wine of the democratic process. 'Everybody does it' is the truest political maxim of them all." And he should know, having carried envelopes of cash to selected candidates, sometimes on orders from the "Maximum Leader."

In the late 1960s when I knew him best, Miller occasionally came back home to the Northwest to lobby on behalf of small lumber-mill owners, many of whom had been his classmates at the University of Oregon. A collection of vivid personalities, they were entrepreneurs dependent on special set-aside sales of public timber for their raw material. The small mill owners were a contrast in personality, dress and wherewithal to the timber giants—Weyerhaeuser, Crown Zellerbach, and very few others—who cut lumber from trees on land they owned.

This was David versus Goliath: Miller working Congress and various state legislatures on behalf of the small mill owners, against what turned out to be the iron laws on free enterprise economics. In other words, impossible. But it was a good fight, made fascinating by the likes of Bob Spence, Alex Cugini, and Sid Leiken, small mill owners who helped shape the Pacific Northwest before Microsoft, Boeing, and Weyerhaeuser, in their attempt to hang on to their diminishing slice of the timber economy.

Joe did his damnedest as a lobbyist and then captured it as a writer.

"Lobbying," said Miller's sometime partner, the astute Maurice Rosenblatt, "is a natural by-product of democracy."

"It beat hell out of hacking for a living on a Seattle newspaper," said Miller. And no regrets. What follows shows you why, as well as how. So much for peanuts before a full-course meal.

PREFACE

I TOLD HIM I WAS WRITING MY MEMOIRS, LOOSELY QUOTING GEORGE Bernard Shaw to the effect that an "old man's only reason for existence is to justify all the time that he has spent on this earth." He sniffed, not sneeringly or disdainfully, but a definite sniff. "It shouldn't take you long," he said. "I wouldn't imagine that you had that much to say." I was incredulous, though I struggled to hide it. He had always seemed to be a kind and understanding person. How could he so cavalierly set aside what was going to be my penultimate contribution to humankind? Everyone, it seemed, had been pushing me to write my story. I had done it all, they flattered me; it would be a best seller. I modestly demurred but secretly agreed that I did have one hell of a story to tell.

After seething about his belittling remark, I realized he had done me a favor. What did I have to say that hadn't already been said? Would my memoir be just another account of a hick newspaperman-politician coming to the Capital of the Free World for adventures and misadventures with the High and the Mighty? Would it be just another vanity-press, name-dropping ego trip? Did I really have anything to say? I had to find out.

I ended up backing into the effort. In June 1993, I attended my fiftieth reunion at the University of Oregon in Eugene. At the class banquet, my impromptu remembrances of our campus days produced waves of laughter. I had been a campus renegade who barely graduated, and now I was being asked for a written copy of my remarks for the alumni magazine. When I returned to D.C., the speech emerged effortlessly from my typewriter, and a plan was born. I would write my memoirs as a series of stand-alone episodes and events and then see if I could fit them together like the pieces of a jig-saw puzzle. Before the year was out, I had a palimpsest of my career on paper, and I was fascinated. I have a reputation for a prodigious memory, and it had coughed up long-forgotten people, places, and happenings. Inspiration came from an "old friend" from college days—Henry Adams—who had written his classic *Education* as a series of episodes from his life. The technique suited me as well. It gave me confidence to realize that I was following in the footsteps of the American Boswell.

Writing made me ask the two questions that comprised the most mem-orable utterance of the 1992 presidential race. "Who am I? What am I doing here?" cried Admiral James Stockdale, Ross Perot's running mate, as he began his televised debate with Vice President Dan Quayle and Senator Al Gore. He never answered the questions, but it didn't matter. He had posed the only questions worth remembering from that lackluster campaign.

Who was I? I was a septuagenarian lobbyist in Washington, D.C., an anonymous foot soldier in an army of special-interest pleaders, lawyers, influence peddlers, and bureaucratic representatives of every socio-economic interest in creation. I was a one-man-shop operator retained by the railroads, forest-products associations, and maritime unions, which I had represented for three decades or more. I had drifted into this arcane trade after fifteen years as a newspaper and magazine reporter and a sometime campaign man-ager and consultant. Many of my contemporaries had backgrounds similar to mine.

I operated out of a four-story townhouse two blocks from the U.S. Capi-tol. My wife Erna and I lived there. For twenty-one years, she had been per-sonal secretary to her hometown neighbor and fellow Norwegian-American, U.S. Senator Henry M. "Scoop" Jackson of Everett, Washington. Over almost four decades, we had come to know every square foot of this "most impor-tant precinct in the world," in addition to a goodly number of the people who had made their living on this hallowed ground since the middle of the twentieth century. Clients hired me because I knew my way around the place and could open the doors that guard the inner sanctums.

I was a small-time operator in a sea of big fish. I probably could have been a big fish—when I started lobbying in 1961, the field was wide open, and I was on the ground floor—but I had no entrepreneurial genes in my makeup. I was content with a mom-and-pop neighborhood store operation. Most of my clients were friends from the Pacific Northwest, and it somehow felt less like impersonal whoring to serve their interests.

My operation was pocket-sized and primitive; but my win-loss record was as good as anyone's, and I knew it. No one was going to upstage me just because he was driven around town in a chauffeured limousine, collected exorbitant fees, and made grand entrances into fundraisers. I had a proletarian working stiff's contempt for that kind of character. Big fees were not my bag either; a good living and the freedom that went with it were ample reward. I had no complaints. Four decades of watching the movers and shakers of the nation at work and play had made me a junkie. Now I owed it to myself to try to capture on paper what I had participated in and observed during those years of work.

A word about my nickname—Smiling Joe. In my day, any athlete worth his weight was blessed with a moniker. He wasn't John Martin; he was "Pepper" Martin, "the Wild Horse of the Osage." He was the Sultan of Swat, the Bambino, Jolting Joe, Jarring Jawn, the Brown Bomber, the Dark Destroyer, the Manassa Mauler, and the Michigan Assassin. My career as an athlete was, in a word, ignominious. I was seldom called more than "hey, you" on the field. But a kindly man named L. H. Gregory, who was sports editor of the Portland *Oregonian*, took a liking to my grit and good nature and dubbed me "Smilin' Joe." It never became a household name, but it sure beat "hey, you," and it fit me.

I came to Washington, D.C., in 1956 to become campaign director of the Democratic Senatorial Campaign Committee, the political arm of the Senate Democrats. I told Doris Fleeson, a syndicated columnist, that I planned to continue writing for the *Reporter* and other political journals. She snorted and gave me this succinct advice: "Quit writing and stay the hell out of the National Press Club bar. You can't do it and work for Lyndon Johnson at the same time." She was right, of course, and I took a sabbatical from the typewriter that lasted almost four decades. It has been satisfying to rediscover rusty old skills and to be able to pick them up after so long.

A grain or two of salt is required with the consumption of all memoirs. It is perhaps natural that they are written with the self as the centripetal force, everything gravitating in that direction. When I asked Wendell Wyatt for advice on rewriting the first draft, his answer was a masterpiece of brevity: "Take the 'I' out of it." That isn't so easy. Although honest introspection forces a person to realize that he wasn't quite the hero he once imagined himself to be, it is hard not to see yourself as the focal point of what you are describing.

I mention these matters to give you some insight into my methodology. I have spent a lifetime trying to understand and control my ego, that strange beast that prowls within us all. Many times I was convinced that I had finally tamed the creature, yet always it broke out and went raging through the jungle of my mind. My ego caused me to do some remarkably stupid things against my rational best interests, but it also has kept me going against the odds, sometimes to surprising success. It has been my worst enemy and best friend and insatiable with demands that never cease. Thank god for its voracity. I would be a placid vegetable otherwise.

One year, while I was visiting Stockholm, a Swedish woman told me: "Scandinavian men live inside invisible boxes sealed off from everyone else. They cannot communicate with each other. That is the message of Ibsen, Bergman, Munch, and Strindberg—our inability to reach out to each other. We live on the surface." Getting under that surface is what this effort is all about. My biggest revelation to myself in writing this is that it is much easier to confess one's indiscretions and inadequacies on paper than it is face-to-face. I was able to put on these pages things that I was never quite able to tell my wife and children. Nothing earthshaking, mind you, but things about which a sense of pride and sometimes shame has lingered for too long.

Many of us simply do not know how to listen. It is a much-overlooked skill. I have been as guilty as anybody in trying to dominate a dialogue. My gentle friend Gaylord Nelson had to tell me to shut up on occasion because I was not letting anyone else get a word in. I was often so full of myself that I did not realize I was monopolizing conversation. I know that my most fruitful moments have come from listening. On a hot 1956 summer night in a Walla Walla, Washington, hotel room, for example, I stayed up all night to hear Senator Warren G. Magnuson's life story. He never told me why he had unburdened himself. It may have been the quart of Crown Royal whiskey that we shared, or it could have been that I asked the right questions. I somehow knew that he needed to tell it and that he trusted me enough to give me the real version, warts and all.

This need to share is a fundamental desire that we are often loath to admit. Yet, it can dominate our direst thoughts and most secret needs—*ergo*, the couch of the psychiatrist and psychoanalyst, the confessional box of the Catholic Church, the best friend or the dear diary on which the inner self tumbles onto paper during the dark hours. The memoir is the ultimate repository of all those impulses and thoughts.

ACKNOWLEDGMENTS

MOST OF THE MATERIAL IN THIS VOLUME COMES FROM MEMORY. All my remembrances would have been discarded had it not been for an angel editor I met by chance: Marianne Keddington-Lang, then editor of Oregon Historical Society publications. She volunteered to edit my outpourings (which I had privately concluded were unpublishable). Two books emerged—this one, the political memoir, and a forthcoming personal memoir.

This book has been a family project. Thank you to my brother Jonathan Miller for his efforts to ensure accuracy in the text and to my daughters, Sue Miller and Nancy Gillen, for their advice and review of the manuscript and the book proofs.

I hope you enjoy the result.—JSM

The Wicked Wine of Democracy

1

A POLITICAL JUNKIE

I WAS BORN TO BE A POLITICAL JUNKIE. A POLITICAL JUNKIE IS distinguished by one universal characteristic—a fascination-absorption-compulsion-passion for politics that sometimes defies rationality. There were periods in my life when my entire being was consumed by politics, as family, friends, food, and sleep were forgotten in the chase for the holy grail of political success. When I emerged from those periods, it was with a sense of shock that I had let myself become so possessed. It is hard to understand until it happens to you.

Political junkies have always been around. From the time of Plato and Socrates, Caesar and Cato, they have been an integral part of the political process, camp followers drawn irresistibly to the flame of potential power. They have come in every form of humankind: the idealists and the cynics, the enchanted and the disenchanted, the lost and the lonely, the dreamers and the pragmatists, the reformers and the plunderers, the dilettantes and the dedicated, the limousine liberals and the hoi polloi—in short, the people, the populace, demos, democracy. Politics is the one game in which everyone can play, and new blood almost always is welcomed.

Motivations are as diverse as the players are. Mine were mixed. I did have a general notion that society's underclass—particularly people of color—was getting the shaft from the ruling class. Otherwise, I was drawn to the political arena by a youthful lust for the action. I wanted to bust the heads of Republicans and businessmen, and I fantasized that success could make me an instant celebrity. Early on, I dreamed of being on the cover of *Time* magazine as "the new Democratic kingmaker." It was a role I craved.

I almost made it. My high-water mark came on September 17, 1957, when the *Washington Post and Times Herald* profiled me as "the Democrats' answer to Madison Avenue." My head inflated like a Macy's parade balloon, and I made some implacable enemies, including Lyndon Baines Johnson and Robert Francis Kennedy. It was not a smart thing to do. Bobby Kennedy and I clashed over the Oregon and Wisconsin presidential primaries of 1960, and I ended up relegated to a meaningless role in the general election campaign. No matter how right I thought I was, it made no sense to challenge the candidate's brother. I had to learn it the hard way. Lyndon Johnson and I took an instant dislike to each other, and things deteriorated from there. During one heated exchange, I lost my temper. He paid me back within a week of assuming the presidency. My two principal clients fired me—at his personal request. I only survived in Washington, D.C., because I had two Oregon clients he didn't know about.

But this is getting ahead of the story, which began on January 1, 1922, when I was born at Manhattan Maternity Hospital under the shadow of the Queensborough Bridge in New York City. My dad, Herbert Rinehart Miller, was a former actor who had left the stage after twelve successful years because his dying father thought it was a wicked place. Now he was a lawyer-lecturer living on the margin. My mother, Dorothy Lillian Spencer, had grown up in affluence in St. Louis, her father the secretary-treasurer of the world's largest shoe company. She had gone to Smith College and aspired to a stage career in New York when she met Dad.

The Crash of 1929 would wipe out the comfortable world in which I was raised. By 1932, we were flat broke, dislodged from a handsome house in the suburb of Mt. Vernon, New York, and living in an apartment house in northern Manhattan. Dad saw the Great Depression as a plot against him personally. Almost fifty and a onetime "golden boy," he had never known adversity, and he was unable to cope with it. He took out his frustration on the person closest to him—my mother. Life at home became hell much of the time.

Mother disappeared in November 1934, taking my four-year-old brother Jonathan with her, and Dad descended into bouts of alcoholism. I was pretty much left to my own devices under the general aegis of "Aunt Delia" Stebbins, a Manhattan schoolteacher who had lived with us. Much of my time was spent learning how to survive. I was the only WASP in a sea of Catholics and Jews, and they took turns beating me up or heaping indignities on me until I learned the ways of the streets. It was a rough but indispensable education. I emerged streetwise and tough.

My cousin Clare Smith was forty-some, pudgy, and balding but still a lady's man. He had left Portland, Oregon, for New York sometime around World War I, some said one step ahead of an irate husband whom he had cuckolded. Clare had prospered running brownstone-front rooming houses on the upper west side of Manhattan. Now, in 1936, he wanted to return to Oregon and show off his twelve-cylinder LaSalle coupe and Isobel, his redhaired mistress, whom he intended to introduce to family and friends as his wife. He took me along to help substantiate the deception.

It was my first exposure to what lay west of the Hudson River, and I was enthralled with our huge and magnificent country, which took us twelve days to cross. The Promised Land was at the end, the Pacific Northwest of soaring white peaks, mighty evergreen trees, rushing rivers, endless white beaches, juicy apples, and leaping salmon. All this and a big family of welcoming aunts, uncles, and cousins.

Clare and Isobel, their deception undetected, went on to California, and I stayed behind to go fruit-picking with my cousins in the Yakima Valley in central Washington. Afterward, I hitchhiked to my aunt's farm on the Olympic Peninsula and lived there into the winter, when homesickness for the Big City suddenly consumed me. I hitchhiked back to New York, arriving shortly before Christmas. It was 1936, and I was a precocious fourteen-year-old, bragging to my street friends about the country I had discovered out there. I was convinced that my destiny, whatever it was, lay out West; and in succeeding years, I hitchhiked back to the Pacific Northwest several times, much like a salmon seeking the stream of its birth. Finally, after more than my share of false starts, failures, and fiascoes, I landed at the University of Oregon in Eugene. I emerged in 1943 with a degree in journalism, a beautiful and talented wife, and a newspaper job in Idaho.

The political bug first bit me at the university in the 1942 race for student body president. It was serious business for us, as we tried to break the fraternity-sorority hold on the university's political system, and we made a spirited but unsuccessful effort. The race rated the front page in many of Oregon's daily newspapers, and the later careers of some of the participants are quite remarkable: U.S. senator from Delaware, governor of Oregon, mayor of Portland, U.S. congressman from California, chief judge of U.S. Ninth Circuit Court, deputy undersecretary of state for political affairs, plus a flock of Oregon state legislators and mayors. My role was minor, but I was hooked. A political campaign is a contest as sharply etched as any sporting event, and it gives the underdog the chance to bloody the nose of the big guy. I started to follow the political news, learning a little about government and imagining the speeches I would give.

I crammed a lot into the years following my college graduation: two-plus years in the U.S. Army, stints on Idaho's two leading dailies and Portland's evening newspaper, one year as music and book critic of the Seattle *Post-Intelligencer*, and another year as its labor and political reporter. As chair of the Newspaper Guild's local, I was in a position to be modestly helpful to the 1948 Democratic candidate for Congress in the Seattle district. He won in something of an upset, and I began to get ideas.

His name was Hugh B. Mitchell, the U.S. congressman from Seattle, and unlike most politicians he had a mission to accomplish—the creation of a Columbia Valley Authority, or CVA. As an appointed United States senator (1945–1946), he had become infatuated by the idea of an agency doing for the Pacific Northwest what the Tennessee Valley Authority had accomplished for the South. The CVA issue had evaporated after Mitchell's 1946 Senate defeat in the Republican congressional sweep, but in 1948 the surprise election of Harry S Truman as president and a Democratic Congress had miraculously revived it.

The League for CVA was reactivated to promote the grassroots campaign and legislative battle ahead, and I left the *Post-Intelligencer* to become its press agent-propagandist. I was thrilled to be in the arena. The League was made up of farm and labor organizations and the individuals who had spearheaded the winning fight for federal dams such as Bonneville and Grand Coulee and for local public power agencies to distribute hydroelectric power to farm and factory at bargain-basement rates. Their efforts were transforming a sparsely settled region into a burgeoning agricultural-industrial colossus.

Alas, the CVA effort was ill-starred from the start, sabotaged as much by turf-jealous bureaucrats inside the Truman Administration as by opposition from Republican businesses. Harold G. Tipton, a political veteran who was my boss at the League, saw that it was a losing cause. One day he received a call from his friend Melvyn Douglas, a movie star whose wife, Congresswoman Helen Gahaghan Douglas, was planning to run for a California U.S. Senate seat in 1950 against a young Republican congressman named Richard M. Nixon. Tipton left abruptly to manage her campaign, and I succeeded him as the League's executive director.

My spirited efforts to breathe new life into the CVA campaign were singularly unsuccessful, and the final *coup de grace* fell on June 25, 1950, shortly after the North Koreans had swarmed across the 38th parallel. What had appeared to be easy re-election races for Congressman Mitchell and Washington Senator Warren G. "Maggie" Magnuson now loomed as dogfights. I segued from the League into the two campaigns. When both men won narrow victories, I tasted the spoils of victory—a federal job that paid three times as much as I had been making at the *Post-Intelligencer* two years earlier. Money was not my goal, but I was happy to get it. My wife and I bought a 1949 Buick and a handsome house in West Seattle overlooking Puget Sound, and I felt less like a renegade child of the Great Depression.

The federal agency that I had joined as regional information director, the Office of Price Stabilization (OPS), was temporary, established to control prices and wages for the duration of the Korean conflict. That was fine with me, as I had no desire to become a permanent federal bureaucrat. The routine work was pretty dull. My boss John L. Salter, the OPS regional director, was on leave from his post as administrative assistant to Washington Congressman Henry M. "Scoop" Jackson, who was planning to run in 1952 for the U.S. Senate seat held by a discredited Republican right-winger, Harry P. Cain. Salter's OPS post was incidental to his real assignment, to lay the groundwork for Jackson's campaign. Salter was short but husky— "one hundred and sixty pounds of speed, guts, and muscle," he liked to brag. With black, curly hair framing a softly etched face, he would have been perfectly typecast as Puck in *A Midsummer's Night Dream*. In fact, he was skating through life with a "what fools these mortals be" attitude, and his wickedly witty tongue often expressed his sardonic cynicism about the ways of the world. I fell under his spell and gloried in his company. Politics was his permanent passion, and he was a master of the game.

Ten years older than I, he had been educated for the priesthood in a California seminary, giving it up two weeks before his final ordainment to come home and help his boyhood buddy, Scoop, run for Snohomish County prosecutor in 1938. Two years later, he managed the twenty-eight-year-old Jackson into the U.S. Congress and accompanied him to Washington, D.C, as his chief assistant. Jackson did the legislative work, and Salter did the politics. A decade in wartime Washington as a handsome young bachelor had endowed him with a myriad of experiences; and, with an Irish storyteller's wit, he described them, over martinis, with great panache. I became his best audience, soaking up great chunks of political wisdom from him. It sure wasn't the way it was taught at the university in Political Science 101.

The crew that Salter had assembled for the campaign included a young advertising man named Gerald A. Hoeck. A World War II marine officer, Jerry had a confident, take-charge persona that I envied. If there was any self-doubt in his psyche, he kept it well hidden. He was a product of the Marine Corps' Japanese language program at Boulder, Colorado, but you would have thought he had come straight from Camp Pendleton, Parris Island, Guadalcanal, and Iwo Jima. He looked like a recruiting poster and had an air of command to back it up.

His most telling contribution to the campaign was the billboard. Never in my subsequent campaign experience did I see a medium create the sensation that the Jackson billboards and posters did when they were unveiled across the state of Washington in August 1952. No one had ever seen anything like them, and they dominated conversation in political circles for days. Artist Rudy Bundas had painted the short, stocky Jackson leaning forward, his hands on a chair—and with a striking resemblance to Jimmy Stewart in *Mr. Smith Goes to Washington*. The poster's message, based on Jackson's twelve-year record in the lower house of Congress, was grandiloquent but believable: "Jackson Will Make a Great U.S. Senator." There was Jackson, in full living color, set against a rich yellow background, demanding attention from the most inattentive passerby. People actually stopped and stared. That billboard led to my first great political lesson.

My wife Rosalie had fallen in love with Adlai Stevenson, the Democratic nominee for president that year, and she was determined to deliver Democratic literature to every house in the affluent Republican neighborhood in which we lived. Day after day, she went door to door and came home in great discouragement. Few of her fellow housewives wanted to accept the handouts. "Don't waste it on us," she was admonished. But they grabbed up the Jackson brochures. Rosalie began to ask why. "I like his looks," they told her. "He is such a fine-appearing man." "He will be a great credit to our state." Rosalie's reports, corroborated by other Democratic doorbell-ringers, represented a real discovery. Billboards and posters on buses and barns, in yards and windows had been Jackson's only media at the time, so they would have been the only thing about him these women would have seen. They had been so effective that they might influence the women's vote.

This was my epiphany. For a fair-sized portion of the electorate, visual images had supplanted the spoken and written word as a primary conveyor of the political message. Unlike Paul on the road to Damascus, the revelation didn't come to me like a divine bolt; rather, it seeped in over time. "Most politics is visual." The evidence was out there for all to see. By the mid-1950s, television had established itself as the primary medium of communications in the nation, with newspapers and magazines trying to develop new color-printing techniques to try to match its blazing visual force.

My principal requisites for any campaign were the visual image of the candidate and the slogan that would theme the campaign—"Muskie Can Do More for Maine," for example, and "Nelson Is Doing a Great Job in the U.S. Senate." Once those two things were decided, everything else fell into place: the brochures, program and policy papers, television and radio spots. A fair percentage of the voting public is not going to expend time or energy to study the issues and a candidate's background. They are going to be influenced by a handsomely-packaged-but-fleeting-image message. As a citizen, I think it is unfortunate. As a political practitioner, I know it is a salient fact of the game to understand and exploit.

My first chance to measure this phenomenon (actually, more a commonplace) came in the 1958 U.S. Senate race in California, my first experience in a mega-state. Clair Engle, a congressman from rural Red Bluff in the sparsely populated north, was opposed by the Republican incumbent governor Goodwin J. Knight. Before the June primary, in which each was uncontested, the Louis Harris polling organization conducted a statewide survey. Engle's name recognition was a bare 12 percent, compared to Knight's 90–plus percent.

There wasn't much money for an Engle media campaign in the primary, so we decided to concentrate what we had on billboards and posters. A remarkable media buy gave us the space to plaster Engle's image-message from Oregon to the Mexican border. Hoeck and Bundas produced a billboard that was even more dominating than Jackson's had been in 1952. Engle was only five feet six inches tall, but with huge shoulders and a magnificent leonine head. From the waist up, he was an imposing figure. A vibrantly colored portrait of the man rose from a billboard, proclaiming, "Engle Will Make a Strong U.S. Senator." Even in media-sated California, the billboard created a stir.

The most startling statistics didn't come out until after the June primary. Harris's post-primary survey showed that Engle's name recognition had leaped from 12 to 67 percent. More importantly, those who were able to identify him were then asked what they knew about him. Sixty-two percent responded with language that obviously was influenced by the slogan on the billboards. "He speaks his own mind," they said. "Nobody can push him around." "He's a tough guy." "We need strong leaders like him." Engle had been in the state only a couple of times during the uncontested primary and had not attracted much attention. The media were absorbed by the race for governor between Republican U.S. Senator William F. Knowland and Edmund G. "Pat" Brown, the Democratic attorney general. Harris's findings confirmed what I knew. Engle's remarkable leap in recognition could only have come from one thing—the beautiful billboards that papered California.

The general election was a replay of the primary, with the billboard again Engle's media centerpiece. There was also enough money for a modest showing of television and radio spots in California's twenty-six media markets. I turned myself inside out to make the television special, using a variety of production gimmicks. It was awful, the worst I ever produced, but it didn't matter a bit. Engle defeated Knight by almost 800,000 votes, running right behind Brown, who engulfed Knowland by a million votes. Late in the campaign, on a San Diego television talk show, Knight had accused Engle of "running the most misleading campaign in California history." When pressed to document the charge, Knight responded, "Have you seen his billboards? They're a fraud. They make him look like a giant, some kind of a god. And he's only a little bitty guy."

This aspect of political campaigns goes to the chimerical heart of the media image-making process: creating a candidate as larger than life. It is apotheosis, an appeal to the idolism instinct of humankind. Every despot and dictator, pharaoh and emperor, sultan and satrap from time immemorial has used his glorified graven image to legitimate and enforce his rule. From Mao in China to Castro in Cuba, the huge posters of Big Boss Watching You are all the ugly evidence needed. Absolutely nothing is new in politics, although each new generation of political practitioners, with its new technological toys, thinks that it has reinvented the wheel. All they are doing is adapting the new "toys" to the politics of Plato and Cato, Montaigne and Machiavelli. Yogi Berra was right. It is *déjà vu* all over again.

Scoop Jackson's election to the U.S. Senate in November 1952 did nothing to save my federal job. A day or so after he took the oath of office, Eisenhower abolished the Office of Price Stabilization, per a campaign promise, and I learned that political patronage was a two-edged sword. With not even a pat on the back, I was on the street, out of work for the first time. Fortunately, my old part-time post as stringer correspondent for *Time, Life,* and the other Henry R. Luce publications was available. Uninterested in returning to any newspaper (only the Portland *Oregonian* made me a hesitant offer), I decided to see if I could make it with Time Inc. assignments and freelance magazine writing.

Never did I work so hard. After my first year, I was excited to find that I had made slightly more money than I would have at the OPS, and I loved the freedom of being my own boss, accountable to no one but faceless editors in New York and Chicago. Working on a *Time* profile of San Francisco's Clem Whitaker and Leone Baxter, the First Family of political advisers, whetted my desire to be a political practitioner again. That married couple, starting with the famous campaign to defeat Upton Sinclair for governor of California in 1934, had made a tidy fortune as the nation's leading political image-makers. I interviewed Clem, a skinny and sardonic former newspaperman whose most memorable line to me was: "Always remember, kid, people buy more corn than caviar in this country." He also quoted a line from Aristotle that he thought was *sine qua non* for political copywriting: "Think like a wise man but speak in the language of the people." Both lines became mantras to me in subsequent campaign efforts.

As 1954 rolled around, I was hungry for a campaign to run myself, one in which I could put into practice all that I had learned from Jerry Hoeck, Johnny Salter, and Harold Tipton. The opportunity turned out to be next door, in Oregon.

Richard Lewis Neuberger was the Pacific Northwest's leading writer of current affairs. Prolific beyond belief, his articles filled the pages of the *New York Times* and other national newspapers, popular magazines such as the *Saturday Evening Post* and *Life*, intellectual journals such as *Harper's*, the *Atlantic Monthly*, and the *Nation*, not to mention a flock of lesser-known publications that nevertheless paid a tidy buck. Although he seemed to be a nonstop writing machine, Dick somehow found time to be the most articulate of a handful of Democrats in the solidly Republican Oregon state senate. He and his wife Maurine, who was also a member of the legislature, had made headlines by passing legislation to legalize yellow oleomargarine against the opposition of Oregon's dairy lobby. It was a coup that had made the Democratic couple heroes to many a Republican housewife.

Dick and I had become close friends in 1946 when I was writing sports for the *Oregon Journal*, and he had been generous in recommending me to magazine editors with whom he had long-standing relationships. Now he was being opportuned by leading Oregon Democrats to run for the U.S. Senate seat held by Guy Cordon, and he wanted my counsel. We spent many hours brainstorming the chances.

Prospects were not that promising. Oregon had not elected a Democrat to the Senate in forty years; and although the sixty-four-year-old Cordon was crusty and colorless, he still was chairman of both the Interior Committee and its Appropriations subcommittee. With the Interior Department in charge of 52 percent of Oregon's land mass, Cordon was in a nonpareil position to help his state, and he was good at it. Any way one looked at it, Dick was facing an uphill fight. Nonetheless, he promised that he would run if I would come to Oregon for the fall campaign to handle media and strategy. From that point on, Dick and I were in touch almost every day. Breathing fire, I couldn't wait for the fall campaign to begin.

2

SOMETHING SPECIAL—
DICK NEUBERGER

THE EARLY MORNING MIST, SMELLING LIKE DAY-OLD FISH, WAS
rising from the saltwater flats of the Port of Tacoma when I pulled my 1949
Buick sedan into the Poodle Dog's parking lot. It was six A.M., September
6, 1954, and I was en route from Seattle to Portland where I was going to
spend the next two months helping Dick Neuberger get elected to the United
States Senate.

The Poodle Dog was an emporium peculiar to the highway. It featured
food, lots of it. Longshoremen and loggers, truckers and travelers were its
customers and, regardless of the hour, the Dog always seemed to be filled
with people, good-hearted in their boisterous greetings and talk. It was the
kind of blue-collar joint that suited my comfort zone, and I always stopped
there when going south from Seattle. Breakfast was three eggs over-easy, a
rash of burnt Canadian bacon, a stack of buttered rye toast, and a mound of
home-fried russet potatoes. I never varied and usually did not even have to
voice an order. Afterward, with a mug of freshly brewed coffee, I settled into
a back booth with a notepad and focused on the task ahead—to conceptu-
alize the campaign we would have to make and the campaign the opposition could make. It would be my bible for the next two months. Two hours
of scribbling gave me a blueprint.

Dick Neuberger was something special. Only forty-one years old, he had
been a well-known figure for two decades as a writer and a politician. The
native Portlander had "arrived" in 1933 when, as a University of Oregon

sophomore, he had traveled abroad to report on "The New Germany" for the *Nation*. It was the first on-scene portrait of Nazism's ugly face, and it created a sensation—"epoch-making," said the *Nation*'s editor, Ernest Gruening (later a U.S. senator from Alaska). Coming at a time when Walter Lippmann and others were sugarcoating Adolph Hitler, the piece established Neuberger's reputation, and he had gone on to become, as his friend Adlai Stevenson told me in 1947, the most articulate and eloquent voice of the Pacific Northwest. Other great reporter-writers had migrated to New York, but Dick had stayed in Portland and had filled the pages of the nation's leading newspapers and periodicals with accounts of the little-known Pacific Northwest.

Politics was part of the reason he had stayed home. The bug had bit him early. At nineteen and editor of the University of Oregon *Daily Emerald*, Dick had displayed his Republicanism in a page-one editorial, "Why I Will Vote for Hoover." Glossing over the obvious fact that he was too young to vote, he denounced the president's 1932 opponent, Franklin D. Roosevelt, as a "demagogic radical" and hailed Hoover as "what the country needs in an hour of distress."

Two years later, FDR had become his political beau ideal, and Dick's articles extolled New Deal dam-building programs to revive the Pacific Northwest. What happened? Steve Kahn, his roommate, had exposed Neuberger to the face of poverty in Portland's poorest neighborhoods, and he had reacted with horror. Elected editor of the *Daily Emerald* as a safe, conservative defender of the status quo, Dick suddenly began attacking everything many students held dear: football and fraternities, compulsory military training, student fees, and homecoming. He became a pariah at the university.

It was a role he learned to relish. Given to self-dramatization, Neuberger took to being a lonely fighter against the regular order and wrapped himself in the mantle of Lincoln Steffens and Upton Sinclair. Running as an FDR Democrat in 1940, he was elected to the state legislature and soon became one of its best-known members. He resigned after Pearl Harbor to enlist in the U.S. Army and came back after the war to be elected to the state senate. Two years later, his wife Maurine joined him in the legislature, and they became Oregon's most famous political couple—"the only political parties who can caucus in bed," he not so tastefully put it.

The 1954 nomination for the U.S. Senate had been his for the asking.

It was no prize. Oregon's Democrats had not elected a U.S. senator in forty years, and the state's unbroken Republican domination was only equaled by that of Vermont. He also was a Jew in a state that once had claimed the largest percentage of Ku Klux Klan membership of any commonwealth outside the Deep South. My Washington state Democratic friends knew Neuberger and did not think much of his chances or his political skills. To a man they advised me not to waste my time. "Those Democrats are a little nuts down there," Scoop Jackson advised. "Something crazy seems to happen to them south of the Columbia."

The Columbia River was the dividing line between two states similar in every respect except people. New Englanders and midwesterners originally had settled Oregon, and its post-Civil War politics had been determinedly Republican. The GOP had controlled the state legislature since 1878 and held every county courthouse but one. Washington, thirty years younger as a state, had attracted a more variegated mixture of people—Alaska Gold Rushers, land boomers, and Scandinavian seafarers among them. Its politics had been populist in origin and some of its elected officials so radical that James A. Farley, FDR's political satrap, had quipped: "There are forty-seven states and the soviet of Washington." My dad, who grew up in both places, called Portland the "Boston of the West" and Seattle its "Chicago."

Guy Cordon was an aspish sixty-four-year-old lawyer from the downstate lumber town of Roseburg. He had been in the U.S. Senate since 1944, and his primary victory over a liberal Republican former governor, Charles Sprague, had been a triumph for the GOP right wing. Senator Robert A. Taft of Ohio had been his mentor and role model.

In the Senate, Cordon was a dull public performer but a shrewd backroom trader. He was content to leave the public pyrotechnics to his colleague, Wayne L. Morse, and quietly logroll federal projects for Oregon. The state had benefited with federal dams, reclamation projects, and power transmission lines from Hells Canyon on the Idaho state line to the sea-wide mouth of the Columbia River.

Seniority had dramatically aided Cordon's power to perform in the just-concluded 83rd Congress. Republican control had made him chair of both the Interior Committee and the Appropriations subcommittee that funded Interior, the U.S. Forest Service, and the Bonneville Power Administration.

With more than half of Oregon's land mass managed by Interior and with hydroelectricity and timber the state's main economic cornerstones, Cordon held the most important congressional command posts there were for his state. This should have made him invulnerable.

He wasn't. In 1948, the year of Truman, the Democrats did not file a candidate for his seat. At the last minute, Manley J. Wilson, editor of the *CIO Woodworker*, paid the $150 filing fee in order to put a name on the ballot. Ignored by the media and with contributions limited to a few local union pass-the-hat meetings, Wilson confined his campaign appearances to the Portland area. Nevertheless, the day after the election Oregon Democrats awoke to learn that Cordon had defeated Wilson by only a three-two margin; a shift of fewer than 50,000 votes would have changed the result. Still, Oregon's Republicanism was as strong as ever, and Oregon was the only western state to go for Thomas E. Dewey.

Oregon Democrats were tentatively hopeful that 1954 might be the year of turn-around. Progressive World War II veterans—led by Neuberger, Howard Morgan, and Monroe Sweetland—had wrested control of what party machinery there was from a conservative old guard and had infused the downtrodden Democrats with new energy. President Eisenhower's resource policies favoring private power companies and executed by his Interior secretary, former Oregon governor Douglas McKay, had proved to be unpopular in a region that was deriving much of its new economic strength from FDR's Grand Coulee and other big federal dams. During the New Deal, Republican leader McNary had been Roosevelt's chief lieutenant in securing congressional funding for these projects, and sweet bipartisanship was the order of the day. No more. Cordon and the Republicans were solidly aligned with private power, and the Democrats were the only hope of public power advocates, many Republicans among them. Underlying the topical questions of the campaign, such as whether to build a high federal dam at Hells Canyon, was the larger one that had been at the root of western politics since the first wagon trains had trudged down the Oregon Trail: what was to be done with the land?

It was a question that most Oregonians took an interest in. Their state contained perhaps the most beautiful and productive land in the nation, and its use had been the issue in 1849 when Samuel Thurston, the newly elected territorial delegate, had gone to Washington, D.C., to help pass the Oregon Donation Act. That legislation determined how land grants would be made to settlers who had been flooding into the territory since President Polk had settled the U.S.-Canada boundary issue at the 49th parallel.

Guy Cordon represented those Oregonians who believed that the federal government should finance access to and development of the land and then get the hell out of the way to let the home folks put it to its most productive uses. The lumber companies, the principal industry, led the list, closely followed by mining, private power, fishing, and ranching interests. Cordon had spent an honorable lifetime advancing their cause, and that alliance had a major stake in his reelection.

All of this had been impressed on me early in the year when an old newspaper mentor invited me to lunch in Seattle. Art Priaulx, an executive of the West Coast Lumbermen's Association, professed to be a friend of Dick Neuberger. "Don't let him run," he urged me. "I know Dick. He is too emotionally fragile to take what will be thrown at him. Cordon is so valuable to Oregon that it will be a bare-knuckles fight unlike any other. Dick isn't equipped to handle that kind of heat. Use your influence to keep our friend from getting hurt." When I reported the conversation to Neuberger, he said: "They're scared of me. I stand for conservation, and they want a blank check to plunder the resources as they see fit. Cordon and McKay have given it to them. This makes me all the more determined to run."

Hells Canyon focused the land-use issue. Deeper than the Grand Canyon, the chasm on the Snake River that bordered Oregon and Idaho was an ideal site for a dam that would be even higher than Grand Coulee. Yet, the Eisenhower administration, spearheaded by McKay, had opted for building three small run-of-the-river dams that the Idaho Power Company had proposed. "Giveaway," cried the public powerites and the Democrats, and the issue was joined.

Recent history favored the high-dam concept. A quarter-century earlier, an almost identical fight had been waged at the Grand Coulee of the Columbia River in Washington state. FDR had opted for the high dam, and it was finished in time to provide the hydroelectric power to produce the aluminum that Boeing used to build the B-17s and B-29s that helped win World War II. Almost overnight, the Pacific Northwest had gained a hydro-based manufacturing industry to augment its traditional economic standbys—lumber, salmon, fruit, and wheat.

With the high dam a symbol for jobs and prosperity, Democrats saw Hells Canyon as a cutting issue, but was the party capable of capitalizing on it? Half of Oregon's thirty-six counties did not even have Democratic organizations, and the state committee seemed to consist of its chair, Howard Morgan, and not much more. My first day in Portland revealed the problems ahead. Some sketchy polling indicated that Dick Neuberger was almost unknown outside the Portland metropolitan area. My media corrective was to be the statewide showing of billboards and posters that had worked so well for Magnuson and Jackson. It was an ideal medium on which Neuberger's youth and vigor could be capsulized with a slogan calling for change.

When I brought a suggested media budget up to his big old house in Portland Heights, Dick shook his head at the entry for billboards. "That has to come out," he said. My protestations were cut short when he went into his study and returned with a copy of the Oregon Voters' Pamphlet. His statement of candidacy began: "I am not a billboard candidate." It felt like a hard punch to the pit of my stomach.

Television was relatively new in Oregon, and everyone was watching. The campaign budget was weighted to video, and Dick offhandedly said that he had agreed to let Ken Rinke, the Multnomah County Democratic chair, produce the campaign spots. I had to fight off the urge to say goodbye and return to Seattle. Dick had assured me that I would be in charge of media without interference from anyone, and I was not happy with the situation.

A day of filming in a makeshift studio with Rinke's crew confirmed my worst fears. When the raw footage came back for screening, Neuberger's head floated eerily in a filmy fog, and his voice was out of synch with his mouth by a full second. I scrapped the footage, pushed back the television schedule, and got rid of Rinke. It cost a few bucks, but it was worth it. It put me back in charge.

The fiasco had demonstrated that the candidate was, at best, a mediocre television performer; and a Hollywood film crew wasn't going to turn him into a star. I was lucky enough to recruit three media professionals as volunteers for a long Saturday of filming. Ten hours later, there was some acceptable footage.

Afterward, Neuberger, the three volunteers, and I headed to nearby Jake's Crawfish House, a famous joint that dated back to my grandfather's day. We were thirsty and famished. The candidate, who had a speaking engagement across town, ate while the rest of us drank beer. He called for the check, perused it carefully, and pulled out his coin purse. "My share seems to be $2.50, and I'll leave fifty cents for the tip," he said. "Thanks for taking the time to help me." And he left. A silence followed. Finally, Ru Lund, an advertising man, gave it the right twist. "Look at it this way," he said. "If he is as careful with taxpayers' money as he is with his own, everything will be all right."

Lund later gave me a way to compensate for Neuberger's weakness as a television performer—radio. "There is so much fascination with television," he said, "that media buyers often forget that there are damned near one million Oregon housewives who have the radio on all day. Time is cheap, and you should have it all to yourself." He was right. Radio also provided a necessary campaign ingredient—a co-starring role for the candidate's wife, Maurine Brown Neuberger. In her second term in the legislature, she had achieved fame by passing a bill to legalize yellow oleomargarine, which was fiercely opposed by the dairy lobby. Until then, only white margarine could be sold in Oregon, and consumers had to mix in yellow powder to make it look more like butter. On the House floor, Maurine demonstrated with a mixing bowl just how hard it was to make oleo yellow, and her picture was on the front page of every Oregon daily and led the local TV newscasts. Overnight, she had become the best-known woman in Oregon.

Maurine's voice was ideal for radio. Its intimate down-home quality conveyed the image of one housewife talking to another over the backyard fence. A typical spot began: "This is Maurine Neuberger, and I want to talk with you for a minute about your family—and mine." John Jones, Dick's campaign chair who had run a radio station in eastern Oregon, checked for reaction and received an enthusiastic response. "Give us more Maurine," people demanded.

With radio as the principal weapon, we were trying to make Cordon's Senate voting record the main issue of the campaign—a chronology of *no* votes on everything from Eisenhower's foreign-policy program and NATO to school lunches, cancer research, and aid to education. It revealed him as a reactionary isolationist in a state where Republicans generally were moderate internationalists. Cordon's record, as well as his political personality, were little known in Oregon. Usually referred to as "Oregon's other senator," he was a self-taught lawyer who disliked the spotlight but loved the backroom maneuvering that produced legislative results on the Senate floor. His crowning achievement for Oregon, as counsel to Senator Charles McNary, had been passage of a bill that had resulted in eighteen western Oregon counties receiving half the revenues from timber sales on the two-and-a-half million acres of the old Oregon & California Railroad timber-lands. Over time, his bill had been a billion-dollar bonanza for the state's counties.

I knew and liked Senator Cordon. His daughters Marge and Carolyn had been friendly to me at the University of Oregon, and I had dropped in on him on my visits to Washington, D.C. He had continued McNary's "Oregon Club," an informal after-hours gathering of Oregonians who happened to be in Washington. Cordon liked a drink and conversation, and I enjoyed his company. But my personal feelings did not inhibit me when it came to crafting a caricature of Cordon as a rank reactionary who was "giving away" the resources of Oregon and the nation to private utilities and Texas oil inter-ests and, for good measure, was opposing President Eisenhower on his foreign-policy ventures. How could Oregon, in mid-century, tolerate such a fossilized troglodyte?

This bushwacking was principally accomplished through a series of radio spots, deceptively titled "Compare the Candidates on the Issues that Affect You." On two dozen or so issues, Cordon's negative votes were compared to Neuberger's positive stands. The senator was on the defensive from the start.

Radio could be produced without the candidate; it was one of its great virtues. There was no such luxury with television. Production facilities were so spartan that the candidate had to be used, mostly as a talking head. For a person who had spent his entire life as a writer-communicator and politi-cian, Dick was curiously ignorant and indifferent to the effect of television on the body politic. Without a television set of his own, he knew little about the video-centered world that had been mushrooming around him.

We immediately clashed. After he had read a script once or twice with the camera running, he was ready to quit. "That is good enough," he would decide after stumbling through a performance. When I demurred, he became huffy. "You are keeping me from campaigning by making me spend all this time in the studio," he complained. My insistence that most Oregonians would only know of him through what they saw on their television sets was greeted with disbelief. When he cut one filming session short by saying that he had a last-minute luncheon speech to make at a neighborhood Lions Club, I blew up.

"How many will be there?"

"From forty to fifty, I guess."

"How many do you expect to vote for you?"

"Not too many—ten or fifteen."

I put my face within inches of his and exploded. "So you would short-change this and come across the tube as a stumblebum to god-knows-how-many-thousands of voters just to chase ten votes. That is disgraceful, and I'm ashamed of you." We had been friends for years, but I never had talked to him so bluntly. His face reddened, and then he grinned. "You're right," he said, and stayed for more filming.

Oregon television was splendidly seat-of-the-pants in those days, and improvisation often was the order of the moment. One Monday morning I took a call from Bill Swing, program director of KPTV, an independent channel. "We just had a cancellation of the fifteen-minute slot after wrestling," he said. "You can have it for thirty-five bucks." Monday night wrestling at Civic Auditorium was the hottest item on Portland television. I bought it and then realized that Dick and Maurine were in eastern Oregon.

Wayne Morse was my only hope. I miraculously caught him as he was leaving his hotel room for a campaign swing to Astoria with Howard Morgan, the Democratic state committee chair. Could he come by and cut a kinescope (the earlier version of videotape) to use in the time slot? Minutes later, he was there and ready to go. Shelley Goldstein, the studio manager, had an inspiration. "Let's use Morgan to introduce Morse and to close out the program."

I was staying with staunchly Republican cousins in Portland, and Monday was the night when the neighbors came in for coffee, cake, and canasta, followed by wrestling on television. Out of courtesy to me, they all watched Morse, an anathema to them for having deserted the GOP for the Democratic party. After it was over, four housewives asked me with one voice: "Who is that handsome man?" They were referring to Morgan, whose rugged good looks had projected remarkably on the fifteen-inch screen. I explained that he had been a Jefferson High School football star who had worked his way through Reed College and had married a daughter of a prominent pioneer family, a rousing success story. "Well," said my cousin Connie, "he is just about the best-looking man I've seen on local television."

I did not have to be hit on the head with a two-by-four. Her remark focused my suspicion that television was changing long-held attitudes toward many things, particularly politics. The idea that my cousin and her three Republican friends would swoon over a Democratic functionary would have been laughable pre-television. A Democratic boss was usually seen as the personification of evil. Now he was Handsome Howard. Guided by this micro-survey, I put more of Morgan on the little screen in the fall than the candidate himself.

Among one of Neuberger's quirks was his insistence on stressing conservation. Oregon's economy was in a slump in 1954, and I didn't think it made much sense to talk about such an esoteric issue when people were worried about their jobs and businesses. "They care about their pocketbook, not saving the wilderness," I remonstrated. He was adamant. "There are enough people who care about the rape of the land, and many of them are normally Republican," he shot back. "Every time they drive from Portland to the Oregon coast for a weekend, they pass through the ugliest clearcuts in creation, all arrogantly perpetrated by Crown Zellerbach and other big timber companies. I want them to realize that a senator like Neuberger will fight this kind of degradation."

As with many other issues, my friend was far ahead of his time. A Conservationists for Neuberger committee proved to be an attractive alternative for Republicans unhappy with what they perceived to be Cordon's lap-dog relationship to big timber. Dick had learned that some of the most hidebound conservatives shared a love for the land and hated to see it manhandled, particularly when it was in their own backyard. It was my first taste of the incipient power of the environmental issue.

It also helped bring in campaign money. National conservationists, sparked by writer Bernard DeVoto, passed the hat among their wealthy friends and came up with a tidy bundle. The National Committee for an Effective Congress—newly formed by *Encyclopedia Britannica* publisher Senator Bill Benton—not only sent substantial funds but also the most valuable of young volunteers, Roy Schotland, a recent Columbia graduate who postponed going to Harvard Law School for the fall campaign. Funds were arriving in chunks large enough to pay for the radio-television schedule, the campaign's principal expense.

Organized labor never had been a dominant force in Oregon, despite a claimed total membership of 215,000, and its support seldom had focused on one candidate. But now it was focused on Dick because he was a liberal Democrat and not a reactionary. Even such hoary antagonists as Harry Bridges's longshoremen and Dave Beck's teamsters were marching in lockstep. Their big effort was the canvassing of labor precincts and a massive get-out-the-vote program on Election Day. And funds poured in from national labor.

My big disappointment was the paucity of Jewish money. I had naively assumed that Dick's religion would open up checkbooks across the country. In Seattle, I learned how wrong I was. Despite my excellent relations with leaders of Seattle Jewry, I struck out when it came to help for their landsman south of the Columbia. Joe Gluck, Washington's Democratic national committeeman, explained why. "He is regarded as an anti-Zionist Jew," Gluck told me. "Being a goy you wouldn't know that American Jews historically have been divided between those favoring a Jewish homeland in Palestine and those thinking we should concentrate on being Americans. Dick is in the latter category, and that's why there is no enthusiasm."

Still, his religion was an issue burrowing at the surface of the campaign. In the spring of 1954, an obscure weekly newspaper in eastern Oregon, the Morrow County *Journal*, editorialized about Neuberger's "financial acumen, typical of members of his race." Another rural weekly offered up similar comments. The Cordon campaign, in a major blunder, circulated the material to editors across the state. An editorial firestorm erupted. The *Oregonian* and its rival the *Oregon Journal*, seethed with righteous indignation, as did downstate dailies from Eugene to Medford and east to Pendleton. The GOP state organization protested its innocence. Yet, calls to Cordon headquarters by Neuberger volunteers posing as newcomers to Oregon seeking information about the candidates yielded a stock answer: he was a Jew and supporter of radical left-wing causes.

Neuberger lived in dread of the kind of smear that Senator Joe McCarthy of Wisconsin had tarred Democrats with across the country. At two o'clock one morning, he called me from Coos Bay, his voice sepulchral with doom. "The campaign is all over," he said. "Charley Porter gave it to the Republicans tonight. Go home to Seattle. I am going to withdraw in the morning. I am working on my withdrawal statement right now."

Neuberger had been at a "candidates' night" in the Marshfield High School auditorium with an audience largely made up of longshoremen who backed Harry Bridges's call for the recognition of Communist China. Aghast, Neuberger heard Charley Porter, the local candidate for Congress, endorse Bridges's demand. Deaf to the longshoremen's cheers, Dick saw the Democrats' campaign self-destructing right there. "The Republicans now have the tool to make Red China the whole issue," he moaned. I promised to call Porter in the morning to keep him from doing it again. (After the election, Porter accused me of costing him the victory; the county in which he endorsed recognition was the only one he carried.) Despite Dick's foreboding, the Republicans never attempted to make any capital out of Porter's declaration, nor did it occasion any media reaction. It was a quietly dramatic manifestation that the "Red issue" had lost its potency.

Porter, who was to win the House seat two years later, was one of a strong group of Democratic congressional candidates that included Al Ullman in eastern Oregon and Edith Green in Portland. Dick asked me to help Mrs. Green with her media. "She can't beat Tom McCall," he said. "But the stronger she runs, the better off we are."

Mrs. Green, a former schoolteacher and lobbyist for the Oregon Education Association, was spunky and articulate. She had a crisp style that adapted to television, and she was a pleasure to work with. McCall, whom I had known casually in Idaho when he was a newspaperman, had a neo-Lincolnesque frame but an upper-class Boston accent that belied his central Oregon upbringing. Although he had been a Portland television newsman, I suspected that his accent could be his Achilles' heel. My Republican cousins and their neighbors had said emphatically that they never could vote for anybody who spoke like *that*. Of such stuff are elections sometimes determined.

The Republican campaign, well financed as it was, seemed to lack focus. Its media was not exploiting Cordon's obvious advantage: his Senate chairmanships and their significance to Oregon. And there was no negative attack against Dick. Coming from Washington state's rough-tough political arena, I was amazed.

The Republicans did know that they were in a race. GOP "stars" from outside the state were campaigning for Cordon almost every weekend. At one appearance, U.S. House Speaker Joe Martin urged the electorate to re-elect his good friend, "Si Gordon." He was not alone in his blundering. Interior Secretary McKay, home to speak for Cordon, was using a teleprompter in a live television speech. When it broke down, McKay lost his train of thought and ended his presentation in a blur of incoherence.

Vice President Richard M. Nixon was next, slated to appear at Portland's Masonic Auditorium in late October. He had been campaigning throughout the West against Democrats, indiscriminately splashing them with Red paint. Earlier that month, the *New York Times* called it a "demagogic spree," and some western newspapers had picked up on the theme. When Nixon reached Portland, the last stop on his tour, a chorus of editorial outrage preceded him.

Dick Neuberger had been in an overwrought state for days, certain that Nixon would hit new depths in smearing him. "He has saved me for last because last will be the worst," he prophesied. We shared his nervousness and had responded by purchasing the identical radio and television time that the Republicans had reserved for Nixon, but on the next night. We even had splurged for quarter-page newspaper ads headlined "Neuberger Answers Nixon."

The Neubergers were in Klamath Falls the night Nixon spoke; Maurine would drive back through the night so that we could kinescope his thirty-minute answer to Nixon in the morning. Hans Linde and I had gone to hear Nixon and picked up the text of his speech so we could write Neuberger's speech immediately afterward. Hans was a University of Oregon law professor on leave for the campaign, a practical intellectual who had made himself indispensable.

Amazement! Nixon did not even fire a popgun Dick's way. He made an obligatory passing reference to "Oregon's hard-working Senator Cordon" and then advanced to a thoughtful speech about President Eisenhower's foreign-policy initiatives. Neuberger or any liberal Democrat could have made the same speech and had it hailed as a splendid bipartisan statement of American purpose. What had happened to Nixon? Hans and I could only speculate that the editorial barrage had chastened the Republican command and Nixon had been directed to end his campaign swing on a positive note.

The answer that Hans and I crafted for the ad in the *Oregonian* the day

after Nixon's speech was a paper tiger, just as seemingly bland and bipartisan as Nixon's speech. But it had a kicker, just the kind of punch we were
looking for to dramatize the chasm that divided Eisenhower and Cordon on
foreign policy. The first eight paragraphs began: "I agree with Vice President Nixon when he said in Portland last night," followed by the appropriate quote. The kicker? "But what Mr. Nixon did not tell you is that Senator
Cordon voted against President Eisenhower on this very issue—every time
it came before the Senate." It came across clearly that Cordon was no Eisenhower Republican. The Nixon speech couldn't have served our purpose better
if we had drafted it ourselves.

Curiously, the Cordon campaign suddenly came alive and began driving home what always had been the senator's principal selling point: re-elect
me because I can do more for Oregon than Neuberger can. That had been
the argument that I always had feared the most, and the Republicans were
plugging the hell out of it. I found out why. Hal Short had arrived to take
over the Cordon campaign. A former Oregonian, Short was a GOP campaign expert whose efforts had produced Senate upsets in Maryland and Kentucky. He and Frank Herbert (later to became a science-fiction author) almost
overnight had refocused their media and recharged their candidate for a run
down the stretch.

Our campaign was exhausted. Too few people had been trying to do too many
things, and it had worn us down. I had lost sixteen pounds, and my mind
was blanking. I badly needed help and found it in the form of a round little
guy with bright searching eyes who I had threatened to kick into the
Willamette River a few weeks earlier. His name was Eddie Stanton, and he
had been assigned to us by the jackleg ad agency that was placing the media.
My impression that he was a no-talent blowhard wise guy had gradually
changed as I saw his rapport with station managers and other media functionaries. He also had a talent for detail and an instinct for improvisation,
the kind of assets a seat-of-the-pants campaign like ours needed. We became
inseparable partners.

There is a time in a close race when every breath, every lunge, every swing
of the whip can make the difference. That is the time for guys like Eddie
Stanton. Neither his energy nor his enthusiasm ever flagged. We would finish
up late at night, too tired even for a well-deserved nightcap. Early the next

morning he was on the phone: "Get your ass out of the sack. You ain't gonna elect Dick there." He was just the kind of jockey I needed.

Our campaign closer was in the can, a patriotic flag-waver designed to end on a high note and take away any bad taste left by our attacks on Cordon's record. But with Cordon revitalized and charging hard, something more was needed. We couldn't jab and dance away in the last round; we had to punch as hard as we could until the final bell.

The medium was radio. As late money had poured in, we had bought saturation coverage on Oregon radio for the Friday to Monday before Election Day. I decided to use all that time on one spot that had been percolating in my mind ever since Nixon had spoken in Portland.

The spot began with the opening chorus of Irving Berlin's "I like Ike," as recorded by Fred Waring and His Pennsylvanians. The music suddenly ended with a screechy snarl. Then the announcer came on: "But . . . does Senator Cordon like Ike? He has voted in the United States Senate against every foreign-policy initiative that President Eisenhower has offered. From the Atlantic Pact to the summit meetings, Oregon's senator has voted against his own Republican President. That is why many thousands of Oregon Republicans are going to vote for Richard L. Neuberger on Tuesday. They know that Neuberger will support President Eisenhower's bipartisan efforts to preserve peace throughout the world." The spot concluded with the final chorus of "I Like Ike" and a voice underneath saying "Paid for by the Republicans for Neuberger Committee."

Later, in a Seattle bar, Frank Herbert described the spot's effect for me: "It was devastating. I had been desperately trying to make an Eisenhower Republican out of a reactionary Taft isolationist, and this one spot drilled us right between the eyes. Calls came into headquarters from all over the state with the same message: It's killing us." Hal Short remembered: "We tried everything to get it off the air. It violated all the copyright laws. The radio stations should have known it was bootlegged material. Hell, who can't recognize Fred Waring? We called Jim Haggerty at the White House. He told Ike, who got mad as hell and told Haggerty to call Irving Berlin. Berlin was furious and was going to send out telegrams threatening to sue every station in Oregon. Len Hall, the Republican national chair, killed that one. He said that it would only make headlines that would hurt Cordon. So that damned spot probably cost us the election. You got away with murder."

Election Day that November was typically windy and rainy, yet reports came in that indicated an unusually heavy turnout for an off-year election, a good sign for Democrats. I slept in and then wandered down to the Boilermakers Building's basement, the command post of Oregon labor's first massive get-out-the-vote effort. Volunteers at telephone banks were busily dialing targeted voters to make sure they voted and offering rides to polling stations. Watching them recharged me, and I began to anticipate hearing the first returns.

The Democratic suite at the Roosevelt Hotel, Portland's only union hostelry, was peopled with a grim-faced lot of folks when I arrived shortly after seven. Cordon had jumped out to a substantial lead, which reached 18,000 three hours later. It appeared to be Democratic *déjà vu* once again. Television and radio remotes from Cordon's Imperial Hotel headquarters conveyed unrestrained joy as Oregon once again proved its dedication to Republicanism. Only Howard Morgan retained any semblance of confidence. "We are getting the count from Republican precincts," he maintained. "They haven't counted the lunch-pail vote yet. That's our vote, and it was big."

Oregon's biggest county, Multnomah (Portland), still used paper ballots, and it was possible that the evening vote had not yet been counted. With over 800 precincts to report, it was possible that many Democratic votes were still to be counted. In addition, the counties along the Columbia River, where Hells Canyon was an issue, were starting to come in, with Dick showing unexpected strength. When I called Dick at home to give him these promising developments, he digested it all in a voice tragic with self-pity. "It's all over," he moaned. "The reactionaries have beaten me with their smears. I am letting them have it in my concession statement. Thanks for everything, and go home to Seattle." Roy Schotland was dispatched to his house to keep Dick from conceding, and the night wore on into the early morning hours. Cordon's lead had been holding at about 15,000, and the returns slowed to a trickle. I turned in at four that morning in a benumbed state.

Seven o'clock found me still numb but awake. After some fumbling around, I called the Associated Press office to get the latest results. My friend Jim Cour answered. I asked him for the vote totals. "Hey," he said, excitement brimming in his voice, "I've got some real news."

"Just give me the count, buddy," I said.

"Okay. Cordon is up by around 12,000. I'm on shift at the Journal Building where the Multnomah County ballots are being tabulated. I just talked the counters into giving me the completed results from five precincts they picked at random. Dick did great with the late lunch-pail vote. I did some figuring. If these precincts are an indicator, he is going to carry Multnomah by about 18,000 votes and win statewide by 2,500. His upriver vote still is coming in strong, and he is doing well in Klamath Falls."

My numbness suddenly lifted like fog in a hot sun. I called Dick. He answered on the eighth ring, his voice eerily despondent over the death of his dream.

"Wake up, senator," I shouted. "You are going to win the election!"

His voice didn't change. "Joe, you are still drunk. Please, let me get some sleep."

"Shut up and listen," I shouted, and told him Jim's projections.

He was not convinced. "It's wishful thinking, a pipedream," he said.

"Think what you will," I concluded. "I am going to the *Journal*. Keep this phone open because I am going to be calling you regularly."

My second call was to Senator Earle C. Clements of Kentucky, chair of the Democratic Senatorial Campaign Committee in Washington, D.C. I explained the situation, and he responded with a great whoop of excitement. Then he told me that control of the United States Senate hinged on the outcome. Republican Clifford Case had finally won in New Jersey by 3,500 votes, making Dick the Democrats' last hope to retake the Senate. I promised to keep Clements posted and headed for the *Journal*'s city room.

In publisher Bill Knight's office, Hal Short and a gaggle of GOP functionaries, all wearing frowns, were conferring. Knight gave me a curt nod; I was no favorite of his. He and Guy Cordon had been law partners in Roseburg, and during my brief sojourn at his newspaper I had helped organize a local of the American Newspaper Guild there.

Hours flew by as votes came straggling in, each new tally shrinking Cordon's margin. Neuberger finally took the lead around four that afternoon by a scant ninety-seven votes. It was the lead story on the national news. Someone handed me a brief bulletin from the Associated Press statewide wire: "The Dalles—Wasco County today gave its votes to Richard L. Neuberger, the first time it has voted for a Democrat since 1864 when General George B. McClellan defeated President Abraham Lincoln."

As afternoon turned into evening, the election hinged on the precincts that still were unreported—something like eighteen in Marion County, fourteen in Lane, eight in Douglas, and some scattered others. With Dick's margin now at about 1,500, the fear arose among us that the election still could be stolen by vote-rigging in those precincts. Senator Clements of Kentucky, where vote-stealing was a tradition, directed us to call out the state patrol to find the missing ballot boxes. Lyndon Johnson, who had won his Senate seat in an 87-vote squeaker, was on the phone offering advice. Howard Morgan and Monroe Sweetland were calling Democrats in the counties where precincts were unreported to go to the county courthouses to guard the ballot boxes. With so many precincts out and the margin so small, the fear arose that something sinister might happen.

Vote-buying and stealing had been common practice in frontier Oregon. So rank had it become that civic-minded citizens had led a movement for sweeping reforms that resulted, in 1908, in Oregon becoming the first state to elect U.S. senators by popular vote. Until then, state legislatures had selected its two solons and many senators had simply "bought" their seats. Oregon's example led the way and, in 1913, ratification of the Seventeenth Amendment legalized the direct election of senators. Oregonians prided themselves in the squeaky clean reputation that their state had acquired as a result.

Like many of my contemporaries, I had brought the morality of sports to politics. Anything went, provided that one wasn't caught. It was like throwing an illegal spitball or running a hidden-ball play. Ethics in politics was for political science professors.

Fortunately for our side, the Republicans simply did not know how to steal the election. Wendell Wyatt, GOP state chair at the time, described a scene of chaos in the Cordon camp that made one thing perfectly clear: they didn't know how to do it, even with control of thirty-five of the state's thirty-six county courthouses and paper ballots to be manipulated. In retrospect, I find that amazing. Public protestations aside, I think either side would have had reason to steal that election because too much was at stake for ethical considerations to prevail. I have seen moralistic politicians rationalize deviations from righteousness for much less reason than control of the U.S. Senate.

The missing precincts came straggling in that Wednesday night. With all the votes in, Dick's margin had risen to 2,462, 38 votes off Jim Cour's prediction. At ten minutes to eleven, when Lawrence Davies, western correspondent of the *New York Times*, handed me the lead paragraphs of the story he was filing, I knew it was over. The *Times* had made it official.

I headed for the Roosevelt Hotel, skipping through the deserted streets of downtown Portland. The lobby was a madhouse. Victory-starved Democrats had left their homes on a cold night and headed for the Roosevelt. I was hugged, mauled, and kissed. A few minutes later, Edith Green, surprise winner over Tom McCall, appeared, and the cheers shook the little hotel. When Neuberger showed up, the place exploded. It was a night that no one who was there would forget. Little Oregon once again had made its mark on the nation's political map.

Dick Neuberger, who died of cancer on March 9, 1960, near the end of his one term, has been dead almost fifty years. One can only speculate on what might have been had he lived longer. After a shaky start, he developed into a senator of the first rank, staking out advanced positions on the environment, public campaign financing and better treatment for America's non-white minorities—issues that dominated the national conversation in the decades that followed. He would have been in the forefront of that dialogue, using his brilliant writing skills for the affirmative position. At home in Oregon, Dick attained such popularity that his widow Maurine, running for his seat in 1960, rolled up what was then the biggest plurality in Oregon history. He would have had a long Senate career and quite possibly would have been the first Jew to run on a national ticket.

I saw him for the last time on January 22, 1960, two days before his final trip home to Oregon. We had dinner at his favorite Washington restaurant, the Old Europe in Georgetown. I dreaded the evening; his situation was grim, and I was unequipped to handle my emotions. My fear was needless. We embarked on a flood of reminiscing, starting with our first meeting in Idaho in 1943, girls we had chased after, our fake Seattle versus Portland newspaper feud, the paranoia of Wayne Morse, the crazy characters we had known on newspapers and in politics, and mostly the good times we had together. Then it was late and time to go. He had a serious message for me. "Joe, let us assume that, for whatever reason, I decide not to file for re-election in March. There is a Neuberger who can run and win, and I don't mean Muffet, our cat. I want you to promise me that you will do everything you can to see that Maurine runs, if the situation arises."

He went home to the big house on Portland Heights, and reports came back that the cancer was in remission and that he was doing well. On March 5, I received a two-page letter from Maurine saying how chipper Dick was feeling and that he was looking forward to getting out on the campaign trail. Four days later he was dead. He was a remarkable human being. There are few days that have passed since then that I have not thought of him and missed him.

3

MAGGIE AND THE TIGER

JERRY HOECK DID ME ONE OF THOSE UNWITTING FAVORS THAT ENDED up determining the course of what was to become my lifetime career in Washington, D.C. He took me to lunch at Seattle's Washington Athletic Club in February 1956 and talked me out of managing Earl Coe's campaign for governor. Hoeck was the advertising man who came to political prominence in 1952 with his innovative media in Scoop Jackson's winning U.S. Senate campaign. Now he was signed up to do the same for Warren G. Magnuson, and he wanted me as his chief honcho in that effort.

Hoeck strengthened what had been my growing doubts about Coe's candidacy. Conceding that Coe had been a phenomenal vote-getter for the largely ceremonial office of secretary of state, Hoeck compared him to a baseball player who could hit .400 in the minors but couldn't make it in the majors because he couldn't hit a sharp curve.

In Olympia, I had come to know Coe as an amiable and eminently decent wheat farmer from southeastern Washington who had been drafted in 1948 to give geographic balance to the Democratic ticket. I had met with the group that Dave Cohn, Coe's chief backer, had collected. Some were nice fellows, but all of them were dominated by a hot-eyed lust for the state contracts and liquor franchises that would be theirs when Coe became governor. Those guys made me uncomfortable.

My experience with politics at the state level had begun when I covered the Puget Sound ferry strike of 1948 and continued in the 1949 session of the state legislature, in which I was a press aide to the House Democrats. The legislature was a cozy place and casually corrupt. During the 1951 session, I was chief clerk to the House Labor Committee, which was chaired by an older, liberal friend of mine from Seattle. On the side, I was wearing another hat as the part-time business agent of the Seattle Nurses Guild, Local 126 of the Building Service Employees Union, a post I had held since I was a labor reporter for the *Post-Intelligencer*. The nurses wanted compulsory arbitration legislation to determine their disputes with hospital administrators, who generally had ignored their complaints. I got a bill introduced with bipartisan backing, hearings were held, and it was ready to be voted out of committee.

One night I asked the chairman when he would report the bill. "I'll give you a break," he said. "It will only cost you a C. Ordinarily, I wouldn't bring out a bill like this for anything less than five." I still was in a state of shock the next morning when I reported the conversation to Evan M. (Ed) Weston, president of the State Federation of Labor. He pulled a one-hundred-dollar bill out of his wallet and handed it to me. "That's cheap," he said. "Go get that bill out."

My education in legislative politics had advanced to the post-graduate level in 1955 when I served as secretary of the Democratic majority in the state senate. In reality, I was press agent-speechwriter for Albert D. Rosellini of Seattle, the Senate majority leader, who already was running hard for governor. I liked Al, but I could not convince myself that he had a real chance to make it. Washington's population was strongly dominated by its Scandinavian Lutheran heritage, and I couldn't see that key group going for an Italian Catholic of raffish reputation. So much for my political judgment. Rosellini easily defeated Coe in the primary and then swept by the Scandinavian Republican, Emmett Anderson, in the November election.

The more I thought about Hoeck's offer to join the Magnuson campaign, the sounder it seemed. State politics was a messy business, and I was much more fascinated by Congress than I was with the statehouse. Irvin A. Hoff, Magnuson's administrative assistant, arranged for me to be payrolled by the United Steelworkers of America, a move that brought me under the aegis of Frank Nordhoff (Nordy) Hoffmann, the union's legislative and political director.

There was no time to waste getting started on the campaign. With three-time governor Arthur B. Langlie already announced as the Republican nominee, the race was going to be nothing short of epochal. He was their best vote-getter and at opposite poles from Magnuson on virtually everything: political philosophy, lifestyle, and personality. It was hard to find two more complete contrasts, even though their backgrounds were so similar. Both were Minnesota Norwegian Lutherans and both had graduated from the University of Washington Law School, Langlie a star baseball player and Magnuson a substitute halfback on a Rose Bowl team. They had dabbled in the law and then plunged into politics, Magnuson elected to Congress in 1936 and Langlie as mayor of Seattle in 1938.

Jerry Hoeck explained the difference between the two. "There are two kinds of Norwegians: the landlubbers and the sea-goers," he told me when I interviewed him for a *Time* magazine cover story on Langlie. "The landlubbers came here from farms in the old country looking for free or cheap land. They generally are pious and humorless, their lives totally dominated by work, materialism, and strict Missouri Synod Lutheranism. Drink is sin, and sex is solely for the purpose of procreation. Langlie is the archetypal land Norwegian. The seagoing Norsk is a total opposite. He is the descendant of the Vikings who plundered, boozed, and raped their way through parts of Europe for three notorious centuries before they feuded themselves out of business. He is a sailor, fisherman, or logger. He works just as hard as the landlubber, but when the final whistle blows, he heads straight for the tavern or whorehouse to blow his pay on a spree. Yet Monday morning, when the work whistle blows, he is there, hungover and broke, but ready to work like hell until next Saturday night. Magnuson is the classic sea-going Norwegian."

Magnuson was the rare politician with whom I could claim a degree of friendship, if there really is such a thing in political relationships. He cultivated newspapermen and was comfortable in their company. "I need them, and they need me," he said. As a result, he had enjoyed an uncommonly good press, even from newspapers whose publishers abhorred his pro-labor liberal politics.

Magnuson's reputation as a senator rested largely on his ability to "bring home the bacon." When he had run for re-election in 1950, his slogan proudly proclaimed: "He Gets Things Done!" With his masculine charm and his non-ideologic political outlook, he was a natural for the Senate backrooms where deals are cut. The southern senatorial barons whose hands controlled the appropriations purse strings generally went along with his understated requests, particularly those to fund Columbia River dam projects. By the 1950s, one in every four federal dollars spent on water projects went to Washington state. The complaint was: "The Columbia is certainly a wonderful river. It waters four states and drains forty-eight."

But federal funds had dried up in the Eisenhower years. Interior Secretary Douglas McKay had decreed a policy called "partnership," which had left hydroelectric development to the private utilities and resulted in four years of stagnation. Langlie was known as the policy's most enthusiastic spokesman. I knew it was his Achilles' heel. My experience at the League for a Columbia Valley Authority, as *Time*'s part-time correspondent, and with the 1954 Senate race had convinced me that "partnership" was a real loser for Republicans. The people wanted federal bucks to build those big dams. Barring a dramatic last-minute conversion, Langlie was stuck with a long record of strident opposition to those dollars. He was a juicy target.

Magnuson's principal weakness was more corrective. He had a reputation for spending more time in the fleshpots of Hollywood, Palm Springs, and Las Vegas than he did in the grimy, rainy timber towns of western Washington and the dusty farm communities of the Palouse. When he did appear in the state that had elected him, he seldom ventured far from his suite in Seattle's Olympic Hotel or the posh Spokane Club in eastern Washington.

I had made a clumsy pass or two at creating a political documentary, writing scripts for Jackson and Mitchell in 1952 that never were produced. In Dick Neuberger's Oregon race, I had crudely spliced stock footage "borrowed" from the Bonneville Power Administration to augment his television performances. It was as elementary as a home movie, but effective enough to show promise. Magnuson was coming out to spend Easter recess going up the Columbia from Portland to inspect the projects he had helped attain. It was a natural for my documentary, and I not only had a professional cameraman but also a producer (Lee Schulman of Seattle's KING-TV).

As much as I had been around the Great River of the West, I never had been on it, seeing at deck level the incredible force of its waters rushing to the Pacific. I knew it had seven times the flow of the Colorado and two hundred times the flow of the Rio Grande, but these were statistics. Tons of water around us was the reality.

Our companions on that slow-paced voyage were as colorful as the river itself. Lew Russell, the barge's owner-operator, had piloted the Columbia for decades and knew every twist and turn by heart. Since 1934, Herbert West, an ebullient Walla Wallan, had been the driving force behind the Inland Empire Waterways Association, the Corps of Engineers' chief lobbying ally for its master plan to build a chain of dams and locks as far inland as Lewiston, Idaho. West, a conservative Republican and former mayor of Walla Walla, was marching in lockstep with Magnuson, the liberal Democrat, to achieve this end. He also was leading the cheers for Maggie on the Republican east side of the state.

Moving to break the Eisenhower administration's blockage of the ambitious project, Magnuson had landed a sneak punch late in the 1955 session of Congress. It had happened in the early-morning hours of an all-night conference of the House and Senate appropriations committees, which were meeting to decide the government's budget for the coming year. William F. Knowland of California, the Senate Republican leader, was on hand to block any last-minute insertions that were counter to the Eisenhower administration's strictures, such as "no new dam starts." But Knowland had health problems and had to leave the conference for a spell. Maggie seized on his absence to slip in a mere million dollars to begin construction of Ice Harbor Dam on the Lower Snake River. Knowland didn't see it when he returned, and the deed was done.

That million, West knew, would open the congressional money gates to complete the project. All the Corps of Engineers had to do was request funding for the chain of four dams. It was a classic Magnuson move. "I learned it from Wesley 'Yakima' Jones and C. C. Dill," he later told me. In 1929, those two Washington state senators had gone to President Herbert Hoover and received his support for a $600,000 study of the Columbia by the Corps of Engineers. Jones, the Republican majority leader, had slipped it into a routine bill. The "308 Report," as it was called, recommended ten dams for the Columbia-Snake system. Now, thanks to "Maggie's million," they would be built.

We docked at The Dalles, ninety-odd miles upriver from Portland and the site of the dam then under construction. Its cofferdam already had drowned Celilo Falls, where Indians had fished for salmon for thousands of years. It was Saturday night, and the Elks Club welcomed us, but we quit before the last round. We were going to film Magnuson at Easter sunrise services and wanted to capture him at his most pious as dawn broke. We weren't going to concede Langlie anything in the contest for the religious vote.

The filming was going well. In one day, Magnuson had been "shot" endlessly against the backdrop of familiar Washington scenes. With the barge trip ending at Umatilla, the site of McNary Dam, our next stop was to be John Goldmark's ranch in the Okanogan Highlands near the Canadian border. Then I learned that he had never seen Chief Joseph Dam, the second largest power producer in the U.S. hydroelectric system. If any dam on the river could be called "Maggie's baby," it was that one. Virtually alone, he had secured its authorization and funding.

The schedule was changed, and I called the home of the dam's manager at Bridgeport. A spirited party was in progress, and he guffawed loudly when I told him that Magnuson would be arriving on the morrow. "That's a good one," he roared. It took me a good while to convince him that I was serious. Suddenly his voice descended several decibels, "Y'all wouldn't be kidding a fella, would you?" No, I assured him.

He was at the Bridgeport airport when we arrived the next morning, quiet and sober. A lanky Arkansan, he gave us a superb tour of the dam, climaxed with a sumptuous lunch. But he was subdued around the senator, and Maggie worked at bringing him out. Finally he relaxed, and a string of uproariously funny stories came from him. The impromptu stop had been a great success. On the way to Goldmark's ranch, Magnuson commented: "That fellow will likely be one of my best supporters in this county. He'll say something like, 'I know that ol' Magnuson, and he ain't a half bad ol' boy.'"

We were at Goldmark's ranch to dramatize Magnuson's opposition to Secretary of Agriculture Ezra Taft Benson's proposal for a two-price system for wheat, one for domestic sales and the other for export. It would have hit the state's farmers right in the pocketbook. Goldmark was hardly your typical Washington wheat farmer. An editor of the *Yale Law Review*, he and his Brooklyn-born wife Sallie had fallen in love with the rural West, and he had passed up a Wall Street legal career in favor of raising a family, wheat, and cattle in the Okanogan Highlands.

We filmed Magnuson, Goldmark, and Buck, his hired hand, sitting on bales of hay piled atop a wagon, discussing the farm situation. The unrehearsed dialogue was going swimmingly, until Goldmark's heifers began attacking the hay, some evading my frantic efforts to shoo them off. One got through and grabbed the bale on which Maggie was sitting. The chair of the U.S. Senate Commerce Committee slowly slid earthward, his right arm going elbow-deep in manure to break his fall. Quickly recovering, he bounced back on to the bale and turned to the hired hand with a laugh: "Buck, that heifer must have thought I was Ezra Taft Benson!"

The first phase of filming completed, I was off to Washington, D.C., to organize the media campaign. The Republicans had named Langlie their national convention keynote speaker, and he was receiving a major media buildup. Eisenhower reportedly had said that Langlie's election was a top GOP priority, a payback for his influential role in securing the 1952 nomination for Ike. Our effort would have to be first class.

One issue that I intended to develop for the campaign was medical research. Magnuson's arrival in Congress in 1937 had coincided with a developing movement to get the federal government into the medical research field. A bill to create a National Cancer Institute, introduced in the Senate by Claude Pepper of Florida and Homer T. Bone of Washington, appeared to have a good chance. Eager to associate himself with a "mother-love" issue, Magnuson introduced the Pepper-Bone bill in the House and spoke on its behalf. When it passed and was signed into law by President Roosevelt, Maggie shared in the credit. But the all-encompassing issues created by World War II and the federal development of Pacific Northwest resources after the war had shifted his focus, and lately he had largely ignored NCI, now a component of the National Institutes of Health. In an effort to redirect his interest, I had written a fanciful puff piece that was published in the Fraternal Order of Eagles national magazine *Eagle*, titled "Magnuson: Congress' Chief Cancer Fighter." I stretched the truth shamelessly, but the article did succeed in mildly rekindling his interest. Still, we needed something special for him to accomplish.

Mary Lasker and Florence Mahoney provided it. They had devoted their lives to promoting medical research and were always alert to new opportunities to further the cause. The Veterans Administration's hospital budget of $600 million was coming to the Senate floor after the Easter recess, they said, and not one cent was earmarked for research. Could I get Magnuson to offer a floor amendment—to provide a modest $10 million for research? I put the question to him the next morning. "Yes, I can do that," he said cryptically. "But you have to get Dirksen to cosponsor it with me. He has several VA hospitals in Illinois, so he should go along."

Charging up to Senator Everett Dirksen's office with the message "Maggie sent me," I was ushered in to see the famous Illinois orator. He dragged hard on a cigarette as I laid out the proposition. "It's a good idea," he allowed, speaking in the softly sonorous voice that a nation had come to recognize instantly. Then he paused and dragged again. "But we must be sure that the VA medics do not use the vets as guinea pigs for something unsavory that would cause bad press. If I can be so assured, I will be pleased to go with my friend Maggie on his amendment."

I reported the conversation back to the Mesdames Lasker and Mahoney, and they said that the VA would provide the assurances that Dirksen wanted. Three days later, on a near-empty Senate floor, Magnuson and Dirksen mumbled at each other from their desks for fewer than five minutes, and the deed was done. Following a House-Senate conference on the VA budget, in which the $10 million was retained, the VA now was in the medical research field just like that. I asked myself: Can it really be that easy to do things around here? For a day or so I was walking on air. Wondrous indeed were the ways of Washington.

When I had arrived at Washington's National Airport in mid-April, Wayne Morse had been there to greet me. I was surprised to see him and embarrassed when he insisted on carrying my bags to his car. He wanted my services in his upcoming senatorial campaign and had found out my arrival time so he could meet me. Hell, yes, I was flattered.

Morse was another prime GOP target. His defection to the Democrats had enraged Republicans. I had run into Eddie Sammons, who had been his finance chairman, and asked him how he felt about it. He was almost apoplectic in his fury. Desertion was a cardinal sin, and Morse had to be politically shot at sunrise to demonstrate that it was punishable by political extinction. Eisenhower had dispatched Interior Secretary Douglas McKay west to do the job, with the promise that he would have all the tools he needed. McKay had been phenomenally popular in Oregon, amassing almost 70 percent of the vote in his last race for governor. Morse, winning twice as a Republican against weak opponents, had come nowhere near that.

Ambitious to build a record for myself, I was receptive to creating Morse's media campaign. He had been almost as successful as Magnuson in obtaining federal funding, and I was convinced that a "he brings home the bacon to Oregon" campaign could work as well south of the Columbia River as it had in Washington. Irv Hoff and Nordy Hoffmann approved my plan to help the Oregon maverick.

Morse had run twice on the notion that he was not a professional politician. "Principle above Politics" was the slogan that had dominated both of his campaigns, and it had become his mantra. It was nonsense. He was a pragmatic and sometimes unscrupulous operator, schooled in the often vicious orbit of campus politics. His real mantra was: "I'll get them before they get me." He liked being known as the "Tiger of the Senate."

I anticipated some protest from Morse to my idea of his running as a common pork-barreler, but it was merely pro forma. He was more than amenable to the idea of being portrayed as the Santa Claus who had brought all those federal dollars to Oregon while he was declaiming from the Senate floor against sin in all its manifestations. Under his cloak of selfless nobility, Morse was more than willing to do whatever it took to win. He was a pol after my own heart.

Putting together a "Morse Gets Things Done for Oregon" campaign was not difficult; in fact, it was largely a rewrite of past Magnuson and Jackson efforts. Later, I would be blessed when Bob Ginsburg, a talented political wordsmith, joined the Morse team in Oregon. As I was to learn many times over, there is nothing like having empathic colleagues when working several campaigns at once. Bob was a jewel and our work for Morse was superbly executed, although the campaign itself was fraught with moments of nail-biting crisis.

In August, Congress closed for the national conventions of both parties, and the focus of the Magnuson and Morse races shifted to home territory. In Seattle, rumors were rife that Langlie was planning to run a smear campaign, similar to his 1952 gubernatorial race against Hugh B. Mitchell. William C. Speidel, a Republican publicist known for "dirty stuff," had been heard bragging in Seattle bars about what was coming to "expose" Magnuson. Irv Hoff was so nervous that he had convinced Maggie that he could not even see his longtime friend in Seattle, a glamorous blonde divorcée named Jermaine Peralta. Jermaine had lived in Hollywood for years with her husband, a movie director, and was as sleekly beautiful as any film queen.

That was the problem. Maggie had had well-publicized romances with a bevy of Hollywood beauties, and Irv feared that Jermaine would just add to the "gone Hollywood" image of Magnuson that Langlie was preaching. So she stayed out of sight.

We learned that the Langlie campaign had ordered a major printing at several high-quality presses in Seattle. It was rumored to be the Magnuson exposé to end them all, a blockbuster that would blow our campaign to bits. On an early Saturday morning in September, I received a call from Bill Gregory, business agent of the Seattle local of the International Typographical Union. "I've got it," he said.

We met in Magnuson's hotel suite later that day. The "blockbuster" was a slick-print, magazine-size pamphlet titled "The Myth That Is Magnuson," and it was filled with pictures of old girlfriends, some scantily clad, and scandal-sheet articles about his playboy proclivities. A quick glance revealed nothing new; it was old stuff. We gathered around Magnuson, sitting in a wing chair, as he began reading the text out loud:

Once there was a senator who loved the purr of Cadillacs, the clink of
high-ball glasses and the rustle of lovely ladies shedding their clothes late
at night. Unfortunately this is no myth. This is the sordid and shocking
story of Washington state's senior senator—Warren Grant Magnuson.

Maggie stopped, an expression of wry disbelief on his broad Scandinavian face. "Hell, who doesn't like these things?" he snorted. "We're going to use this ourselves. Let's pass them out at our meetings. I'll say, 'Those of you who don't approve can leave, and I'll talk to the rest of you.'" And so the Langlie "bombshell" was defused. When it was mass-circulated in a statewide mailing by Langlie, little attention was paid, and its only impact was its documentation of the message that Langlie was conducting an ugly negative campaign.

Langlie next hit with a half-hour speech on statewide television, assailing Magnuson for "making false claims" about his record, in particular his role in shaping the fishing section of the treaty with Japan that closed out World War II. "John Foster Dulles wrote that treaty," said Langlie, "and he tells me that he doesn't even know Magnuson." Langlie's speech ended with two challenges to Magnuson: Reveal your income-tax records for the last five years and debate me on the big issues such as the power program.

Alone among our campaign-strategy team, I was strong for accepting the debate on the power issue. Certain that Magnuson couldn't lose on it, I wanted to see him draw a bucket of Langlie's blood. More mature heads wisely said: We're ahead. Why give him a big audience he couldn't otherwise get? They were right, but I still got my wish. At a Spokane reception, Magnuson encountered Lou Wasmer, manager of television station KREM, who challenged him: "Why are you afraid to debate? Everyone is talking about it." Stung, Magnuson snapped back: "Who said that I was afraid? I'll debate him." Wasmer quickly closed the deal. "I knew you would, Senator. I'll make the arrangements, and it will originate from KREM." Then he slipped off to call the local bureau of the Associated Press to announce it. The next morning it was front-page news.

"The Chiefs" met in emergency session, almost unanimous that anything should be done to get out of Magnuson's rash promise. My stance, that we had more to lose by chickening out, finally won converts, and eventually we agreed that there was no alternative. I was assigned the role of the candidate's "handler," with the warning to head for the Idaho line and keep going if it turned out badly.

I wasn't worried. Langlie had opposed just about every federal and local public power development within recent memory, even being hostile to the burgeoning aluminum industry that had located in the state to take advantage of a source of cheap, plentiful power. It was documented in newspaper stories and headlines that I had blown up to use in the debate. My own jousts with Langlie in my CVA days had convinced me that he would rattle when confronted with evidence he didn't expect.

KREM's small studio auditorium was packed with a predominantly Republican audience when we arrived. The governor presented his case first and, sure enough, took credit for just about every power development in the state, giving Magnuson an ideal opportunity to counterpunch his claims with the headlines. But as he began, I realized that he was confused about how to use the props I had created with the blown-up headlines and news stories. Standing off-camera, I cursed my frustration to Lou Wasmer.

Lou had nerve. "Crawl under the camera and hand the right ones up to him," he directed me. On hands and knees, I crept under the podium and passed the props up to Magnuson. If looks could kill, Langlie would have zapped me. Maggie caught fire and superbly demolished the governor's claims. The debate was as good as won. I crept back to Wasmer, relieved that Langlie had not had the presence of mind to ask that the camera be directed at me handing up the props. (Later he described the incident in speeches to show that Maggie needed a "servile stooge" with him at all times. The phrase became a term of endearment for me.)

Langlie did not issue anymore debate challenges after Spokane; and when I returned to Seattle, "The Chiefs" informed me that I had been damned lucky. They were right.

Howard MacGowan was *primus inter pares* in a raffish collection of hangers-on who Maggie had collected around him over the years. His official position was U.S. Collector of Customs for the Seattle district, a political job, but he was principally known as Magnuson's eyes and ears. With a patch over the eye that he had lost in China dominating a shrewd, sharply etched face, Mac looked like the buccaneer he professed to be. He had an idea a day, most of them off the wall. When more orthodox advisers complained, Magnuson silenced them by saying: "Yeah, Mac has ten ideas a week and nine are lousy, but the tenth is a beaut. And when was your last good idea?"

Mac was the master of what he called the "magoozle," a word that he claimed to have coined. Roughly interpreted, it was an unorthodox ploy or a trick play that completely fooled the other side. This time, he had two "magoozles" up his sleeve.

The Reverend S. C. Eastvold, president of Pacific Lutheran College in Tacoma, was the state's leading Lutheran cleric. He also was the father of Washington's attorney general, who was a Republican candidate for governor in the coming September primary. Donald V. Eastvold had come to instant television fame ("beware a young man with a book") when he defeated Senator Dirksen at the 1952 GOP convention on the procedural vote that opened the gate for Eisenhower's nomination. Now he had become notorious in his home state for his consumption of alcohol and his sexual exploits. His current inamorata was Ginny Simms, once a popular vocalist with Kay Kyser's band, who the candidate had taken around the state with him while his wife and their eight children remained at home. Eastvold was trailing the sedate and respectable Emmett Anderson in the polls.

The Reverend was desperate to do anything to help his son, and he found a "helper" in MacGowan. A letter was drafted that pointed out that only two true-blue Lutherans were running who should be supported: Republican Eastvold and Democrat Magnuson. (Langlie, like "Scoop" Jackson, had left the Lutheran Church to become a Presbyterian.) The letter, signed by Lutheran laymen, was sent to a list of some 70,000 Lutherans that Reverend Eastvold controlled. It didn't help his son, who lost. It was a classic Mac-Gowan "magoozle."

Mac's next one was even more audacious. The Reverend Oral Roberts had been spending his summers preaching in a huge tent near Renton, a blue-collar suburb of Seattle that housed the main plant of the Boeing Airplane Company. With many Boeing workers coming from the rural South, Roberts had drawn as many as 20,000 people to his Sunday gatherings. Mac scheduled Magnuson's appearance at Roberts's tent the Sunday before the primary, and the reverend introduced him with language that he normally reserved for Our Savior Himself. After Magnuson finished speaking and was leaving the stage, Roberts suddenly shouted: "Come back here, Brother Magnuson." When the perplexed senator did, Roberts threw his arm around his shoulder and proclaimed to the audience: "Brother Magnuson was too modest to tell you what he did for us poor preachers. He took the government tax off bus, train and plane tickets so that we could afford to come here and bring you the Lord's word."

Magnuson enjoyed needling Langlie's religious pretensions. He would read aloud from the Republican's literature, which was filled with hyperbolic adjectives such as "selfless," "God-fearing," and "pious." His audiences rocked with laughter as he sonorously rolled the words out. Then came his punch line: "It looks to me as if we'll have to watch this fellow at Easter-time."

Suddenly, it was mid-September and Primary Day, the day when we would learn where we really stood. Washington State has the nation's most open nominating system, the so-called blanket primary. It means that a voter can vote for anyone on the ballot, without regard to party affiliation. With Magnuson and Langlie both running unopposed, the primary vote would be a true indicator of what the November balloting would produce. The result exceeded our most hopeful expectations. Maggie carried thirty-eight of the thirty-nine counties, swamping Langlie by 155,000 votes. Neither Eisenhower's coattails nor some cooked-up scandal could salvage Langlie now. He had thrown his meanest punches, and they had boomeranged to hit him back.

Even so, there was to be no letup in our campaign effort. The Thursday after the primary, Magnuson was leaving in the campaign bus, a vehicle of 1938 vintage painted blue and gold, for a two-week tour through the state's smaller towns. My last "maverick" contribution to the campaign involved that bus.

John Cherberg, the deposed University of Washington football coach who had won the Democratic nomination for lieutenant governor, called me Wednesday to ask: What do I do now? I had an idea. John had been a longtime leader in the state high school coaches association and knew every coach in the state. Maggie already had expressed apprehension about going to towns where he had seldom been and didn't know anybody. Cherberg not only would be an ideal traveling companion, but he also could contact his coaching friends to make sure there were people on hand in every town to meet the bus. John said he would be ready to go on the morrow. When I told "The Chiefs," there was a roar of rage. This time I had gone too far. Irv Hoff had laid down the law: no deals with other Democratic candidates; "The Boss" is running on his own. But I held my ground and refused to call Cherberg and cancel him. No one else would either, and he went on the bus.

When your luck is running, it is running. Back from the bus tour, Maggie pulled me aside and said: "Keep Cherberg with me for the rest of this campaign. He knows everybody, and they like him. He had coaches and players there to meet us in every town. It made the trip."

Jermaine Peralta surfaced in Magnuson's suite election night, and we were happy to see her. She had borne her banishment with good grace, and Maggie's joy in her presence convinced me that it was a serious thing (they were married in the White House in 1964). Except for an occasional look at the television, no one but Scoop Jackson was paying that much attention to the vote. The only question was how big the margin would be. In the end, Magnuson won by 268,000 votes, a total made all the more remarkable because of Eisenhower's 145,000–vote margin in the state over Adlai Stevenson, the Democratic presidential nominee. It was an unprecedented triumph.

Next to Magnuson, I probably was the happiest fellow around that night.

Wayne Morse had easily defeated Doug McKay in Oregon, and thirty-two-year-old political novice Frank Church, my "sleeper" candidate, had overwhelmed Idaho's senator, Herman Welker, even though Ike had swept both states. It was my first political trifecta, a three-horse parlay, and I was drunk with joy well before I touched my first drop of liquor. Now I was certain that I had the formula that would elect Democrats anywhere that I chose to go. I humbly accepted congratulations, but I knew that I was the new political king of the mountain.

I watched Magnuson that night, suddenly sad that all of us would be parting company. He was not given to braggadocio, but I knew the satisfaction that the victory had brought him. The circumstances of his birth and upbringing had scarred him with an underlying insecurity, a nagging doubt as to whether or not he really belonged. He was only really comfortable with people outside the so-called establishment. Langlie had tried to exploit this vulnerability by challenging his legitimacy as a true representative of the state. Now the people, in a mighty outpouring from every county, had removed any doubt that might have lurked in his mind. They wanted him. How sweet it was. Garcia Vega cigars and chilled Smirnoff vodka had never tasted better, with Jermaine again by his side.

A couple of days after the election, Maggie called us together and announced that he had his income-tax returns ready for release to the media. Why now? we chorused. "Because I don't want anyone to think that there is anything suspicious there," he said. "I just didn't want to give Langlie the satisfaction of having forced me to do it." Johnny Salter looked them over carefully. "Hell, Maggie, I thought you were rich," he scoffed. "You're a piker, just like the rest of us." The story, buried inside the state's newspapers, went totally unnoticed.

4

FROSTY

COMING UP ON THE 1956 ELECTIONS, I HAD A SCORE TO SETTLE
with someone over something that had been simmering in my psyche for
some time. Curiously, the object of my animus would have only vaguely recognized my face and certainly not my name. My *bête noire* was Herman
Welker, Idaho's junior senator. Elected in 1950, Welker—a former movie-
industry "fix-it" lawyer—had been Joe McCarthy's leading acolyte in the Senate. Politicians in those years were black or white to me, and no one was
blacker than Herman Welker. His record and general deportment had been
outrageous, so much so that even conservative columnist Holmes Alexan-
der had written of him: "He mercifully should be retired by the voters of
Idaho."

My abomination of him, however, was not political; it was financial.
When I had left Idaho in August 1946, I had passed on my $25–a-month
retainer as stringer scout for the Pittsburgh Pirates to Tom Tuttle, baseball
coach at Payette High School (which later was to produce the home-run
slugger Harmon Killebrew). He knew of my abiding, almost proprietary interest in Vernon Law and my hope that he would sign with Pittsburgh when
he graduated from Meridian High School in May 1947. A covey of major-
league scouts had other ideas. Vernon had been discovered. Tuttle called
me in Seattle, where I was the music and book critic of the *Post-Intelligencer*,
and asked if I could come to Boise for Vernon's graduation weekend, when
he most likely would be signed. Six other major-league clubs were offering

48

contracts, Tuttle said. He wanted me there because "Mrs. Law likes you." I did not drink coffee or smoke cigarettes, and my mother had taught me deferential manners, especially in the presence of older women.

A horde of scouts was clustered in the lobby of the Hotel Boise when Tuttle and I walked in—Joe Devine of the Yankees, who had discovered Joe DiMaggio, Tony Lazzeri, and Frankie Crosetti; Johnny Moore of the Boston Braves; Howie Haak of the Brooklyn Dodgers; and my Ogden, Utah, friend, George "Highpockets" Kelly of the Cincinnati Redlegs. Tuttle and I felt like army recruits tossed in with a bunch of Congressional Medal of Honor winners.

Bing Crosby, who was from Spokane, Washington, and a major investor in the Pirates, had heard about Vernon Law, and he wanted to come up with a good player from his home digs. Before leaving the Pittsburgh organization, Babe Herman, the Pirates' chief western scout, had persuaded Crosby that the Mormon youngster was a hot prospect. Crosby had contacted Welker, who had returned to Idaho following his eight-year sojourn in Hollywood as a law partner of Jerry Giesler, a famous "fix-it" operator, and authorized him to do whatever it took to sign Law.

The Law family was what we called "true Mormons." They followed the teachings of founder Joseph Smith to the letter; and alcohol, coffee, and tobacco were taboo. So just about every one of the big-time scouts disqualified himself in the Law kitchen by lighting up a cigar or cigarette or maybe asking for a cup of coffee. Tuttle and I were hellers, but one wouldn't know it from looking at us. Tom looked like a pietistic Baptist deacon out of Oklahoma, which he once was. One of my more sardonic girlfriends used to call me "Jack Armstrong, the All-American boy," which gives you an idea. Besides, we had a hole card that the other scouts did not have. The Pirates had a farm team of the Class C California State League at Visalia, which was heavily populated with Mormons. By sending Vernon and his brother there, the Laws could be sure their teenage son was in good hands.

How much we influenced the signing I have no way of knowing, but I am sure that it was a lot more than Welker did. He was florid and Hollywoodian, and too much exposure to the senior Laws could have queered the deal. I went back to Seattle before the deed was done, and left Tuttle as the closer. Tom later told me that all he got was a $100 bonus from the Pirates and that Welker submitted a statement to them for $5,000. I was paid plane fare and the hotel. Tom was philosophical; he and his kin had suffered a lot worse in the Oklahoma droughts, he said. For years I burned with the injustice of it, and every time Welker did something outrageous in the Senate it fanned my ire.

I had seen Welker one other time. In June 1950, Bing Crosby had thrown a party at his home at Hayden Lake in north Idaho, where Welker announced his candidacy for the Senate seat held by Glen H. Taylor. Taylor had been Henry A. Wallace's running mate for vice president on the Progressive Party ticket in 1948, and prominent U.S. Communists had been among their supporters. This renegade foray was presumed to kill Taylor in Idaho, even though he had been a surprisingly good "pork chop" solon, adept at scrounging federal dollars for Idaho projects and people.

At Crosby's party, Welker's handlers had collected a crowd of American Legion and Veterans of Foreign Wars patriots interspersed with red-white-and-blue Republicans, and Welker delivered a stemwinder on fighting to save all we had won in World War II against the One Worlders and those Iscariots who would grovel to the Monsters of Moscow. I was on hand as a *Time* correspondent, and Welker paid cursory attention to me. I gathered that he regarded Henry R. Luce, *Time*'s publisher, as one of the One Worlders. (Welker was to win easily in the November election.)

In January 1951, I had been named information officer for the Pacific Northwest region of the Office of Price Stabilization (OPS), newly created to control prices during the Korean War. The appointments were controlled by Magnuson and Jackson, who was planning to run against Republican Senator Harry Cain in 1952. Jackson's strategy team saw the OPS as a heaven-sent vehicle to set up an embryonic statewide organization. Jackson's administrative assistant and best friend, John Salter, was named deputy regional director. Because OPS regulations required that each state have at least one high-grade official in the directorate, I was a "two-fer," used to represent both Oregon and Idaho. Salter and I went to Boise early on in Jackson's campaign to check out the OPS setup in Idaho.

Harry Yost, former Boise postmaster and longtime Democratic state senator, had been appointed state director, with D. Worth Clark, a former U.S. senator of dubious reputation, as counsel. We all went over to the Lamp-post Club in the Hotel Boise. Yost said he was going to hire two young lawyers who he thought were political comers: Carl Burke Jr. and Yost's niece's husband, Frank F. Church, a recent Stanford law school graduate and winner of the national American Legion oratorical contest. Church's nickname was Frosty.

So I at least knew who Church was when I read on the Associated Press regional wire in early 1956 that Church had announced for Welker's Senate seat, with Carl Burke as his campaign manager. He was thirty-one years old. His principal opposition was Glen Taylor, attempting yet another comeback as a "spoiler" with enough following to win a crowded primary but not enough to carry a statewide election.

At the time, I was the Pacific Northwest political agent for the United Steelworkers of America, and I had a sharp interest in the Idaho race. The USW was going after the membership of the International Mine, Mill and Smelter Workers, the successor to the Western Federation of Miners and a union that had been expelled from the CIO for "being under Communist domination." Much of Mine Mill's membership was located in Idaho's Silver Valley of the Coeur d'Alene. A Steelworkers' organizing drive could be helped by a friendly U.S. senator, and its legislative-political director, Nordy Hoffmann, was acutely aware of that possibility. My contacts with newspapermen and Idaho Democrats convinced me that Church had a real chance.

I arrived in Boise a couple of days after the August primary, which was still an undecided cliffhanger. While Welker had narrowly turned back Bill Holden, the Republican challenger, Church was hanging on to a 170–vote margin over Taylor, achieved through a late surge from Elmore County, a mining area south of Boise. Glen Taylor was screaming that major vote fraud had occurred in Elmore, and Republican Governor Robert E. Smylie was promising an investigation.

Meanwhile, Frank Church was the Democratic nominee—sort of, and just barely. That was the situation when we convened on U.S. District Judge Chase A. Clark's sun porch in Boise to plan the fall campaign. Clark, a former Democratic governor, was Church's father-in-law and a shrewd old hand in Idaho politics. Present were my old friend from Lewiston, Democratic National Committeeman Harry Wall; George Greenfield, the party's state chairman; Carl Burke Jr.; Church; and his wife Bethine. I wasn't too happy about the last entry; it had been my experience that wives offered little to such deliberations.

My trepidation about Mrs. Church was quickly confirmed. Early in my presentation of the media campaign, I recommended a heavy use of billboards. Her jaw set. "Democrats do not use billboards in Idaho," she informed me, rather grimly. "They are absolutely out." I was a veteran of three successful Senate campaigns and wasn't about to be second-guessed by some housewife, even though she did come from Idaho's most prominent political family. I commented that I hadn't come from Seattle at my own expense to sit through amateur night. Judge Clark eased the impasse by firmly suggesting to his daughter that her mother needed her help in the kitchen. She glared at me and left. The billboards stayed in the budget, and Bethine stayed in the kitchen.

Theming the campaign became the most important task at hand. I had sold the group on the idea that the campaign should be centered on a simple, saleable theme that would be believable to the people of Idaho. But what? How could the voters be convinced that a thirty-one-year-old tyro nicknamed Frosty, never elected to any public office, could properly represent the state in such an august and important body as the U.S. Senate? Claiming too much, that he "would make a great U.S. Senator," could backfire.

Harry Wall came up with the key word: pride. It had been suggested to him, he said, by Irv Hoff. Idaho once had had a senator in whom they had pride—William Borah, who had represented Idaho to the nation, even the world. Since then, the state had been held up to national ridicule by the likes of D. Worth Clark (Church's uncle-in-law), Taylor, and Welker. Young and inexperienced though he might be, Church—who came from a well-respected Idaho pioneer family—would not disgrace himself in the ranks of the high and the mighty. Thus, "Idaho Will Be Proud of Church in the U.S. Senate."

The theme caught on, as quickly as I ever have seen a campaign slogan take hold. "This kid may be young and inexperienced, but he's got good stuff," was a generally expressed comment. "At least, he won't disgrace us like the others have." The billboards that blazoned the pride message across the length and breadth of Idaho were a smash hit, even with the most anti-Madison Avenue Democrats. Mrs. Church never commented. (I later came to admire her political shrewdness and her total dedication to her husband's career. We eventually made up.)

We also used television, which was in its infancy in Idaho. With no live network programs to dominate scheduling, programming was either by film or live local shows. It made for a bonanza for the political shopper, as five- to fifteen-minute segments could be bought for a song. With Church's forensic ability, the medium was a natural for him, as long as he concentrated on speaking in conversational tones.

He could. The series of five-minute segments, which were filmed in the most primitive of conditions, turned out to be the finest political television I ever have been associated with. They were produced off-the-cuff—no scripts, no teleprompter, an amateur cameraman using a rudimentary single-system sound machine. Their initial showings established Church as a political heavyweight.

The best of the series was one that I vehemently opposed with all my conventional political wisdom. "Frank," I argued, "you can't touch foreign policy. Borah was the arch-apostle of isolationism. Idaho has to be the most parochially backward state in the nation on this issue. All we can do is ignore foreign policy and hope it never surfaces in the campaign." He shook his head. "Bethine and I went to all of the state's forty-four counties in the old Studebaker," he said. "Attitudes are changing. Television is largely responsible. Idaho people, even in the most remote areas, are discovering that there is a world out there and that we all are part of it. Besides, I think I have a way to make pragmatic internationalism palatable in the context of Idaho history."

The segment was filmed in Judge Clark's library. Church's only props were a globe, a basketball, a baseball, and a golf ball. His discourse went somewhat this way:

When the late and great Senator Williams Edgar Borah represented Idaho in the United States Senate, the world was this big [picks up large globe]. We thought we could mind our own business and let the rest of the world mind its business. It was a valid theory. It was a big world and we were three thousand miles away from almost everybody.

Senator Borah, my boyhood hero, died as World War II was beginning. That war proved that the isolationist theory was no longer valid. The technological advances it unleashed had shrunk the world to this size [picks up basketball]. Whether we liked it or not, we had to be involved with the rest of the world. The United Nations came out of this kind of thinking, and Republican Senator Arthur Vandenberg of Michigan—who had inherited Senator Borah's isolationist mantle—now led the USA into the UN.

Now, further technological advances have shrunk the world to this size [picks up baseball] and more is coming to make it even smaller [picks up golf ball]. In our lifetimes, developments we cannot imagine—such as those taking place in outer space—may shrink the world to the size of a pea.

We may not like it, but we cannot stop it. Idahoans understand and recognize that we have to live with this situation. Idaho's elected representatives must get their heads out of the sand. That is why I am running for the United States Senate.

The spot caused less of a furor in the isolationist heartland than I ever would have imagined. Church was right. Isolationism pretty much was dying of its own accord in the go-it-alone areas of the nation. Church had the courage and the conviction to stake out a position that not only turned out to be politically sound but that also helped eliminate a longstanding bug-a-bear from the American electoral scene.

I was determined to stay out of sight during my time in Boise. The basic reason: Jim Brown, general manager of the *Idaho Statesman*, still had it in for me for organizing the union there ten years earlier. I stayed out of old haunts, didn't contact friends, and generally laid low. But I did not go unnoticed. One night the phone rang in my room at the Hotel Boise. It was John Corlett, Idaho's most influential political columnist. "Joe," he said, "kick the dame out. I'm coming up." I cursed silently. John was a great guy and an old buddy, but the *Statesman* was all-out for Welker and now I was sure to be made an issue.

He put my mind at ease as he strode into the room. "I'm here to do anything I can to help you beat that rotten ex-roommate of mine," he declared. It turned out that he and Welker had bunked together in the Kappa Sigma fraternity at the University of Idaho in the early 1930s, and Corlett had some horror stories to tell.

Following law school, Welker had gotten himself elected attorney for Valley County, in which was located a beautiful resort area named Payette Lakes.

It was a great favorite with the Hollywood crowd, particularly the male stars on the Metro-Goldwyn-Mayer lot. One of them had impregnated a local fifteen-year-old girl—a clear case of statutory rape. Welker saw his way out of Idaho and into the glittering world of Hollywood, and Corlett told me that Welker had quashed the case. M-G-M made its payoff to the parents; and not a word appeared in the press. Welker's price was a partnership with Jerry Geisler, one of Hollywood's most prominent insider fixer attorneys. He had vaulted to the big time.

As with many aspiring newspapermen in the Depression, Corlett was not having an easy time of it. Three years after Welker had left Idaho, Corlett was in McCall, Idaho, promoting a Frontier Days fair for the local merchants. He had an inspiration. He called his old roommate in Hollywood and asked if he could get the actor—the one who had been responsible for the statutory rape—to be grand marshal of the parade. Welker called back. The actor would be delighted to come, and M-G-M's publicity department sent a raft of promotional material. The fair was rolling, its success assured.

Two days before it was to open, Corlett said, Welker arrived in McCall and met with his old roommate. "John," he said, "I want twenty-five hundred dollars in cash on the line, or there will be no star here for your parade." Corlett was forced to go to the merchants and raise the money, and he had detested Welker ever since. Now he was determined to pay him off.

One morning I inadvertently walked by the Welker headquarters. I looked in and saw C. A. Bottolfsen, the former governor, sitting at a desk, alone. I introduced myself and reminded him that I had covered him in Lewiston several times when he was governor. He brightened at that and asked me what I was doing now. I told him that I was a regional correspondent for *Time*, the *Reporter*, and the New York *Daily News*, all of which was true. I added that I was planning to write a piece on the Idaho Senate race and wanted to interview him. His title, I noticed, was campaign director. He was delighted to talk.

I asked him what Welker's biggest problem seemed to be. "The people of Idaho don't seem to know the senator," he confessed. "His record has been terribly distorted by this young fellow Church, and we haven't been able to get the true facts across. It has been particularly bad in south Idaho where the Mormon church is so strong. The papers down there use headlines like, 'Church Assails Welker Record' or 'Church Attacks Welker.' So people think that the LDS Church is against the senator. We are having an awful time with that one. I have told all the editors, but they keep doing it." I did my best to look sympathetic, but it was hard to keep from laughing.

Despite all these favorable developments, campaign contributions were not keeping Church's treasurer up late at night depositing checks. The entry of Glen Taylor into the race as an "independent" candidate—it was generally assumed he was financed by Welker to be a spoiler—had discouraged Democratic money men who assumed that Church didn't have a chance.

Florence Mahoney, a medical research lobbyist I knew in Washington, D.C., owned a ranch in the beautiful Stanley Basin north of Boise and had a strong interest in Church's campaign. She advised that we needed a private poll or survey to substantiate the contention that Church could win. I don't know how it was financed, but in record time the Louis Harris organization produced a survey that exceeded our wildest expectations. According to a sample of eight hundred randomly selected voters, Church easily defeated Welker, with Taylor running a distant third. Taylor's candidacy actually had helped Church by establishing him as the middle-of-the-roader.

The poll had broken the financial logjam, and the money flowed in. Maurice Rosenblatt and the newly created Committee for an Effective Congress sent checks almost every day. Organized labor, led by the Steelworkers union, came through handsomely. Irv Hoff called from Seattle to report that Bobby Baker and Scotty Peak were on their way to Boise with at least $10,000 for the campaign. Baker was Lyndon Johnson's chief operative on the Senate floor and had the reputation of being LBJ's "dog robber"—a scrounger and hustler. Peak was his sidekick, an assistant to Senator George A. Smathers of Florida. I thought of them as the Rosencrantz and Guildenstern of Senate Democratic politics. Carl Burke met with them. After much palaver and a recitation of their own importance, they turned over $7,500. Carl fixed a cool Norwegian eye on the money. "Where's the rest of it?" he demanded and proceeded to let the messengers know that Hoff had told him what to expect. After a bit of sputtering, the missing money was produced.

Suddenly there was plenty of money to close out the campaign with a bang. It was apparent that I would not be a campaign issue, so I called my old friend Robert F. Smith, public-relations director of Morrison Knudsen, the global contractors headquartered in Boise. He suggested that we meet for a drink. When I arrived at The Lamppost, there was a message that he would be late, so I settled into an easy chair with the newspapers. As I did, my eye caught those of a young woman reading a magazine. She smiled— radiantly. She was one of the most beautiful sights I had ever seen, auburn-haired with a heart-shaped face and glowing skin. I was unable to focus on what I was reading. I took another peek. Again, a dazzling smile.

Not much at barroom pickups, the third smile forced my hand. I put down the paper. "I am waiting for a friend, and I presume you are, too," I said. "Can I buy you a drink while we wait?" She said she would be delighted.

We were well into the second drink by the time Bob Smith arrived. When she left for the ladies room, he turned to me, wide-eyed. "Where did you find that?" he demanded. "I've lived here ten years, and I've never even seen anyone remotely resembling her. I'm going to get out of here. I'm the third man. But you have to promise me that you will tell me all about it in the morning."

He was gone when she returned. She didn't seem to notice, nor did she say anything about the lateness of whoever was supposed to meet her. After another drink or so, I tentatively suggested the idea of food. "There is a wonderful place across the street," she said. "It has a good combo, and we can dance." I pinched myself. This sort of thing just didn't happen to traveling salesmen or itinerant political operatives; it was the stuff of pulp fiction. We had a softly lit table in a corner, and the combo was playing Gershwin and Rodgers and Hart. She was soft and yielding on the tiny dance floor.

As the wine flowed, some cold realities, bit by bit, began to surface. Her voice slurred and rose in strident decibels as she poured out her hatred for "this lousy hick town" and its "crummy people." It finally turned out that she was married to an employee of the U.S. Weather Bureau who was stationed in Boise. "Dumbest thing I ever did," she said. She staggered a little as she went to the ladies' room again. My ardor by now thoroughly chilled, my thoughts centered on how I would get out of this one.

When she returned, she barely picked at her food. I tried to get her to eat, which inspired her to turn her ire on me. I was just like all the others, she slurred. Her skin was blotched and her eyes unfocused. I was afraid to leave her. How would she get home in that condition? While she was gone, I had looked up her address in the phone book. She lived on The Bench, a new area of Boise that I knew pretty well. She had her own car, she said, so I decided that I would drive her home and walk back to the hotel, which would help me sober up. After some argument, I took the wheel of her Buick Roadmaster, and she huddled against the door in the front seat. As I turned on to Main Street she lurched at the door. It suddenly swung open and she tumbled out, screaming as she hit the pavement.

It was past midnight, and the street was almost deserted. A group of people gathered on the sidewalk and stared curiously as I picked her up and put her on the front seat. I was asking an older passerby the quickest route to St. Luke's Hospital when the Buick suddenly revved up and off it went, both doors open. She raced the car down Main to Capitol Boulevard and careened around the corner. I walked back to the Hotel Boise, sick at the pit of my stomach. I envisioned the worst, a psychotic woman with a vengeful husband—who knows?

I locked the door to my room and called the Boise Police Department to describe what had happened. When I identified myself to the officer who answered the phone, he asked, "Do you happen to be the Joe Miller who was sports editor of the *Statesman* some years ago?" I was. He told me that he had been one of the high school all-stars whom I had picked in 1946 for the All-American Boys Game competition. My tense body unwound. He said he would send a car to check her house. A few minutes later, he called back to say that the car was in the driveway and that all was quiet. I thanked him profusely and fell into a troubled sleep.

The phone rang early. It was Bob Smith. "How was it, buddy?" he leered. I filled the phone with expletives. He laughed, mockingly. Subdued, I went back to Seattle for the windup of the Magnuson Senate campaign.

Harry Wall called me from Boise early election night to say that Frosty had won. The Harris poll turned out to be right on the money. As it unfolded that night, Church's surprise victory turned out to be the factor in preserving the Democrats' one-vote majority. The young senator-elect would go to Washington, D.C., with good credentials. Herman Welker never went back to Idaho. He died in December 1957 at Bethesda Naval Hospital of a brain disease that had been affecting him for some time. He was only fifty.

A few months later, we went on a Sunday picnic in Rock Creek Park with several couples, including the Churches. Later, I observed to John A.

Carver, Church's new administrative assistant, that "Frosty didn't seem much changed" from his Senate exposure thus far. Carver, a marvelously acerbic lawyer from Boise, gave me a sardonic smile. "Don't kid yourself," he said. "They all wear the invisible toga. It goes with the territory, just like that carapace of conceit that they put on once they are sworn in. It's the system around here."

I was to learn that it was all too true.

5

PROX

WISCONSIN SENATOR JOSEPH R. MCCARTHY HAD DIED A FEW DAYS
before, on May 2, 1957, and I was being ushered into Lyndon Johnson's baro-
nial office in the Senate wing of the Capitol by a curvy brunette with a smiling face. It was to be my first meeting with The Maximum Leader of the
Senate Democrats. I had arrived that week from Seattle with my family, ready
to take up my new job as campaign director of the Democratic Senatorial
Campaign Committee (DSCC), the election arm of the Senate Democrats.
I quickly learned from LBJ that I had to hit the ground running.

"Here's the situation in Wisconsin," he said without any warm-up. "It
looks as if we are going to be stuck with the same asshole for a candidate
who lost the governorship three times in a row, twice to Governor Walter
Kohler, who likely will be the Republican nominee. We tried to get Congressman Henry Reuss of Milwaukee to run in this special election, but he
did a damn fool thing. He met with Clem Zablocki, the senior Democrat in
the Wisconsin delegation, and said he would defer to him if he wanted to
run. Zablocki had no idea of running, has no chance, but damned if he didn't
get the bug—thanks to Reuss. So now we are going to be stuck with this
loser, what's his name? Proxmire."

"The reason we are in this is this," he continued without pause. "Now
there are forty-nine Democrats and forty-six Republicans in the Senate. A
Republican win in Wisconsin by itself would not affect our majority. But
what very few people know—and don't let it out of this room—is that Sen-

ator Matt Neeley of West Virginia is out at Bethesda Naval Hospital, and he's not coming back. How long he holds on is anybody's guess, Matt is a tough old bird, but when he goes, West Virginia has a Republican governor named Underwood, and he will appoint a Republican. That will create a 48–48 tie, Vice President Nixon will vote to break the tie, Bill Knowland will become majority leader, and your padrone, Senator Magnuson, will have to step down as Commerce Committee chairman." Once again, and for the third straight election, control of the U.S. Senate was being placed in my managerial hands.

Johnson did not waste any more time on me. He got up abruptly and headed for his inner chambers. "By the way," he said in parting, "my birthday is August 28, the day of that special election. I expect you to bring back what's-his-name to me as a birthday present." He half extended a limp left hand for me to shake and left.

I went back to the Senate whip's office shaking my head. It was inhabited by Earle C. Clements of Kentucky, who had been Johnson's hugely popular whip until his surprise eyelash defeat in November by Thruston B. Morton. Michael J. Mansfield of Montana had succeeded Clements as whip but wanted little part of the oft-onerous duties of that role. Johnson had cajoled Clements into staying on as director of the Democratic Senatorial Campaign Committee and keeping his old office. I was to become Clements's main campaign man.

Clements wasn't in the office that day, but his twenty-three-year-old daughter Bess Abel was. She looked up from her typewriter and asked, "What did you think of the leader?" Magnuson had forewarned me: "Johnson is absolute King of the Hill, more powerful than any Bourbon king. He expects to be treated as a demigod, particularly by staffers. Don't forget it." I gave Bess the correct answer: "great," "brilliant," "awe-inspiring." She gave me a mocking smile. "Joe, I bet that you're a lousy poker player," she said.

I was relieved to learn from Clements that I did not have to take the next plane to Wisconsin. Zablocki was opposing Proxmire in the primary, and the DSCC had to stay out. So I settled my wife and two daughters in a big house overlooking Rock Creek Park and began interviewing everyone I could find who knew anything about Wisconsin politics.

Andy Biemiller, former Democratic congressman from Milwaukee and now the legislative director of the newly merged AFL-CIO, was the most insightful. He and everyone else to whom I talked expanded on what LBJ had crudely intimated—that William Edward Proxmire was indeed an *avis raris* in American politics, one who played completely outside the established rules of the game. From a wealthy Lake Forest Park, Illinois, family, Proxmire had moved to Wisconsin after Yale, Harvard Business School, and the J.P. Morgan Company for the express purpose of carving out a political career in a state that he had analyzed as ripe for the election of a Democrat. Not long after going to Madison as a reporter for the supra-liberal *Capital Times*, Proxmire had gone door-to-door to win a seat in the state legislature. In the next election, in 1952, he had captured the Democratic nomination for governor in the first of three losing tries for that office. In the process, he had alienated just about every Democratic stalwart in the state.

I arrived at Milwaukee's Billy Mitchell Field on the late afternoon of the primary election. A gray-mustached, imposing man was ushered off the Northwest Airlines flight ahead of the rest of us and was greeted at the foot of the ramp by a gaggle of newspaper photographers and television cameramen. I recognized him as Victor Johnston, executive director of the Republican Senatorial Campaign Committee and my opposition. The waiting reporters hustled him inside for interviews, and I exited quietly. LBJ had made it clear that staffers should keep their names out of the papers.

Philleo Nash, the Democratic state chairman, was there to meet me. I recognized his rotund form and white hair from past Democratic national conventions. Even though the polls had yet to close, he informed me that the Milwaukee *Journal* already was projecting Proxmire as an easy winner. The candidate was eagerly awaiting me, Philleo said, in his victory suite at the Antlers Hotel. I was not naive enough to think that it was my charming personality or political brilliance that he was awaiting. Clements had given me a substantial batch of campaign contributions (mostly checks) to be made out to the winner of the primary, and Proxmire knew that I had them. Clements had promised that all checks coming through the DSCC would be sent to me. I had heard a multitude of stories about Proxmire's refusal to take professional direction and his insistence that he would run his campaign his way. I had my own ideas, tested in five winning Senate campaigns, and I knew that I had to control the money if I was going to put my ideas into effect on this new political battlefield.

The Antlers turned out to be a fleabag. Proxmire's regular room, the "victory suite," cost $1.50 per night. It was filled with greasy-haired youths in jeans and black leather jackets—the Young Democrats, I was informed. The refreshments consisted of bite-sized pieces of Wisconsin cheddar cheese, washed down with half-pint cartons of Wisconsin milk. After exchanging a few meaningless banalities with the victorious candidate, I drew Philleo aside and said, "Let's get the hell out of here." Philleo's smile was cherubic.

Minutes later, we were on the street. "Where is Zablocki's headquarters?" I asked. "Serb Hall on the south side," he said. "Let's go and commiserate with Clem. At the least we'll get some decent drinks there."

It turned out to be a brilliant political stroke. We walked into a scene of stoic resignation as Proxmire's plurality kept mounting. Zablocki had seen it coming and was consoling his supporters as we arrived. He was delighted to see us. "Here's the state chairman and LBJ's man from Washington," he shouted to his supporters. "They're not with Proxmire tonight. They're here because they want to be with us!"

Suddenly, Philleo and I were celebrities. We must have shaken a jillion Polish hands and hoisted almost as many horns of Milwaukee's finest that night. At least I felt that way the next morning in my Pfister Hotel room, my head throbbing when the phone rang. It was LBJ and Clements demanding a detailed analysis of Proxmire's prospects based on my eleven hours on the scene. I mumbled on, faking it until Johnson asked, "What's the candidate like?" "Just like you said, Leader, an asshole," I replied. He indicated that I should show more respect. "What do you think of a guy who eats birdseed and drinks sauerkraut juice for breakfast?" I said. He did not have an answer for that one.

My showdown with Proxmire came later that day. He had asked me to meet him in Watertown, where he was doing a talk show on a local radio station. Leonard Zubrensky, one of his few real supporters among mainstream Democrats, drove me there. A labor lawyer with a wicked sense of humor, Len was completely candid about his candidate. "He is not a normal human being as you and I know one," he told me. "He will do anything, say anything, sacrifice anyone or anything in order to succeed. Nothing else, not even his wife or his children, matters to him when it is measured against political success. You must know that."

Prox, as everybody called him, and I sat by ourselves on a bank overlooking the Wisconsin River. "I have my campaign all planned," he began. "We have some real good television buys in fifteen- and thirty-minute segments."

I cut in quickly. "Bill, it is summertime. People are swimming and fishing. The Braves are in a hot pennant race. Who is going to listen to, pardon me, a three-time loser talk for fifteen or thirty minutes about things they really don't give a damn about?"

He clouded over. "I am going to run my own campaign. I will not take outside dictation from anybody, and that includes LBJ and his minions."

Pulling the batch of campaign checks from my pocket, I replied: "It's a free country and that works both ways. I am not going to waste my time and these campaign funds on the kind of foolishness you are talking about. Say the word, and I will throw these checks into the river and be on the next plane to Washington."

It worked. He would immediately issue a press release announcing that I was running the campaign. I nixed that one. Could I work with his wife Ellen, who had always run his campaigns? I could. She had impressed me as the most sensible and least reverent person around him. We went to his old house in Blooming Grove on the outskirts of Madison. Ellen mixed a large shaker of martinis (Prox did not partake) and cooked a good meal, and we ended the long day with a working relationship. I gave Ellen the checks.

My first target was organized labor, which we had to have with us. Andy Biemiller, the AFL-CIO lobbyist, had warned me to expect some discontent with Prox, but nothing like the hostility I encountered. Charley Schultz, a 250–pound autoworker who headed the Wisconsin CIO, was loud and profane in the Eagles Club bar as he told me what "a double-crossing, ungrateful son-of-a-bitch" Proxmire was. The smartest tactic, I decided, was to make no rejoinder. Schultz did give me what I wanted. He agreed to call a meeting of the state CIO executive board to decide whether or not to endorse Prox.

As a past vice president of the Washington state CIO, I was invited to the meeting to present the case for Proxmire. My pitch was brief. "I am not here to make a case for the candidate. Instead, I am speaking for the self-interest of the labor movement." I described how the Republicans would take over the Senate if Kohler were to win. "You may not like Senator McClellan and Bobby Kennedy running the Senate labor rackets committee," I ended, "but how would you like it run by Barry Goldwater and all those right-wing Republicans?"

There was a silent moment. Then John Giacomo, a razor-mustached steel-worker, brought a ham-sized fist down on the conference table. "Move to endorse," he thundered. It was unanimous. The campaign was off the ground.

It was tougher with the AFL (that body had yet to merge with the CIO on the state level). George Haberman, a surly plumber who was president, gutturally told me: "I hate him so bad I won't even say his name." And the endorsement that we eventually hacked out of them at their Green Bay con-vention did not mention Prox by name. Still, it was enough.

The Republicans were not without their own troubles. Kohler, a mod-erate, had narrowly won his primary against Congressman Glenn Davis, the current darling of the Wisconsin right-wing McCarthy crowd. Davis, refus-ing the customary concession and endorsement of the winner, had gone back to Washington, D.C., in sullen silence. His supporters were sitting on their hands.

Zablocki, despite his cordiality to Nash and me, was also sitting it out. This was serious. We had to win big in his fourth district to have any chance at all. It was a Slavic enclave—Polish, Serbian, Croatian, Slovenian. Though they were solidly labor and Democratic, Joe McCarthy's class war against Ivy League, State Department "traitors" had made its inroads. Prox was hardly a "shot and a beer" type of candidate with whom they were comfortable.

This was clearly evident in the project that Philleo Nash had embarked on with his sidekick Rod Riley, a former public opinion analyst with the Elmo Roper organization. Riley had designed a one-page questionnaire, to be carried on a clipboard, and Young Democrat chapters in Wisconsin's ten congressional districts had taken on randomly interviewing people in shop-ping centers. The results were stunning. Prox and Kohler were in a virtual dead heat, and the undecideds were concentrated in what could be called the "Joe McCarthy belt"—Catholic Democratic south Milwaukee, Racine, and Kenosha, up to Fond du Lac through the Fox River Valley, and into Appleton and Green Bay. Winning this bloc back onto the Democratic col-umn was the key to the election. It was that simple.

We had had all kinds of offers of campaigners from outside—senators Hubert Humphrey and Estes Kefauver and governors Soapy Williams and Orville Freeman, among others. I said no to all of them. "They're old hat here and won't swing a vote," Paul Ringler of the Milwaukee *Journal* had warned me. There was only one outsider that could do Prox any good—the "poster boy" of the 1956 Democratic convention, Senator John F. Kennedy of Massachusetts. He had lost the vice-presidential nomination by an eyelash to Kefauver and by doing so had made an indelible impression on a nationwide television audience. The Proxmire campaign had to have him to swing the largely Catholic undecideds.

CIO leaders, led by the Steelworkers' Walter J. Burke, were coming alive to the possibility of a political coup. The rudimentary machinery existed for a massive get-out-the-vote (GOTV) effort with union members and their families in Wisconsin's industrial centers, including Milwaukee. It never had been tried, but we decided to push our chips into GOTV. At that moment, a heavenly creature dropped into our laps—Esther Higgins Murray, women's activities director of the AFL-CIO's Committee on Political Education, or COPE. A one-time congressional candidate, Esther brought know-how and charm into the GOTV effort. She soon had two shifts of labor unionists working from eight in the morning to midnight, and she worked with them every second. Enthusiasm began to percolate among cynical veterans who hadn't seen a Democrat elected to a major statewide office since New Deal days twenty-five years before. Every day brought more volunteers to work the banks of phones we had installed for the effort. You could feel something building.

Proxmire had been traveling the state, shaking hands at plant gates, shopping centers, and ballparks, pounding out press releases on his portable Royal typewriter in the back seat of an old Nash. The press releases were published—on the back pages of the state's newspapers—but there was little media interest in the campaign. That was fine with us. We wanted the Republicans to be complacent, to go through the motions of a campaign.

Money for the all-out closing days of the campaign was beginning to materialize. Clements called me one day in great excitement and said that I, and only I, was to meet a courier at Billy Mitchell Field on a Capitol Airlines flight at ten o'clock that night. I did, and he gave me a thick envelope. It contained $10,000 in $100 bills, an under-the-table contribution from a corporation that was angry with President Eisenhower for vetoing a natural-gas deregulation bill in 1956. It was Proxmire's largest contribution.

Jerry Bruno was becoming indispensable to me. A roly-poly, rumpled Italian American of irrepressible humor and native political sagacity, Jerry was on unpaid leave from his $90–a-week job as a forklift operator at the Nash Motor Company in Kenosha. He took tough assignments and kept coming back for more. Example: I needed a spy at Kohler headquarters (I always had one in the opposition camp), and Jerry recruited his sixteen-year-old nephew. Every night, the youth brought us Kohler's daily schedule, press releases, internal campaign memos, anything he could pick up. We knew everything they were doing—which wasn't much.

As our GOTV program began to take shape, Bruno brought me a jewel—a sallow, chain-smoking reporter from the Kenosha *Evening News* named Gerard Clark. "He knows where our votes are," Bruno said by way of introduction. Clark showed me the most remarkable set of precinct maps I had ever seen, all coded and marked to show where the historic Democratic votes were to be found. They turned out to be as pinpoint accurate as a satellite camera, and Clark quickly became the master navigator of our GOTV.

More good news. Zablocki, while still harboring bad feelings about Prox, was coming aboard with his organization. He had agreed to sign an endorsement letter to be mass-mailed in his district and to turn loose his people in the closing drive.

Jack Kennedy remained a problem. I wanted him for at least one day in the campaign's last week, but he hadn't committed to a date to LBJ, the master persuader, or his best friend Senator George Smathers, the new chairman of the Democratic Senatorial Campaign Committee. We already had planned the day, and I was starting to bite my nails. Figuring that he couldn't turn us down, we projected a dawn-to-midnight day from Milwaukee to Green Bay so full that there would be barely enough time for him to relieve himself. The morning before The Day, the sword fell. LBJ called me to say that Kennedy had said no. "The rackets committee has Jimmy Hoffa on the stand, and Jack wants to get the TV coverage," Johnson, obviously disgusted, said. "I gave him both barrels, but he wouldn't budge."

The conversation was ending, and I was desperate. "Do you mind if I call him and explain the situation from the field?" I asked. I could sense his disbelief. If he couldn't do it, how could a mere staffer and new kid on the block? He grunted and hung up.

I took it to be an assent and called Evelyn Lincoln, Kennedy's personal secretary. I went right to the point. "Mrs. Lincoln, we both know that Senator Kennedy is not running for vice president in 1960. You as a midwesterner know the tremendous importance of the Wisconsin presidential primary. Just look at what happened to Taft, Willkie, and MacArthur. Now, as to this situation, the Dems have their first chance to win a Senate seat in twenty-five years, and they are excited about it. I would hate to have to tell them that the senator refused to come out and help them in their hour of need because he was going to get some television coverage."

It was blunt talk, but I could sense that Mrs. Lincoln was receptive. "Give me your number, Mr. Miller," she said, "and the senator will call you back in ten minutes. He is at the rackets committee now."

I barely knew Kennedy. In Idaho the year before, Carl Burke and I had talked him into an extra campaign appearance at Twin Falls for Frank Church on the assurance that Church would upset Senator Herman Welker. He had, and I hoped that being right would enhance my status with Kennedy. He remembered all right. "I am still quivering from that miserable private plane flight from Twin Falls to Reno that you and Burke talked me into," he began. "Now, as to Wisconsin, I have been reliably told that, one, Prox-mire is a prime horse's ass and, two, he can't possibly win. So what's the purpose of my coming?"

"I won't argue with point one," I replied. "He is. But, as to two, you have been misinformed. He has a real chance." He then asked probing and inter-ested questions and, suddenly—*mirabile dictu*—I knew that I had him.

It was a beautiful late August morning at Mitchell Field, a cool breeze blow-ing off Lake Michigan. The Young Democrats were there with a band, flatbed trucks, and pickups with banners to stage a parade onto Mitchell Street in south Milwaukee, the Great White Way of Slavland.

The parade's first stop was at a park to allow Kennedy to place a wreath on the statue of Thaddeus Kosciusko, a Revolutionary War general from Poland. "What do you know about him?" Kennedy whispered to me as we accompanied a bemedalled and bannered band of Polish-American Alliance officials to the statue. "Revolutionary War hero," I muttered. Kennedy was masterful. "Noble Polish patriot carrying the torch of freedom from the Old World to the New. From a land that has known the cruel tread of the con-queror to help the people of a new land shed their shackles." It went over big with the Polish-American Alliance crowd. Zablocki was beaming.

Mitchell Street thronged with people. The crowd surged along with the lead car, Prox shaking hands and Kennedy smiling, with Zablocki glowing like a *pater familias* at a family banquet. "Who are those two guys with you, Clem?" came a holler, and the crowd laughed.

When we reached the Pfister Hotel, Kennedy went into a private meeting requested by the leaders of Milwaukee's small but influential black community. He had been the only Northern Democrat to vote against bypassing the Judiciary Committee, chaired by arch segregationist James O. Eastland of Mississippi, and taking the 1957 voting rights bill directly to the Senate floor. I was nervous but shouldn't have been. His explanation came across plausibly, and he charmed the black leaders almost effortlessly. The luncheon in the hotel ballroom was an overflow sellout, and Kennedy's low-key pitch for Prox was so compelling that all I could think of was television. We've got to get this on the tube, I decided, and play it as much as possible.

Afterward, our entourage headed for the A. O. Smith plant gate, so that Kennedy and Proxmire could shake hands with the workers at the shift change. Proxmire was missing, and Bruno left on the run to find him. At the plant, Kennedy turned out to be adept at trading quips with the departing workers. Prox finally showed for picture-taking, and we left for a suburban airport to fly to the Republican Catholic strongholds of Appleton and Green Bay. I broached the idea of Kennedy filming or taping some TV spots. He responded warmly. "It seems to be my best medium," he said. Luckily, WBAY, the Catholic Brothers station at Green Bay, had recently installed the latest in taping equipment. Kennedy did the spots off-the-cuff, in one or two takes, and right then and there I decided that I had found my candidate for president in 1960.

Election Day, August 28, was overcast but comfortable. To get away from the telephone I went to our get-out-the-vote phonebank operation and hung around, bringing coffee to the phone operators and driving senior citizens to the polls. It gave me something to do and calmed my usual jitters. Late that afternoon, I headed over to the Milwaukee *Journal* city room with Frank Wallick, editor of the *Wisconsin State CIO News*, to see what they had.

The city edition was on the street, and most of the editorial staff had gone home for supper. The political writers—Ed Bayley and Paul Ringler—and managing editor Wally Lemieux had stayed and you could see excitement on their faces. The rural precincts upstate, which closed at five and six o'clock, were reporting in on the teletypes—and it was all Proxmire. The election was over before the polls in the Democratic strongholds of Milwaukee, Madison, Kenosha, and Racine had closed. Richard Scammon, a noted analyst of voting patterns, shouted as the teletypes kept bringing in more upstate returns. "Look at this. The LaFollette progressive vote is going en bloc to Proxmire. I've never seen anything like it."

I headed for the Wisconsin Hotel and our election-night party. Jerry Bruno had hustled several kegs of beer out of the Pabst Brewing Company, and the hotel, a comfortable fleabag in which I had been staying in a $16–per-week room, had offered us its ballroom, bar, and lobby rent-free for the party.

The place was throbbing. Numbers were coming in fast, and it was all Proxmire and more Proxmire. The CIO's GOTV effort was producing spectacular numbers in Jerry Clark's targeted precincts, Jack Kennedy had led the Catholic, ethnic, and blue-collar Democrats back to the fold, and Prox's lead topped 100,000 by nine o'clock. The bartenders couldn't pour drinks fast enough.

Victory-starved Democrats, many who hadn't been seen for years, flooded into the hotel. They overflowed into the rainswept street, where a musicians-union band was playing "Happy Days Are Here Again" over and over again. The hotel's ancient switchboard was jammed with phone calls, many from big-name Democrats trying to find out what kind of weird political earthquake had taken place in a solid Republican state that had given Eisenhower a 400,000–vote plurality just ten months before.

One of the hotel's phone operators reached me in the crowded lobby. "Joe," she said, "Adlai Stevenson has been waiting in a country store in Ontario for two hours to find out what happened. Please talk to him." He wanted a cogent analysis of what had happened, and I, a little drunk, was unable to provide it. "What were the factors at work to cause such a massive vote shift?" he wanted to know. "Hell, governor, Proxmire talked to the LaFollette progressives in language they could understand. Jack Kennedy talked to the Catholic McCarthyites in language they could understand. We identified our vote and got it out. That's about it." He wanted more for his two-hour wait in a country store, but it was the best I could do.

The crowd finally thinned out, and I went to bed near dawn, the adrenaline still pumping. I was awakened after an hour or so of sleep by a call from Clements. It was the last day of the first session of the 85th Congress, and

Bill Knowland, the minority leader, had graciously agreed to waive the usual formal certification of election to allow Vice President Nixon to swear Proxmire in if we could get him there. The national media finally had discovered the Wisconsin campaign. The *New York Times*, *Time*, *Newsweek*, CBS, and NBC—they were there to find out what had happened. *Life* magazine had sent two of my old colleagues, photographer Howard Grey Villet and reporter Jane Estes, who told me that *Life* had slated Prox for the five-page lead story in the next issue.

I had hardly seen Prox on election night. I went up to the room where he and Ellen were staying and told him about the *Life* story. "That settles that," he said to Ellen. "Your kids can't go with us. The picture captions in *Life* will have to say that the children are yours by a former husband and will probably point out that we both have been divorced. I can't afford that. I have to run again in fifteen months and they will be out to get me."

Ellen dissolved in tears on my chest. The phone rang, and he went to answer. He was on for a long time as she sobbingly told me that she had promised her young children a trip to Washington, D.C., to stay with their grandparents if he won. Proxmire got off the phone with a bemused expression on his face. "That's how those *U.S. News and World Report* interviews are done. I would have thought they would have at least given me warning." He ignored Ellen's agitated state. "Let's take the four o'clock Northwest flight," he continued. "It gets us in a little after six. Lyndon told me they'll be in session late."

Washington National Airport looked like a movie set with klieg lights illuminating a big crowd and spotlights probing the sky as the plane taxied to the terminal. Just about every Democratic senator from Eastland to Douglas was there to greet Prox, who bounded down the ramp like a conquering Caesar. A U.S. Marine band was playing on the steps of the Senate as we entered to a gala reception that Johnson had thrown together to enable the Senate and selected insiders to meet the newest hero. It was a magic night, and the glow was still there when I turned out the lights at four in the morning.

Clements and I met the next day. We knew that something big had happened in Wisconsin, but what was it? Our best guess: the political momentum was shifting to the Democrats despite President Eisenhower's recent drubbing of Adlai Stevenson. With twenty-two Senate Republicans, mostly reactionaries, and only eleven Democrats up for re-election in 1958, the prospects for a Democratic surge were more than promising. Clements and I eventually traveled from Maine to California seeking candidates to exploit the possibilities. The Democrats ended up winning a record sixteen new seats and made similar gains in the House of Representatives.

Kennedy's prospects for the presidency were greatly enhanced. His role in Proxmire's campaign was widely publicized, and he quickly became the Democrat most in demand as a campaigner. Even though he had a nominal race for re-election in Massachusetts in 1958, he campaigned across the country that year in his own plane with all the hoopla and trappings of a presidential candidate.

The one day Kennedy spent in Wisconsin provided him with the nucleus of a strong campaign organization that ultimately enabled him to beat Hubert Humphrey in the first significant primary of 1960. He took my advice and hired Jerry Bruno as his man in Wisconsin, and Jerry went on to earn his reputation as the best advance man in politics. Organized labor found its future major role in politics in Wisconsin. The AFL-CIO produced a documentary on the GOTV effort called "The Wisconsin Story," which it used to educate its membership. Esther Murray and Jerry Clark, now political director of the AFL-CIO's biggest union, the American Federation of State, County and Municipal Employees, traveled the country telling local labor bodies how to do it.

Proxmire's victory encouraged State Senator Gaylord A. Nelson to run for governor in 1958 against incumbent Vernon Thomson. His conservation program for Wisconsin, paid for by increased tobacco taxes, won plaudits from liberals and conservatives alike and eventually propelled him to the U.S. Senate, where, as the creator of Earth Day, he made ecology and the environment a cutting-edge issue for the national agenda.

As for Proxmire, he went on to serve almost thirty years in the Senate, a strange loner who ran to work every day, sponsored no major legislation, and is most remembered today for a cheap publicity gimmick called the Golden Fleece award, which was nothing more or less than a mindless attack on the idea of research.

Sic transit gloria.

6

WINNING BIG

BILL PROXMIRE'S SURPRISE VICTORY IN WISCONSIN BROUGHT ME
onto the Washington political stage with a fanfare. Before that, not one line
of type had been printed about my campaign efforts. That was by design. A
provincialism in American politics had made the outside "expert" a sinister
figure who manipulated local candidates as a ventriloquist or puppeteer would.
Campaigns were supposed to be free of "foreign" influence, so political gun-
slingers like me were sometimes put up in obscure hotels under aliases and
hidden in the campaign closet. We were the faceless people of politics.

That kind of anonymity was denied me by an event on August 28, the
night of the Wisconsin special primary. It also was the night of Philip Stern's
bachelor party. As news of Proxmire's victory was reported, Phil, research
director of the Democratic National Committee and a Sears Roebuck heir,
was being feted by Washington's Democratic power elite. My name was mentioned, and Alfred Friendly, managing editor of the *Washington Post*, asked
who I was. He called his city desk, and the next morning I was anonymous
no more.

The political writers began analyzing the election's startling results, and
I fared quite well in their accounts. "Political wunderkind" and "media magi-
cian" were among the descriptions used. Lyndon Johnson did not appreci-
ate such mention of his minions, but I shrugged off his frowns. I loved coming
out of the campaign closet. The *Post* capped my "press run" with a profile by
Carroll Kilpatrick, its political writer, topped by a five-column headline:

"Democratic 'Find' Helps Win Six Senate Elections." I was flatteringly described as "the Democrats' answer to Madison Avenue."

Invitations poured in—cocktails with Averell and Marie Harriman, a dinner party with Adlai Stevenson, and numerous Georgetown gatherings. Roger Stevens invited me to the opening of his newest Broadway play, and Thomas K. Finletter gathered some wealthy liberals to discuss the political future at '21'. The newly formed Democratic Advisory Council welcomed me, and I became an *ex officio* member of the Democratic Study Group, the congressional liberals organized by Minnesota Senator Eugene J. McCarthy as a power bloc to check the conservative southern "barons" in the House of Representatives. Being inside that world was exciting, no doubt about it, and I reveled in it.

Traditionally, Democrats had scorned the Madison Avenue media manipulation of the political process. The television and radio spot announcements used on President Eisenhower's behalf had been derided as "political pabulum." There was a growing realization that Adlai Stevenson "talking sense to the American people" had impressed Walter Lippmann and James Reston but didn't seem to win elections. Groping for a new approach was now in vogue.

After the 1956 campaign, I had written a sixteen-page paper on the changes that I thought were occurring in the political process. In a nutshell, it said: "Politics is visual." The paper centered on an obvious truism—that because of television and *Life* magazine-style journalism, people were looking at politicians as well as hearing and reading about them. What they saw could determine how a significant portion of them voted. Thus, it was an imperative that the candidate be packaged as prettily as possible to appeal to that segment of the electorate. The paper's other main point was that all most people could remember about a candidate was a simple central idea, a theme that registered favorably. Continually bombarded by competing entertainment and information, many citizens were not up to absorbing anything more complex than a simple slogan that resonated with their self-interests.

It was nothing new. Americans had been influenced by political imagery and slogans since the inception of the republic. Every schoolboy was taught about William Henry Harrison's "hard-cider" campaign of 1840, in which a patrician Virginia plantation owner was transmogrified into a log cabin-born frontiersman, running under the most appealing but meaningless of slogans: "Tippecanoe and Tyler, too." That flimflammery was only equaled by the fledgling Republican party in 1860 when an Illinois railroad lawyer was presented as "Honest Abe, the Railsplitter."

So, what was new in my paper? Nothing. But many Democratic politicians had not taken into full account the postwar developments of both television and the flight to the suburbs and the corresponding decline of the old city neighborhoods. This political generation found it difficult to believe that it was on the verge of being superseded by a new generation of "bosses"— the media operatives. The paper was also written in language anyone could understand.

It made me into a minor prophet, a guru of the new-style media campaign. Philip Graham, publisher of the *Washington Post,* asked to print the paper in its Sunday editorial section. Lyndon Johnson said no; it was the property of the Democratic Senatorial Campaign Committee. I agreed. Like every new hotshot, I thought I had invented the new round wheel and wasn't eager to share it with the hoi polloi. LBJ's view was that operatives such as myself were merely technicians who had no right to public attention. What did we know about the real game of politics—organizing precincts, herding voters to the polling booths, paying off preachers, and dealing with *padrones?* We were just glorified press agents, lowly scriveners who were at the bottom of the political ladder.

Johnson's distaste for me was evident. With my paycheck coming from the United Steelworkers of America (a violation of the Taft-Hartley Act), I was an outsider on the inside. He did not, as he liked to put it, "have my balls in his pocket." Nor did I conform. My biggest sin was to look the other way when he would rattle his empty glass at our cocktail-hour gatherings. It was his signal to a minion to refill his glass with Cutty Sark whiskey. I did it once, felt like a flunky, and vowed never to do it again. My refusal helped classify me as a not-to-be-trusted outsider.

For all that, my close relationship with Earle Clements qualified me for de facto standing in the Johnson circle. It included some figures of real stature: George Reedy, Gerry Siegel, Solis Horwitz, and Harry McPherson on staff and the downtown lawyers Abe Fortas, Jim Rowe, and Tommy (the Cork) Corcoran. These were people who had been playing big-time politics and government for years. They must have seen me as a bumptious de facto, a bit player who had gotten lucky. They were not far wrong.

The meeting places for this group were the ornate suites of offices that bordered the gallery of the Senate, Johnson's as majority leader and Clements's old whip's office, in which I had a small cubbyhole. The steady stream of visitors ranged from Harry S Truman and John Steinbeck to Clements's Kentucky political cronies. Senators regularly came in from the floor for a drink and to share gossip. Clements usually included me, and I was bedazzled to sit in with the high and the mighty. It beat the hell out of hacking a typewriter in Seattle.

The event of the week was the Friday staff luncheon, held in the conference room of Secretary of the Senate Felton (Skeeter) Johnston of Mississippi. The room somehow reminded me of William Randolph Hearst's imposing dining hall at San Simeon. There was a pecking order in the seating—Johnson, of course, at the head and Mike Mansfield of Montana, the whip, at the foot. I sat near Mansfield, who seldom spoke and whose pipe never seemed to leave his mouth.

LBJ was habitually, and perhaps ritually, late. When he swept in, like a great wind breaking the calm, Bobby Baker would leap to his feet and proclaim, "The Leader." Everyone else, save Mansfield, rose and chorused greetings. Once I irreverently suggested to George Reedy that we should practice some *seig heils*. He gave a rueful shrug and didn't comment. Reedy, the press secretary who had been a highly regarded United Press capital correspondent, was a reliable guide to LBJ's moods. When Johnson was in good spirits, George was ebullient and forthcoming with marvelous stories about the institution he revered, the U.S. Senate. When a story or editorial comment, particularly from the Leader's chief tormentor the *Texas Observer,* had outraged LBJ, George was subdued, even downcast.

One afternoon I ran into George coming out of the Senate Office Building. Wordlessly, he gestured toward the Carroll Arms. We went into an empty bar, known as "the sewer." Flo, the Alabama waitress, brought the martinis. George silently downed his with one gulp and beckoned for another. His face was chalk-white. After he knocked off the second martini, he spoke his first words: "Miller, you haven't really lived until you have been banished from the human race by Lyndon Baines Johnson." George recounted the torrent of abuse that Johnson had just subjected him to because of some story, but by the third martini he was laughing and tolerant about the Leader's tirade. Despite Johnson's tyrannies and sometime cruelties, his lieutenants saw him as a larger-than-life force of nature (James Reston's apt phrase) and, with wry humor, put up with his occasional indignities. Gerry Siegel, the brilliant Democratic Policy Committee counsel, was the one exception. His spirited wife, Helene, had given him an ultimatum: "You cannot be married to me and Lyndon Johnson at the same time." Gerry opted for Helene and took a professorship at Harvard Law School.

The question hanging over the Johnson circle in 1958 was the 1960 presidential contest: Would Johnson run? With him commanding headlines and flattering magazine cover stories, there was a cocky, euphoric confidence being expressed by Bobby Baker and other acolytes about the chances. "He's got most of the Senate Democrats in his pocket," bragged Baker. Older hands such as Clements and Corcoran knew that senators seldom controlled politics in their states and that Johnson's style, so successful in the Senate, might not go over well in the country at large. LBJ himself blew hot and cold on the subject.

Nineteen-sixty was too far in the future to interest me. The 1958 election was ahead, and it was consuming all my waking hours. There were eleven Democratic and twenty-two Republican incumbents up, and many of the Republicans appeared to be walking on Achilles' heels. Driven by partisan bloodlust and dreams of more glory, I envisioned the biggest collection ever of senatorial scalps: Fred Payne of Maine, J. Glenn Beall of Maryland, Chapman Revercomb and John Hoblitzell of West Virginia, Charles Potter of Michigan, Ed Thye of Minnesota, Bill Jenner of Indiana, Alexander Smith of New Jersey, Frank Barrett of Wyoming, Arthur Watkins of Utah, George Malone of Nevada, and John Bricker of Ohio looked like the ripest targets.

Clements and I knew that unparalleled opportunity was ahead. Yet, we had only sketchy knowledge about who our Democratic challengers might be and no funds to attempt to find out. Johnson flatly turned down Clements's request to use committee funds for such travel. I raised the money from labor sources, and Clements and I made trips to twenty states. We met with everyone who counted, and I took copious notes, which later turned out to be invaluable. My reportorial training was a blessing.

Wyoming, where we started out, had a unique "institution," one that we would encounter in other small states. Around a huge, round table in the restaurant of the Plains Hotel in Cheyenne, Wyoming's establishment—the governor, leaders of the legislature, Democratic and Republican state chairmen, and leaders of the state chamber of commerce, the cattlemen's association, and the state AFL-CIO—met every weekday morning for the coffee hour. Clements, no stranger to state capital politics, couldn't believe that people representing such disparate interests could meet in such apparent comradery.

The influence that Clements brought to bear was manifest in these smaller states. Nevada, for example, was a state normally Democratic, but it was represented by an eccentric Republican: George (Molly) Malone, high on *Time*'s list of "most expendable senators." When asked to recommend a Democratic challenger, Nevada's other senator, Alan Bible, suggested the mayor of Las Vegas, one C. D. Baker. Clements and I spent two excruciating evenings with him on his home turf and found his right-wing views appalling. Compared to him, Malone was a statesman.

LBJ had Clements, Bible, Mansfield, and me to lunch to hear our report on the western states. Clements gently made it clear to Bible that his putative candidate wouldn't do. The gracious Nevadan easily accepted the assessment and then advanced another name: E. L. Cord, manufacturer of the once-famous Cord automobile and now state senator from Esmeralda, a Nevada county with the brag that it had "more jackrabbits than people." Mansfield stiffened. "Alan, is that the same Cord who gave $5,000 to my last opponent and who contributes to every right-wing cause in the country?" Bible allowed that he was but protested that he had promised to quit such contributions if the Democrats gave him the nomination. "And he will finance his entire campaign," Bible threw in. Mansfield, who hardly ever spoke at these meetings, almost bit off his pipe stem. "He won't do, Alan," he barked. "He won't do." There was no further mention of E. L. Cord.

An obvious choice would have been the state's lone congressman, Walter S. Baring, but no responsible Nevada Democrat wanted him. Originally elected as an orthodox moderate, he had turned to the far right and had incurred the wrath of Speaker Sam Rayburn and the House Democratic leadership. Yet, if he ran for the Senate, he undoubtedly would win the nomination and might beat Malone. Clements saw such a happening as a calamity. He called me in one morning and said, "We've got to come up with $10,000 in cash. Don't ask me any questions. Just help me raise it." The money was raised, and Clements put it in an attaché case. Then he called Baring and invited him to a private lunch in his ornate, chandeliered office. Shortly before the Nevadan arrived, Clements said, "You might as well sit in. You may learn something about human nature and, besides, I probably need a witness."

Baring waddled in wearing a blue double-breasted suit. As Clements talked, Baring gorged himself. After the final bite was consumed, Clements turned pitchman. "Walter," he said unctuously, "you are one of the most valuable members of the other body. You are a vital presence on the Interior and Labor committees. Your value there is beyond compare." Baring nodded, a self-satisfied smirk emerging from his jowls. Clements picked up the attaché case and opened it on the table. "Walter, you are so valuable where you are that some of your friends have raised this money to encourage you to run for re-election. It will be yours the moment after you so announce. I will have it here for you in my safe." Baring's eyes almost came out of his face. "You can count on me, Senator," he said. The next morning a messenger brought a press release from his office announcing for re-election. I was not there when he came for his money, nor did I wish to be. I had seen enough of naked greed. Later Clements said, "That was ugly. But keeping him out of the Senate may be my best contribution to the campaign. His kind do not belong." I felt good about being under his tutelage.

Still, we did not have a Nevada candidate. Finally, Bible came up with a good one—Fred Anderson, a noted Reno surgeon who had been elected in a bruising statewide race for the chairmanship of the University of Nevada board of regents. I went to Reno and helped him set up both an organization and a media campaign with Joe McDonald, a topflight pro, to run it. It made all the fuss over Nevada worthwhile, we thought. Dr. Fred had the makings of a real senator.

I was in Augusta, Maine, with Governor Ed Muskie on the day filings closed in Nevada when Joe McDonald called me with a bombshell. A fringe Las Vegas political figure named Jack Conlin had gone to the Nevada capitol to file his candidate for either governor or attorney general. There, he learned that Grant Sawyer had filed for governor. "Scratch that one," Conlin muttered. "We can't beat Sawyer." Roger Foley, filing for attorney general, also looked too strong. Conlin's candidate, Las Vegas City Attorney Howard W. Cannon, had run statewide once and finished fourth. But Cannon wanted to run for something and had given Conlin *carte blanche* to file him for whatever position he had a shot at winning. Conlin paced up and down. Fred Anderson was a personal friend who once had saved Conlin's life in an emergency operation. But friendship had no place in politics, he reasoned. "The world belongs to the bold," he told himself. "We can beat Fred." He filed Cannon for the U.S. Senate. Nevada has eighteen counties, and Anderson carried seventeen; but Cannon won statewide by sweeping his home county of Clark (Las Vegas) and went on to easily defeat Malone in November. He served for twenty-four years, losing in 1982 because of his alleged role in a Teamsters Union land scandal.

Two seats that appeared to be ours for the plucking were in normally Democratic West Virginia, where intra-party feuding had resulted in the anomaly of the state being represented in the U.S. Senate by two Republicans, Chapman Revercomb and John Hoblitzell. Hoblitzell had attained notoriety one day when he strolled into the Senate chambers wearing a sport coat. In a body where frock coats, wing collars, and string ties once had been the norm, his impropriety caused such a stir that the *Washington Post* put it on the front page.

Clements's eyes twinkled as he described one of our candidates. "For a young fellow, you have seen a lot of different political types," he said. "But never one like this. He is a mountain boy. He is basically suspicious of anyone who doesn't come from his holler or isn't from his clan. West Virginians are called mountain men. This one really is."

We went to see the Sixth District's young congressman, Robert Carlyle Byrd, in his rabbit warren of an office in the Old House Office Building (now called the Cannon HOB). Byrd settled down to a long session, in which I was explaining a media campaign to him. He reached down and pulled a page from a huge pile of scrapbooks on the floor. "I've always made up my own ads," he said. "This is the first one, when I ran for the House of Delegates in 1946. I drew it and wrote the poem." The quarter-page advertisement consisted of his drawing, a scabrous, vulture-like bird with wings extended. Byrd's photograph was pasted on the head of this sorry-looking creature. The only text was:

Byrd by name
Bird by nature

Let's send Bob Byrd
To the legislature

I said that it was "original" and left, lugging the six scrapbooks he insisted that I take. I found them fascinating. An orphan, adopted by a childless couple named Byrd, he had documented every aspect of his life. Unabashedly included was all the material accumulated when he was the young Kleagle of a Klu Klux Klan chapter in Sophia, where he had grown up and begun working life as an apprentice butcher. His belief in education as the Aladdin's lamp that would enable him to rise from poverty was clear on these pages. He had carefully preserved scraps of favorable comments from grade-school teachers, and his efforts to seek higher education while working were documented through letter exchanges with West Virginia colleges. He was someone I could identify with, and I liked him.

The other Democratic nominee was going to be Jennings Randolph, a rotund Capitol Air Lines vice president who had served eighteen years in the House of Representatives. A politician of the old school, he had a personality as unctuous as his voice, a version of Illinois' Everett Dirksen but without his self-deprecating humor. His virtue was that he was acceptable to all of West Virginia's feuding Democratic factions.

Clements decided that the two Senate campaigns had to be joined to guard against another split. I suggested that all the media feature pictures of both of them and headline them as "The Team for West Virginia." In Rudy Bundas's series of flattering layouts, Byrd and Randolph looked like the Bobbsey Twins.

I was learning that politics was a great laboratory in which to learn about human nature, particularly the fundamental truth that nothing is dearer to a human's heart than his own image. Dress up a candidate in color with a halo, and you had him with you when it came to the arguments with his inner circle. It was an "edge" that I often needed, because the outside expert is generally an automatic target for the local wise guys. And there were always those.

Clements and I had functioned remarkably well as a team in these encounters. He was the wise old patriarch who had been everywhere, done everything, and seen it all in the political world and now was imparting his hard-won wisdom to help a new generation of Democratic politicians. I was the young technician who knew the media world and was experienced in using polling data, a new weapon for the campaign arsenal. We had persuaded the AFL-CIO Committee on Political Education to finance Louis Harris surveys in the states where there were Senate contests, and the polls were an impressive "calling card" to take with us when we visited.

It was late spring, and Clements and I were splitting up after being together for almost a year. With family along, I was leaving for a six-month sojourn on the campaign trail, beginning with a month in Maine for Ed Muskie's bid to become his state's first Democratic senator in a century. Then it would be Michigan with Philip A. Hart, Ohio with Steve Young, Indiana with Vance Hartke, Minnesota with Eugene J. McCarthy, Nebraska with Frank Morrison, Wyoming with Gale W. McGee, Utah with Frank Moss, Nevada with either Fred Anderson or Howard Cannon, Arizona with Ernest W. McFarland, California with Clair Engle, and, finally, Alaska's first election as the forty-ninth state, with E. L. (Bob) Bartlett and Ernest Gruening as our U.S. Senate nominees.

I had spent considerable time convincing Muskie to run. In evening sessions in his study at the Blaine House, the governor's residence, he had continually talked of his desire to make some money. He had been offered $25,000 a year to be counsel for the Hathaway Shirt Company, located in his hometown of Waterville just up the road from Augusta. Another $15,000 would come from a printing firm owned by the brother-in-law of his assistant, George Mitchell. With the potential of making much more, he already was guaranteed twice a senator's salary without the expense of living in Washington, D.C. "I would be a fool to turn it down," he kept saying. Growing up poor as the son of Polish immigrants in a class-conscious Yankee state, he had tasted the good life as governor, and the money was the route to more of it. It was a hard argument to rebut.

Yet, I knew that he loved government and the political spotlight, and, perhaps even more important, so did his wife, Jane. Waterville was dullsville compared to Washington, D.C., where the future for such a stunning couple could be limitless. I worked on her harder than I did on him.

We wanted him because his September victory would energize our campaigns across the country, and we wanted to use his superb campaigning abilities through the fall. The deal we finally cut was my services for one month and our promise to raise $100,000 for the entire Maine Democratic ticket. In return, he promised to spend two months on the road for Democratic Senate candidates after his September victory. It was a bargain.

When my month was up, it was time to head the car west—to Michigan, Ohio, Indiana, Wisconsin (Proxmire revisited), Minnesota, Nebraska, Wyoming, Utah, Nevada, Arizona, and California. One week per state, with round-the-clock days, seemed to work. It was a brutal but exhilarating pace, and I did not get tired.

The media campaigns were grounded on my basic formula: a theme-line that fit the situation. The slogans were by no means original. If Muskie "can do *more* for Maine," so also could Steve Young "do *more* for Ohio" and Frank Morrison for Nebraska. Such theme-lines also were adaptable for more specialized appeals: "Steve Young can do *more* for Ohio's farmers" (or teachers, senior citizens, or whomever). The theme-line, along with the candidate's larger-than-life portrait, was the centerpiece of the media billboards and posters, television-radio spots, direct mail, and newspaper advertising. I was so enamored of the concept that I demanded that the line-and-logo be printed on every scrap of paper leaving campaign headquarters. Negative campaigning was covered by the "compare the candidates" concept popularized in Dick Neuberger's 1954 campaign. All such comparisons naturally had our candidate upholding virtue and his incumbent opponent revealed with an appalling record of error.

It was a struggle to vary these media campaigns so they did not appear to come from the same cookie-cutter mold, and I did not always succeed. When I reached Eugene McCarthy's headquarters at the Capri Hotel in St. Paul, for example, he took me aside. "I want to change our motto," he said. "I would rather be 'great' than 'strong.'" His theme-line was a standard of mine: "McCarthy Will Make a *Strong* U.S. Senator."

"Changing it poses a real problem," I replied. "Minnesota borders on Michigan, and Phil Hart already is 'great.'" McCarthy laughed and forgot about being "great." Later, he called me when I was in Wyoming and reported: "We still have to change the slogan. Hubert saw it and raised a real ruckus. He claimed that we were implying that he wasn't 'strong.' Now it reads: Minnesota Needs Two Strong U.S. Senators.' Hubert is happy."

The victory-starved Democratic organization of Nebraska had scheduled a press conference for me in Lincoln. My protest that I was strictly a back-room operator was waved off by Bob Conrad, the state chairman. "You are just about the first national Democratic party official to stop here since Bob Hannegan in 1944," he said. "Like it or not, you are news." Frank Morrison, the Senate nominee, agreed, so I met the press. The next morning, I received an irate call from Bernard Boyle, who informed me that he was Nebraska's longtime Democratic national committeeman. "How dare you come into my state without clearing it with me?" he demanded. I drove to Omaha to soothe his ego. Without Clements to watch over me, my igno-rance of political protocol was showing.

Arriving in Utah, I told Calvin Rawlings, the courtly national commit-teeman, that there was a Democratic wind blowing across the country. He sniffed and said, "If so, it will jump over Utah and not stir a breeze here." Informed of his negativism, a prominent Democrat commented: "The worst day of Cal Rawlings's life will be the day a Democrat is elected to the U.S. Senate because then he will lose his influence." It was to happen that Novem-ber with Frank Moss's victory.

Arizona was a political minefield, and I walked gingerly lest I trip a booby trap set by the wily Steve Shadegg, Barry Goldwater's campaign guru, or Eugene Pulliam's statewide newspaper, the *Arizona Republic*. Earlier in the year, I had gone there to confer with Governor McFarland, who was itch-ing to avenge his 1952 defeat at Goldwater's hands. I was picked up at the Phoenix airport and whisked to an obscure motel on Scottsdale's outskirts. McFarland and his staff arrived, and we huddled until two in the morning. When they left, I was warned not to call anyone in Phoenix and to await further instructions.

The next morning I went outside to the pool to soak up some desert sun-shine. Out of the next cabin came the silverhaired "Gray Fox of the G.O.P.," my counterpart, Victor A. Johnston, executive director of the National Republican Senatorial Committee. He also had been stashed out here incognito and had met with Goldwater and Shaddegg at the same time I was meeting with McFarland. Vic was a good guy. We laughed over the irony of our being hidden side-by-side and spent a couple of hours in the sun, drink-ing Bloody Marys and gossiping about the campaigns we were involved in.

Los Angeles was my end of the line. I arrived there in mid-August nurtur-ing an idea that I had been mulling for some time: finding a production studio to which I could bring candidates to film their final television spots and programs. The idea came from my correspondence with Michael Levee, vice president of the Music Corporation of America. After Proxmire's victory he had offered help, and now I was ready to take him up on it.

He could not have been more gracious when I visited MCA's colonnaded, Southern-mansion headquarters on Santa Monica Boulevard, which had everything but Scarlett O'Hara coming down the grand staircase. There was just one problem. Neither Mike nor I had any practical ideas on how to harness the creativity and technical skill of Hollywood to the exigencies of media campaigns in Minnesota or Maryland. Mike took me to lunch at nearby Chasen's Restaurant several times with different groups, and it was always the same: much good and expansive talk but nothing that would work.

I had produced some television with Clair Engle, a fifteen-year House veteran, in the cozy little House of Representatives studio, and his ruggedly handsome western looks had projected well, with the country twang of his voice just as appealing. Now, with a huge soundstage that Mike had arranged, we were going to try and capture those qualities in a Hollywood production. It was, in a word, a disaster. The stage was huge and intimidating, with Engle looking like a tiny bird in a huge sky. Blinded by the klieg lights, he could hardly see the text on the teleprompter. When the endless session mercifully ended, not one usable foot had been filmed. Even worse, the candidate's confidence had been shattered, and his wife Lucretia had vowed vengeance on all those responsible.

At that moment the man whose name was on my retainer checks from the United Steelworkers of America came to Hollywood, and I discovered Allendor Spotlight Films. David J. McDonald, the Steelworkers' handsome and dandified president, had studied for the stage in his youth and had even had a screen test. He never got over it. Forced to take a union clerk's job, his acting ability had aided his remarkable rise to the presidency of one of the nation's largest unions. Now he got his kicks coming to Hollywood to film messages to his far-flung membership.

At Allendor Spotlight Films on North LaBrea Avenue, I found what I was looking for: a small studio with a professional staff capable of doing quality production at one-quarter the cost. The manager, Al Blanchard, was Boston Irish, political to the core, and ready to deal. The production costs were ultimately hidden in the Steelworkers' account and didn't cost the candidates a cent. Before the disclosure laws, burying such costs was not uncommon, and one of my strengths was an ability to find ways to pass off costs to groups or people who could absorb them. It was illegal, of course, but we reasoned that everyone was doing it, even the straight-arrow, good-government types.

I moved to the Allendor studio and began shuttling candidates in at a dizzying pace. "Today is Tuesday," quipped Blanchard. "It must be Ted Moss of Utah." We produced the television and radio media for eight Senate candidates, including Moss and Engle.

Muskie had won easily in Maine's final September election, and I joined him during his campaign swing through the West. He had been a wise investment. Our new "Abe Lincoln" was drawing big crowds and pumping enthusiasm into the campaigns. Muskie had the wonderful, understated ability to reach a first-name, I'm-just-one-of-the-guys rapport with local politicians, and they loved him for it. And he could do it without sacrificing his dignity or gravitas, the neatest trick of all. Ed Muskie was my hero of 1958, and possibly beyond. As a judge of political horseflesh, his potential as a future FDR excited me. He had much more than his resemblance to Lincoln.

The October days now flew by, filled with a myriad of detail and crisis calls in the middle of the night from campaign managers. I got involved in some Hollywood fund-raising, mostly through a suave, well-connected Beverly Hills lawyer named Paul Ziffren, who was California's Democratic national committeeman. I enjoyed going to the mansions of Bel Air and Brentwood, seeing famous faces, and making my pitch on what pure and lovely liberals we had to offer in places such as Utah and Nebraska. Money was raised, and Ziffren took care of its distribution.

My other fund-raising efforts were on the somewhat shady side. The Teamsters Union, discredited by the recent revelations of the U.S. Senate Rackets Committee, had money to contribute. The trick was getting it into the campaigns without being tarred by the source. I participated in several schemes, mostly involving direct payments to companies performing services for the candidate. Once, in Arizona, Democratic Chairman Joe Walton inadvertently gave me away, but I got away with it—barely.

Oil money was in the same shady category. Howard Keck, CEO of Superior Oil Company and earlier involved in an alleged "bribe" of Senator Francis Case of South Dakota, wanted to raise oil-industry funds for our candidates, but he wanted written assurance that they would support the oil-depletion allowance. I played the role of middleman. Only one candidate rejected the offer out of hand—Ted Moss of Utah. I told this to Senator Paul H. Douglas of Illinois, scourge of the oil-depletion allowance, in hopes he would use it to raise some liberal money for Moss. Douglas told Columnist Drew Pearson, and I received some unwanted publicity as a "middleman" for oil interests. "Part of the game," said Clements.

Suddenly Election Day arrived, and it was all over. I spent the day on the phone in a rented Hollywood Hills house, gazing out on a panorama of clouds drifting across the Los Angeles basin. I was totally relaxed for the first time in months. To paraphrase Harry Truman's favorite axiom, I knew that I had done my damnedest. It was now up to the voters. All I had to do was wait for television reports of the early returns from the East.

The California Democrats were having a huge party at the Ambassador Hotel on Wilshire Boulevard, but I decided to stay and work the phones. As dusk fell, my first call came in. "Joe, this is *Senator* Ted Moss," cried an excited voice. "I want you to be the first to know." The polls had closed early in Utah, and the first returns showed him a certain winner. His call was an augury of what was to come. When the national networks finally closed shop in the early-morning hours, the nation had the greatest Democratic congressional victory in an off-year election since 1934. When the 86th Congress convened on January 7, 1959, there would be sixteen new Democrats in the Senate and forty-eight in the House of Representatives.

For my family, it meant leaving a place that we had grown to love in the three months we had been there. My wife Rosalie and I had found a beautifully furnished house that had been designed in 1930 by a Frank Lloyd Wright disciple and came complete with a lush citrus-fruit grove. My daughters, Sue and Nancy, had been attending wonderful schools near the Paramount Pictures lot on Melrose Avenue and were teary-eyed about leaving them. But Washington, D.C., was where the action was, and I had to get back there.

7

REVENGE IN KENTUCKY

EARLE CHESTER CLEMENTS DID NOT SPEND MUCH TIME SAVORING the great Senate election triumph of 1958. He had a big score to settle back home in Kentucky. The Bluegrass state's Democratic gubernatorial primary was on May 30, 1959, and there was no time to waste. Clements had been defeated for re-election to the Senate in 1956 by Republican Thruston B. Morton by 7,200 votes out of more than a million cast. Actually, it was Governor Albert B. "Happy" Chandler, a fellow Democrat, who had done Clements in. For decades, the two had been feuding in Kentucky Democratic politics, the political equivalent of the Hatfields and the McCoys. Kentucky Democrats were for one or the other, with little room in between.

At the time, Lyndon Johnson was *hors de combat* with a heart attack, and Clements was acting majority leader in the Senate, a role that limited his usual careful attention to his home state. Chandler had attempted to take advantage by running his handpicked candidate in the primary, but Clements had beat him two to one. Nevertheless, Happy was tenacious. With President Eisenhower running—he was remarkably popular in Kentucky—the general election might be the place to trip up the unsuspecting Clements. It was, and Chandler openly exulted in the political demise of his longtime rival.

Chandler, serving his second term as governor (his first was 1935–1939), was ineligible to succeed himself in 1959. His handpicked candidate was his able lieutenant governor, Harry Lee Waterfield, who came from western Kentucky and had much strength in that Democratic stronghold. Clements's candidate was the same one Chandler had upset in 1955—Bertram T. Combs, a taciturn "mountain man" from the Big Sandy River country of eastern Kentucky. A shrewd lawyer and highly regarded former judge, Combs nevertheless gave the impression of being fresh out of Butcher Holler.

But there was a wild card in the picture—Wilson Wyatt, former mayor of Louisville, President Truman's housing administrator, and national campaign manager of Adlai Stevenson's 1952 presidential effort. Wyatt had little chance of being elected despite the support of the Louisville *Courier-Journal*, but he could be a spoiler. Clements had hired Louis Harris to survey Kentucky's Democrats, and the result confirmed what he already knew: if Wyatt stayed in the race, Waterfield would be an easy winner. Wyatt, a wealthy corporation lawyer, had an ego as long and broad as the 400–mile length of Kentucky itself—and he could talk. He stayed outwardly confident that he could use his mellifluous, musical baritone and urbane charm to beat Kentucky's political arithmetic. Clements's dream of revenge depended on dealing Wyatt out.

The "Old Coach," as I called Clements (who in the 1920s had coached Morganfield High School to within a touchdown of the state championship), had more than his share of political guile. He came up with a scheme based on our success with Senate nominees Byrd and Randolph in West Virginia in 1958. Clements reasoned that Wyatt could be induced out of the gubernatorial race and into the lieutenant governor's contest as Combs's running mate with a ploy aimed at his ego. Accordingly, our layout artist Rudy Bundas designed a series of billboards and poster and newspaper display ads that featured Combs and Wyatt in portraits of equally heroic size. The slogan or—as I called it, tent-line—was "The Team You Can *Trust* to Build a Better Kentucky."

In late January, lugging our layouts, I accompanied Clements to Louisville's Standiford Field airport, where the two groups were to meet at a nearby motel. The outcome was a foregone conclusion, I thought. As the talks wore on endlessly, Wyatt's eyes would surreptitiously slip to the posters, undoubtedly imagining them dominating the highways and byways of Kentucky. There is nothing more surefire than appealing to a man's vanity.

What finally emerged was the Combs-Wyatt ticket—Bert for governor and Wilson for lieutenant governor. I thought Wyatt came out of it pretty well. The post of lieutenant governor had some authority and carried with it all the trappings—personal staff, a limousine, and even a mansion—and it was the traditional one-term steppingstone to the governorship. Everything in the campaign—staff, headquarters space, advertising—was to be divided equally between the two camps. The campaign chairman, Dr. Bob Martin, the state superintendent of public instruction, would be the mediator of any disputes.

The next few days were the most incredible vortex of activity that I can ever remember in a campaign. Despite the attractiveness of the ticket, it still was deemed an underdog effort. It is an uphill task to oust an incumbent administration in Kentucky. Not only does the incumbent have all the machinery of government at his command (until recent days, this included the voting apparatus), but he also controlled large sums of money—at the time, state employees "contributed" a percentage of their salaries to the administration's political fund. The state's powerbrokers—business, farm, and labor, for example—were wary about crossing such a powerful force.

Clements was a man possessed. He and I were sharing a suite at the Seelbach Hotel in Louisville, from which he forayed across the state in a private plane to pull the two organizations together and pick up the fence-sitters in the most important of Kentucky's 120 counties. One night, as I was wearily turning in after a grueling day, he returned. He had been without sleep for fifty-four hours, but his eyes were glitteringly alive and his voice vibrated as he reported his successes.

"Coach," I pleaded, "get to sleep. You're sixty-three years old. You will kill yourself." Finally, he turned out the light. Maybe an hour or so later I heard the phone ring. The next thing I knew he was dressed and heading for the door. I staggered up and tried to stop him from going to Ashland for a breakfast meeting. "You can't," I said. "You've got to get some sleep." He grabbed me and, with a look I'll never forget, roared: "I'm all right. Boy, this is my life. God, I love it." And he was gone.

He had left me behind in Louisville to organize the media campaign. The reasoning behind the theme—"The Team You Can *Trust* to Build a Better Kentucky"—had come from Lou Harris's polling research. There was a powerful feeling on the part of a majority of Kentuckians that they wanted their state government to build better roads and offer better schools and public services. They even would be willing to pay for it if the taxes were fairly apportioned. They were tired of being near the bottom in every category of rankings among the states. "Thank the lord for Arkansas and Mississippi" was the rueful saying.

Harris's other major revelation was that there was a considerable degree of distrust for the Chandler-Waterfield administration (we always hung Happy around Harry Lee's neck). And no wonder. Even by the old *outré* standards of southern politics, Chandler was outrageous. During World War II, for example, Senator Chandler, who virtually controlled military contracts in Kentucky, had allowed a Louisville contractor to use 6,000 pounds of war-rationed materials to build a swimming pool as a "gift." When the shoddy deal was exposed, Happy shrugged it off. "The people of Kentucky aren't going to get mad at me over a little old pool," he protested. Episodes of this nature had not been uncommon with Chandler, and it was apparent that he had worn out his welcome with many Kentuckians.

If you were typecasting, you couldn't have come up with a more ideal contrast to Happy Chandler than Bert Combs of Prestonsburg, located hard in the hills of eastern Kentucky. Despite Bert's college and law school education, he remained a homespun product. Sandy-haired, lean, and taciturn, his twangy drawl was almost unintelligible at first hearing. Despite our dissimilar backgrounds, Bert and I took to each other immediately.

My status as media guru led me to my first error. I had had success with television by filming candidates as "talking heads"—that is, a use of tight close-ups when a candidate uttered his most sincere and noble words. I had written the scripts, and they were in the teleprompter ready to go. Warwick Anderson, the resident advertising agency chief handling the campaign, did not think the technique would work with Combs. "He is a mountain boy and head-on filming won't work with him," he said. I dismissed the warning. I could make an orangutan a television star, I said—or something as ridiculously silly.

Three days of filming in a studio outside Louisville's Bowman Field was excruciating. Despite an excellent film crew and an imported teleprompter expert who had worked with Lyndon Johnson, Combs simply could not mouth the simplest words and phrases. "Our state" came out sounding like "Uristedd." The more he fumbled, the more he froze. I was too stubborn to admit failure. With "main strength and awkwardness," to use an old Kentucky saying, we stumbled through all the scripts. It would be charitable to describe the finished product as mediocre. My persona as the omnipotent outsider was considerably bruised.

Clements had told us not to cut corners, to put everything but the capitol dome at Frankfort into the budget. Kentucky was adjoined by seven states, and to cover it media-wise meant buying television and radio in Cincinnati, Nashville, St. Louis, and Huntington, West Virginia, among other places. Clements dismissed the cost. "It is the money men's job to raise whatever we need," he said. "They will get it back ten times over when we win." The total came to a whopping $935,000, an almost unheard-of sum for those days. I had been in some expensive campaigns, but not one of them, including California, had cost over $300,000.

We made our presentation to the candidates and the money men in the campaign's master suite in the Seelbach on a balmy Sunday morning. The money men, headed by a bluff businessman from nearby Versailles named Bill May, hardly blinked as we ticked the expenses off, item by item. At the conclusion, one of them spoke up. "I do believe that you've forgotten the money for the sheriffs," he said. Clements nodded. "Just scratch in another $100,000, and that will take care of it." It was another one of Kentucky's political "traditions" that the 120 county sheriffs (or at least those who weren't irrevocably committed to the other side) would receive "walking-around" money to protect the sanctity of the ballot boxes on Election Day. We now had a million-dollar campaign.

With the machinery of the campaign appearing to be functioning smoothly, Clements and I returned to Washington in late February to resume our preparations for the 1960 Senate elections. Actually, most of his days were spent on the phone to Kentucky. At the office cocktail hour, he would update me and his two secretaries, both Kentucky transplants, on the day's developments. Our horses appeared to be doing well in the backstretch.

One day, Clements grabbed me with a growl: "They are screwing up our campaign. We've got to go back." Kentucky had been cursed with an outmoded constitution since 1891. In his term as governor, from 1947 to 1950 (when he resigned in order to be appointed U.S. senator), Clements had concentrated on modernizing the constitution and shaking and cajoling recalcitrant lawmakers to support his reforms. He had succeeded, and he envisioned the Combs-Wyatt team as a continuance of his reform policies. Now, as we flew through a thick fog to Louisville, he was in a rage because,

as he put it, "They have been sitting on their asses in the Seelbach thinking they have it won."

Clements took over the master suite at the Seelbach and began sum-
moning those he deemed the "guilty parties"—starting with Combs. I ran
into the gubernatorial candidate after his session. He was rueful and white-
faced, but he laughed: "I ain't had such a hiding since Pa whipped me for
using the Model A without his permission." Wyatt was next. No one was
spared in Clements's three-day reign of terror. He hided one and all with
the brutal impartiality of a Torquemada or Tammerlane sacking an enemy
village.

There was method in Clements's "Mad King Ludwig" routine. He
believed that two campaigns, Combs's in 1955 and his in 1956, had been
thrown away because of overconfidence. Big leads in the polls had lulled the
candidates and campaign staff into complacency, and they had been nipped
at the wire in the stretch. Each campaign's bar bill at the Seelbach told the
story, Clements held. It had been excessive for the last two weeks of both
campaigns. Now, not only had Clements designated the bar as out of
bounds, but he also repopulated the campaign staff with the oldest and least
attractive set of females I had ever seen in a campaign.

Finally, the reign of terror ended. Clements returned to his normal civil-
ity, and a relieved staff was relaxing with him in the campaign suite. Suddenly, he shouted at Dr. Bob Martin, the campaign chairman: "Martin, what
are you doing about the Greek vote?" Martin was speechless. He was just
finding out that there was such a thing as a "Greek vote" in Kentucky. "We
are going to find out about the Greek vote," Clements commanded. We followed as he strode imperially down dark streets toward Louisville's riverfront.
We arrived in the foyer of a Greek restaurant, an inviting, softly lit place,
where the proprietor, bubbling with pleasure, greeted Clements effusively.
"Senator, you do us great honor."

Clements was returning the effusiveness in kind when his eye fell on a
button the proprietor was wearing: Waterfield for Governor. His cherubic
face reddened. "What's this?" he demanded. "You can't be supporting that
common son-of-a-bitch." The proprietor pulled himself up, his dignity
affronted. "Senator, it's a free country. A man can support anyone he wants
to." Clements glared. "Yes, it is a free country, and a man can eat wherever
he wants to. Goodnight." Whereupon we marched back to the Seelbach in

silence and ordered room service. There wasn't another word said about the Greek vote.

Clements's calculated implosion had galvanized the campaign. Lights burned late in the campaign offices, and long lunches and barroom strategy sessions were a thing of the past. After a few days of this regimen, I became restive. Enough was enough, and, besides, I had not been a sinner in the 1955 and 1956 campaigns. I decided to test authority at the top. Clements's longtime secretary and trusted Girl Friday was the comely Cattie Lou Miller of Horse Cave, Kentucky, now the campaign's den mother.

"Come on, Cattie Lou," I said late one afternoon. "I want to test some campaign ideas with you, and we might as well do it in the bar over a martini." Her brown eyes glistened with anticipation. "Do we dare?" "Dare, hell," I retorted. "I'm in charge here. It's an order."

We went to the bar, and one martini led to ten or so. In the course of that wonderful marathon, she told me everything there was to tell about Earle Chester Clements, from his childhood in Morganfield through his gubernatorial administration. I was fascinated. Clements was my political godfather, my hero. I loved the man, and so did Cattie Lou.

Even though he was downstate somewhere, Clements found out that Cattie Lou and I were in the bar, and periodically someone from the headquarters came to our booth with instructions to return to our posts. They were airily ignored. Hell, we were going to be shot anyway. Finally, it was closing time, and I walked Cattie Lou to her room. When I indicated a willingness to come in, she smiled and shook her head. Not only was she a lady, but she could also hold her liquor. I went to my room and happily slept it off.

Clements didn't speak to me the next day. I didn't care. The gin hangover was severe enough to make me question whether or not I really wanted to live, let alone give a damn about the election. The next day, however, he and I had to fly to Paducah. A chilly silence prevailed for the first few minutes. Finally, he spoke: "You and Miss Cattie Lou certainly made spectacles of yourselves drinking those Eye-talian passion drinks (his definition of the martini) in front of God and everybody at the Seelbach. You were downright disgraceful." When I admitted that he might have a point, he softened, and his curiosity got the better of his anger.

"What in heaven's name were you and Miss Cattie Lou talking about all that time?" he asked.

"Mostly you, Coach, mostly you."

He huffed and puffed. "Me," he snorted. "How could you have talked about me all that time?"

"You're a fascinating man. It was easy."

"Well, what were you saying?"

"All kinds of things. How you are a political man in every fiber of your being. For instance, Cattie Lou told me that you had never even sought feminine companionship unless you had some definite political purpose in mind."

Clements leaned back and looked at the DC-3's ceiling, mulling this one over. Then he came forward with a growling chuckle and clapped a huge hand on my knee. "My boy, I do believe that she is right. I do believe that she is right."

Clements's goading was evident everywhere in the campaign. The Combs-Wyatt team, infused with new energy, came down the stretch with flying colors and defeated the Chandler-Waterfield organization by 40,000 votes. The Republicans were routed in November, and Combs was sworn in as governor. Clements, to my sadness, took what I thought was a minor post as director of the Highway Department. When I expressed my disappointment, he said: "I made some commitments, my boy. I've got to keep them."

In less than a year, the *Courier-Journal* was savaging Clements for awarding contracts to some of the money men, and Combs didn't lift a finger in his defense. Clements resigned, returned to Washington, and hated Bert T. Combs to his dying day at the age of eighty-eight. So passionate was his detestation that he made up with Happy Chandler and, in 1963, managed his campaign against Combs's handpicked successor, Edward T. (Ned) Breathitt, who won by fewer than 10,000 votes.

Wilson Wyatt had forfeited his chance for the governorship by losing a 1962 Senate race to the incumbent Thruston Morton, Clements's victorious opponent in the 1956 race. Wyatt was never a major factor in Kentucky politics again. He did attract some attention, however, as part of a business syndicate formed to guide the fortunes of a young amateur boxer from Louisville named Cassius Clay.

Combs delivered on most of his campaign promises and is generally regarded as one of Kentucky's two best governors of the twentieth century (the other is Clements). Appointed by President Lyndon Johnson to the U.S. Court of Appeals for the Sixth Circuit, he later resigned for another try at the governorship. Clements, in his last hurrah, helped Lt. Governor Wendell H. Ford deny him that opportunity. As the old judge said, politics in Kentucky indeed are the damnedest.

8

HAWAIIAN ODYSSEYS

AROUND THE SENATE, I HAD ACQUIRED A LARGELY UNDESERVED reputation as an expert on matters Hawaiian and Alaskan. It had come about because my home-state senator, Henry M. (Scoop) Jackson of Washington, was chairman of the territories subcommittee of the Interior Committee. Its principal issue was the longstanding matter of statehood for both territories, and I got involved.

Alaska's former territorial governor, Ernest Gruening, had devised a way to force the hand of Congress. He used what had been known as the "Tennessee Plan," because that state—while still a territory—had elected its own "senators" and "congressmen" to send to Washington to clamor for statehood. The maneuver had succeeded in 1796, and other territories had followed the same course during the nineteenth century. Alaska elected its delegation, including Gruening, in 1956.

But politics and race were befouling the matter. The South's senatorial barons—such as Richard Russell of Georgia and James Eastland of Mississippi—were unwilling to admit Hawaii because they did not want to sit in the same chamber with Japanese American senators. I know because I heard them say it. Thus, the statehood issue had languished for a decade despite the incessant pleading of Alaskans and Hawaiians for admission.

The 1956 election that produced Alaska's "senators" had another territorial surprise: the victory of Hawaii Democrat John Anthony Burns as a nonvoting delegate to Congress. The territory had voted Republican for a half-century, and Jack Burns was only the second Democrat ever to represent Hawaii in Congress. He also had plenty of street sense, quickly seeing that Hawaii's only hope was to let Alaska go first. But before he agreed, he won Lyndon Johnson's promise to back Hawaiian statehood after Alaska had been admitted. "It was a roll of the dice," Burns told me at the time. "If they come up, I'm a hero. With LBJ's support, I liked my odds."

They came up. Johnson kept his promise. Alaska was admitted, and Burns assured the Southerners that he would rig the Democratic ticket so that Japanese American candidates for the Senate would not be on it. When the bill came up on March 11, 1959, it went through the Senate in four hours, with only fifteen senators against it. President Eisenhower signed it, and Hawaii's first election as a state was set for July 28.

During these years, I had become involved with the fortunes of both the new states and their emissaries. I had spent part of World War II in the Alaska-Aleutian theater, and my hometown of Seattle had been Alaska's principal point of contact with the mainland since Gold Rush days. Hawaii was our American dream of tropical paradise. We had all heard Bing Crosby sing "Blue Hawaii" in *Waikiki Wedding* and listened to Harry Owens and His Royal Hawaiians on the radio.

The friendships I had made and my position inside the Senate leadership structure turned me into a self-appointed go-between for the emissaries from Alaska and Hawaii. Thus, after the bill admitting Hawaii to the Union had passed, I was not surprised when my secretary informed me that I had visitors from the Hawaiian Islands. Dolores Martin, Hawaii's Democratic national committeewoman, was in Washington to attend the party's annual meeting. She was also in town to formally invite Lyndon Johnson to a celebration over the Fourth of July weekend that would kick off the Democratic campaign for the two Senate seats, governor, and all the state offices. She had asked the Leader at a bad time, and he had emphatically said no. "Haven't I done enough for you people?" he had complained. "I'm tired. I want to go home to the ranch that weekend and lay on a rock like a lizard in the sun, not fly halfway around the world to watch a bunch of hula girls."

"Who can we get?" Dolores sounded desperate. Anticipating the likelihood of an LBJ turndown, I already had sounded out Ted Sorensen about Jack Kennedy, and he had been enthusiastic. I called JFK's secretary, Eve-

lyn Lincoln, and asked for an appointment. Minutes later, Dolores and I were
meeting with Kennedy. He accepted immediately and said he had not been
to Hawaii since he had convalesced at Tripler Army Hospital in 1943 after
his PT boat was attacked in the Solomons. As we were leaving, he took me
aside. "I want you to go out there with me," he said. "I have noticed you
with the Hawaiians. You have a standing with them that will be helpful."

In late June, I learned that there was no Democratic Senatorial Campaign Committee money to send me to Hawaii—or anywhere else—with
Jack Kennedy. LBJ, who guarded his turf fiercely, had said no. I explained
the situation to Evelyn Lincoln, who told me to show up at Washington
National Airport at the appointed time. "The senator will have a ticket for
you," she said.

When we arrived at the Honolulu airport with Jack Burns, who was returning home, we found a good-sized Kennedy contingent that included the omni-
present Sorensen, Jean and Steve Smith, and Paul "Red" Fay, Kennedy's PT
boat buddy. There was also a big crowd waiting as the DC-7 taxied up to the
modest green wooden building that served as the terminal. JFK by now was a
world-class attraction, and Burns was making his first appearance since statehood. A band was playing, and leis were being draped around everyone in our
party. The Hawaiians knew how to make a person feel at home and then some.
Jack Burns looked like Julius Caesar returning from a great victory in the hin-
terland, Kennedy and "Red" Fay like young princes come to induct a new outpost into the realm. I had a cold, and the leis were making me sneeze. Kennedy
saw me discarding them and came over. "For heaven's sake, don't violate the
local customs," he muttered. I answered with a smiling obscenity. A Honolulu *Advertiser* photographer captured the moment in a picture that I treasure.
It is the Jack Kennedy I remember with aching fondness—lighthearted, irreverent, and endlessly curious. It also is the person I remember best as myself—
crewcutted, grinning Irish mug, usually willing to laugh at myself. Kennedy
complimented me by picking up on my old football nickname, "Smiling Joe."

Our tour of the Outer Islands began with a spectacular luau at Hilo on the
Big Island of Hawaii. The next day we toured the Hilo waterfront and pine-
apple plantations and motor-caravanned through perfumed miles of floral
beauty to Hawaii's only national park, Mauna Kea, a volcanic peak that
jutted 13,796 feet skyward. It was a stunning work of nature and made one
forget, if only briefly, grubby and mundane things such as politics.

That evening we congregated for an al fresco dinner at the Volcano House, a venerable hostelry that had been a favorite hangout of Robert Louis Stevenson. I went into the barroom and found my friend Jonathan Rinehart of *Time* magazine draped over a martini. Jon informed me that he now was *Time*'s Pacific bureau chief and that the magazine was going to do a cover story on the winner of the upcoming governor's race. I was delighted to find a kindred journalistic spirit to pal around with. A diet of politicians could turn out to be hard to digest. I still considered myself a newspaper-man, practicing politics as a temporary avocation. An irreverent attitude toward candidates and their followers was an emotional necessity that most politicians did not understand. Jon understood the need to be able to debunk the high and the mighty without being accused of lacking the proper fealty to the cause.

The culminating event of Kennedy's four-day visit came on the evening of the Fourth of July at Waikiki's newest hotel, the Princess Kaiulani. Jack was at his oratorical best that night. His speech, tying America's oldest "cra-dle of liberty" (his Massachusetts) to our newest one in the Pacific, was a forensic triumph. Applause and cheers reverberated through the packed ball-room long after he had finished. Afterward, we went upstairs to the suite of Vincent Esposito, a Connecticut native who had been a controversial speaker of the territorial legislature. Waiting was a group of Hawaii's intel-lectual elite, including writers James A. Michener and William Lederer. They were there to quiz Kennedy on his views on American-Asian relations.

The next day, after brunch at the Royal Hawaiian Hotel, Kennedy and his party departed for a few days' vacation on Kauai. I moved to the Alexan-der Young Hotel on Bishop Street in downtown Honolulu and checked in at Democratic headquarters, located in a vacant store on South King Street. After a few days of tourist Hawaii, the reality of this place came as a shock. I was no stranger to crummy campaign headquarters, but this one took the cake. It could have been a stage set for *Rain*, Somerset Maugham's drama of degeneracy in the South Pacific. Next to the encrusted door sat an ancient switchboard manned by a huge Hawaiian woman who doubled as receptionist, greeting one and all with sugary terms of endearment. Her children played contentedly at her feet. Although the switchboard frequently jammed, it didn't affect her broad smile or composure. She was a good antidote for hyper-kinetic *haoles* such as me.

The cavernous main floor was crowded with rickety tables and desks occupied by people wrapped around antiquarian desk phones. They scribbled furiously and then took their notes into what passed for the *sanctum sanctorum* of the operation, the office of Jack Burns's brother Ed, the campaign manager. Ed, a relaxed real-estate broker, cheerfully told me that this was his first political experience. He led me upstairs to a loft that contained a few rickety cribs that looked like rabbit warrens. "Looks like a River Street whorehouse," I said, referring to Honolulu's famous World War II whorehouses featured in James Jones's bestselling book *From Here to Eternity*. "I wouldn't know," he answered, somewhat primly. I selected one and sat down at a wobbly desk to ponder how this seeming formlessness could be pulled together into a cohesive campaign.

The recent primary had left the Democratic ticket in some disarray. Jack Burns, keeping his promise to the southern senators that they would not have to serve with a Japanese American, had selected two elderly figures for the Senate on his ticket: seventy-year-old Oren Long, an erstwhile Kansas missionary schoolteacher who had been territorial governor, and Bill Heen, a Chinese Hawaiian senator in the territorial legislature. Frank Fasi, a young Democratic maverick, had upset Burns's plan by defeating Heen in the primary. The International Longshore and Warehouse Union (ILWU), whose leaders detested Fasi, had immediately endorsed his Republican opponent Hiram L. Fong, a move that had the tacit approval of the union's chief political ally, Jack Burns. That worthy could have had one of the Senate seats simply by filing for it, but, with more than 500 appointments to be made by the new state's incoming chief executive, the governorship was The Big Prize. It was the post where Hawaii's political future largely would be decided, and Burns had no doubts in agreeing with ILWU leader Jack Hall that he had to go for it.

The tall, Montana-born *haole* was a paradox in many respects. Coming to the islands with his parents at age four, Burns had grown up in a working-class, multi-ethnic neighborhood in which white kids were a small minority. After St. Louis High School, he had managed a year at the University of Hawaii in 1930–1931 before the Great Depression ended his educational aspirations. Landing on the Honolulu police force in 1934, he had been exposed to the gritty side of island life that wasn't seen in the promotional posters of the Hawaii Travel Bureau. From the first he sympathized with labor activists seeking to organize the poorly paid work force, most of them of Japanese, Chinese, and Filipino heritage.

Pearl Harbor was to focus his future role in life. Now a police lieutenant, he had made many friends in the large Japanese American community and had become convinced of their loyalty to the United States. He emerged as a go-between for the military and Japanese Americans and, later, as a participant in the early discussions that led to the creation of the two Hawaiian all-Nisei U.S. Army combat units that won celebrated honors in the European campaign of World War II. That success—and the success of the ILWU in organizing in 1944–1945—had given Burns ideas. The ink was hardly dry on the Japanese surrender aboard the U.S.S. *Missouri* when he resigned from the police department to attempt to create what Hawaii never had—a real Democratic party organization. Republicans had dominated since Hawaii's annexation by the United States in 1898. The Hawaiian and Alaskan statehood bills had been entwined because new states had been customarily admitted with balancing or off-setting political characteristics, Alaska Democratic and Hawaii Republican.

The orthodox Irish Catholic Burns was a politician to the core, and he knew how much World War II had changed things. Hawaii, which before the war had been a white, sugar-plantation oligarchy, was quickly becoming a democratized multi-ethnic community in which the *haole* ruling class was a distinct minority. Pass statehood and politicize the majority, and Hawaii would be permanently Democratic with a big D. That was the way Burns saw it.

As the fledgling party's leader, he was able to forge a political instrument out of the two basic elements of change: the Japanese American war veterans and the ILWU. The old AFL craft unions were being left behind. Labor organizer Harry Bridges and his honcho in Hawaii, Jack Hall, were married to Nisei, and they related to the ethnic group that was rapidly becoming Hawaii's emerging majority.

Burns's easy victory for the post of nonvoting delegate to Congress in the Republican year of 1956 was the first manifestation that a political earthquake was rocking the islands. That, and the sweep of the territorial legislature by Nisei veterans running as Democrats, clearly signaled what was ahead. The Republicans did not intend to give up without a fight. Their gubernatorial candidate was the territorial governor appointed by President Eisenhower, a charming young Irish American named William F. Quinn. With only ceremonial functions to perform, he had been campaigning every day, and he had one priceless talent that Burns could never match. He could sing. Lord, could he sing. And he did, wherever he found two or more voters. "If he sings 'The Hawaiian Wedding Song' one more time," I muttered to Dan Aoki, "I am going to slice his larynx." Burns shrugged Quinn off. "The singing fool," he called him.

Burns's contempt for Quinn disturbed me. "I'll beat him going away" was his stock boast, reiterated over endless cups of coffee with cronies and hangers-on in the coffee shop of the Alexander Young Hotel, in which he was spending much of his time. As the hero of the statehood campaign, he seemed to feel that people should come to him. "We've got to sandblast him out of the coffee shop," I told Aoki. "He's got to work some precincts, go to teas, ask people for their vote. Media alone won't do it." Aoki nodded in agreement, but nothing happened. No one was inclined to tell the emperor that he was naked.

Burns's party, if not naked, was wearing clothes rent by some ugly tears. His faction's near-domination of the primary had left a legion of bruised losers in its wake, including such significant names as Spark Matsunaga, Tom Gill, and James Michener. When I first met him, Michener wasted no words in telling me that he considered Burns "more dictator than democrat." I learned that he was one of a number of influential Democrats who intended to sit out the general election, despite what was at stake. Their principal plaint was over Burns's alleged "messiah complex." As a Burns partisan, I nevertheless believed they were largely right. He demanded unblinking adherence and did not seem comfortable with the dialogue of equals.

Every aspect of this rift was exploited by the newspaper that was going all-out to beat Burns, the Honolulu *Star-Bulletin*. Its attack was focused on the Democrat's tight relationship with the ILWU and Jack Hall, who had been convicted in federal court for having ties to the Communist Party (the conviction was subsequently overturned). Right after the statehood bill had passed Congress, Burns had gone to the ILWU convention in Seattle to praise the union for "bringing the foundations of democracy to Hawaii." That speech and his failure to come home to Hawaii infuriated conservatives, and the *Star-Bulletin* trumpeted that it showed his "slavish adherence" to the union. Since Harry Bridges was currently negotiating a possible merger with Jimmy Hoffa and the Teamsters, the fear of those two with a potential stranglehold on Hawaii was real to many people. Memories of the 1949 strike that tied up the islands still were vivid. Burns shrugged it off. "The *Star-Bulletin* has been crying Red for years," he said. "Nobody listens to them any more. Why dignify it with an answer?"

I was an inveterate worrier during campaigns and had been losing sleep over these problems, so much so that I had almost forgotten that Jack Kennedy was still around when Jon Rinehart called to tell me Kennedy's party was leaving Honolulu that afternoon. "Let's go see them off," he suggested. I was more than willing. Anything to get out of that crummy headquarters for an hour or so.

Kennedy's flight to the mainland was only minutes in the air when the event for which a goodly crowd really had gathered took place. A Qantas Air Lines 707 direct from Sydney, Australia, landed and rolled up to the tiny terminal, the first commercial jet to arrive in Hawaii. "This really is the start of the big change here, more so than statehood," Rinehart said. "In a few years these jets will be landing every couple of minutes, spewing out hordes of tourists from Keokuk and Okanogan. And Hawaii's unique laid-back charm will be history."

With jet-produced tourism on the verge of booming and Hawaii short of facilities to handle it, the high-rolling developers were out in force, most of them playing both sides of the political street. They were going to make a killing, and they needed to be able to expedite the building permits, the easements and rights-of-way, the roads and sewers to turn the gorgeous beaches into a Pacific version of Miami Beach.

I became warm friends with one of the developers, Chinn Ho, president of the Capital Investment Company, into which most of the island's Chinese had put their life savings. He liked to cruise the Waikiki bars on balmy evenings and at his favorite, the Tahitian Lanai, he would tell me of his plans. Pointing to a grungy area bordering Ala Moana Park, he said, "I am going to build the first locally owned luxury hotel there." (And he did. The Ilikai, built in the early 1960s, still is a Waikiki showplace.)

I sensed from Chinn the land hunger that was endemic among Hawaiians. There wasn't much available for sale because The Big Five controlled it and, instead of selling it in fee-simple lots, held it through life or long-term leaseholds. Jack Burns thought he could break up their land monopoly through market-value taxation; tax it at the going price for land, and the big estates would be forced to sell. But Quinn trumped him in the campaign's home stretch. He called for a "Second Mahele," a plan to sell public lands on the Neighbor Islands with a limit of one acre to a family at the bargain-basement price of around fifty dollars an acre. His proposal had historical appeal; in 1818, King Kamehameha III had divided lands between royalty and commoners in his "Great Mahele." The enthusiasm with which Quinn's gambit was received finally upset the Olympian disdain with which Burns had dismissed Michener and his other detractors. Now I had a green light to "get them in the campaign."

Negotiations took place at Michener's table in the beachfront bar of Waikiki's most "native" hotel, the thatched-roof Halekulani. He was finishing his massive novel, *Hawaii*, in his apartment on nearby Lewers Street and lunched regularly with a group that included Chinn Ho, Bill Lederer (co-author of the best-selling book *The Ugly American*), aspiring Democratic hopefuls Tom Gill and Vince Esposito, plus Jon Rinehart and me. It was both a skeptical and stimulating bunch, and I pressed—sometimes stridently—the argument for Burns with them.

A fear that Burns's victory would result in unrestricted and unplanned growth bothered all of them except Chinn Ho. Michener wanted Burns to support a proposal that would limit the height of new buildings to that of the Aloha Tower. Although Burns did not commit himself to the idea, Michener finally gave in and made an inter-island speaking tour for him, and the other holdouts pitched in at the end.

Compared to the hurtling tempo of most stateside races, time—that insistent dominator of the political process—did not seem to matter. Burns had had a primary opponent, a native Hawaiian who had run simply because he believed that an indigenous citizen—now only 19 percent of Hawaii's population—should become the state's first elected governor. He had garnered enough votes to warrant putting him on television to endorse Burns. I slated him for a five-minute segment in prime time and gave him a script to work from. Hawaiian television was live in those pre-videotape days. The Hawaiian, ignoring the script, meandered for four minutes before he even mentioned Burns's name. But then he became positively lyrical. "I should have bought more time," I moaned to the producer, a tall young Nisei behind the camera. He winked. "Don't worry about it," he smiled. The Hawaiian rhapsodized on for nineteen minutes, and we paid for five. I cursed myself for all the time I had spent producing Burns's filmed television to the precise timing that was demanded by mainland stations. Here they didn't seem to give a damn.

One night, I got together with Victor Johnston, the executive director of the National Republican Senatorial Committee. He and I had campaigned against each other all over the country, and we had become strangely good friends. He was in a pretty expansive mood when we met in his suite at the Royal Hawaiian. It was clear that Hiram Fong, endorsed by the ILWU, was going to beat Frank Fasi, and so he would be going home with a Senate seat that the Republicans had not expected to win. In our boozy rendezvous, Vic and I found ourselves in agreement on the essence of the campaign in which we, as outsiders, had been swept up in. "It was," he said, "the nakedest, most clear-cut, unalloyed struggle for power" he had witnessed in thirty-one years in national politics. "Who gets what and how much is all that matters," he said. "The rest is meaningless window dressing." I had been romanticizing the race as the downtrodden rising up to smite their oppressors, a traditional mindset that I had been carrying from one campaign to the next. Now, my perception focused by Vic's twenty-year-old Scotch, I realized how right he was. From Burns on, my guys really only were interested in one issue—power. It was the birth of my political maturity. The only question was: Who was going to run things?

I wasn't going to be there to find out. A nationwide steel strike had begun, and my presence was being demanded by the United Steelworkers of America, the union that was paying my way in politics. The thought of missing election night in Honolulu didn't disturb me a bit. I had become convinced that Burns was going to lose an election that he should have won, and I didn't want to be around for the recriminations. Jon Rinehart raced me to the airport to catch a flight to New York, and suddenly I had the feeling that I was escaping from a seabound incarceration. Hawaii was great, but after awhile it became claustrophobic.

Dan Aoki called me late at night at the Roosevelt Hotel in New York to tell me that Burns had lost to Quinn by 4,000 votes. He was my first loser since a Seattle mayoralty race in 1954, and I felt the pain.

9

A STATE THAT TIME FORGOT

LYNDON B. JOHNSON CALLED ME TO HIS OFFICE TO GIVE ME AN assignment. "Go to North Dakota," he said. "We can pick up a seat there." If so, it would almost be a first. North Dakota once had elected a Democrat to the Senate, but he had died two months after assuming office. Although the state was at the epicenter of radical agrarian populism, its politics had remained respectably Republican, although sometimes of an unorthodox variety. Many years before, the Senate's Republican leader, George Higgins Moses, had exasperatedly called fractious senators from the Great Plains "Sons of the Wild Jackass," and the prairie's radical solons had proudly adopted the label.

Now the last of the "Sons" had died, which is why Johnson had called for me. William Langer, senator since 1940, had breathed his last on November 8, 1959, and, pursuant to state law, Governor John E. Davis had scheduled a special election for June 28, 1960, the day of the state's regular primary. The winner would serve out the remainder of Langer's term, to January 3, 1965. It was the first real chance in decades for the Democrats, and they were blessed with a bona fide challenger: Congressman Quentin N. Burdick, elected as a Democrat in 1958 to succeed his Republican father, Usher L. Burdick, who had occupied the seat for twenty years.

"I understand the Burdick boy isn't much of a campaigner, the kind his daddy was, and so he's going to need help," Johnson instructed. "Find out what the situation looks like and report back to me."

I was doubly surprised by Johnson—first, that he had an interest in North Dakota and, second, that he had sent for me. I deduced that he still respected my campaign skills, even though he resented my cocky attitude toward the senatorial barons, principally him. But why his interest in North Dakota? I discovered that Langer had been a Republican who Johnson had been able to count on in a close-vote situation. And Johnson thought of himself as a son of the Great Plains, which stretched from the Rio Grande north to Canada's prairie provinces. "The only difference between Texas and Dakota is climate," he said. "It's the same land and produces the same things: wheat, cattle, and oil. The people are the same—tough, independent, and ornery—and they don't like the money-boys and snobs in the East. Our politics are the same, only the Civil War made us Democrats and them Republicans."

LBJ knew his political history. The two Dakotas had been admitted to the Union in 1889 to counterbalance the admission of Montana and Washington, which the Senate Republican leadership suspected of having strong Democratic leanings. Four GOP senators from North Dakota and South Dakota would even it up. There weren't enough people in Dakota Territory to make one state, let alone two, but politics is politics. Politics turned out to be a passionate game as practiced in the frigid northern climes. Since 1915, North Dakota had been aroused by the Non-Partisan League (NPL), a unique body that had come into being chanting the war cry of Arthur C. Townley, its Socialist Party organizer-founder—"the tools of production should belong to the producers."

What this was all about was wheat. Prior to 1915, the flour-mill magnates of Minneapolis and the railroads had combined to hold the German and Scandinavian farmers of the Great Plains in economic bondage. With grain prices rising because of the Great War that was ravaging Europe, Townley capitalized on the farmers' desire to get their share. The Non-Partisan League emerged overnight to capture the governorship and the lower house of the North Dakota legislature. Townley and his allies could not handle instant success, and feuds and a plunge in wheat prices after the war crippled the League. Nevertheless, it survived to remain a potent force for forty years, achieving its principal goal of liberating the farmers from the domination of the Minneapolis flour barons.

Its exemplar was Langer, a Columbia University-educated lawyer who had so much brass that he was universally known as "Wild Bill." When the

NPL's support propelled him into the governorship in the terrible year of 1932, Langer forever endeared himself to farmers by decreeing a moratorium on farm foreclosures and evictions, saying, in words that made nationwide headlines: "The big business interests know that as long as I am governor . . . the moratoria are going to remain in effect, even though I have to keep calling out National Guardsmen three times a day, as I did last Saturday. As governor I am not going to permit eviction or oppression of debtors, whether they be farmers or small businessmen; and if the only way the big business interests figure they can get rid of the moratoria is to remove me, they are right."

His action was patently unconstitutional but dramatized to the nation that farmers were in desperate shape and needed emergency relief. But "Wild Bill" paid a price when the state supreme court removed him from office in 1934 and put him in jail. The setback was short-lived. The voters overwhelmingly returned him to the statehouse in 1936 and sent him to the Senate in 1940, where he stayed until his death in 1959.

The man who aspired to his senatorial robes was like Langer in political outlook but utterly different in temperament. Burdick had grown up in the shadow of his successful father and had been affected significantly by the experience. I found him almost excessively shy and self-effacing, devoid of the up-front ego that earmarked most politicians. I liked him immediately, which meant that I was going to bust my tail. And he was willing to put himself in my hands.

Despite his shyness, Burdick had the makings of an attractive candidate. He was a widower with three daughters and a son. He had a craggy, lived-in face that shone with an open optimism despite a life that had known tragedy—he had lost a wife to cancer and had raised three children alone—and humiliation—until 1958, he had had a long string of dreary political defeats and financial setbacks. Recognizing this election as "make-or-break," he was determined to devote every fiber of his being to the campaign. He took to my strenuous regimen with enthusiasm.

Burdick was remarkably naive. Early on, I asked him how much money he thought it would take to win. "I can put on a terrific campaign for $10,000," he answered. When I said that $100,000 was around what was needed, his eyes widened in disbelief. "I just can't conceive of there being that much money anywhere," he said. It was understandable. He had begun law practice in Fargo in 1932, the year that North Dakota went flat broke. His legal fees were paid with chickens, sides of beef, and bushels of corn and peas. Still, his life had been comfortable. He had followed his father to the University of Minnesota as a football star, where Usher Burdick still was remembered for captaining the Gophers to victory over Michigan in 1904. Politics hadn't particularly interested him until he saw the plight of his farmer clients. He became counsel to the North Dakota Farmers Union, an emerging political force organized by George Talbott and his son Glenn. After World War II, at their urging he became executive director of a revamped state Democratic Party and organizer of a farmer-labor coalition called the Farmers Union Progressive Alliance. But nothing had shaken rural loyalties to Langer, and North Dakota continued in the GOP column.

From my Seattle newspaper days, I knew about North Dakota and its politics because so many Dakotans had migrated west during the Depression and World War II to seek work at Boeing Aircraft, Seattle's shipyards, and Weyerhaeuser's lumber mills. I knew a number of them and had heard their stories of politics on the prairie. So I was prepared for the inevitable wise guy who would say: "You don't know anything about the unique politics of our state." It was a line I had heard many times.

I arrived in North Dakota as the spring wheat was peeking above the ground. Bismarck, the capital, was a placid little burg dominated by its "skyscraper" of a state capitol building and without the amenities common to the state capitals I knew. I felt very much at home. I had last been here in my youth, hitchhiking my way across the country to stay with family on Puget Sound, and I still had a feeling for the territory. "How's Casey Finnegan doing these days?" I asked of the longtime North Dakota State football coach. And "Does Jack Hurley's brother still run that religious bookstore?" It was important to let the locals know that I knew their turf.

Burdick had told me that I would be working with a group of untried young people, but I was not prepared for what I encountered at Democratic state headquarters—a spartan two-room office in the basement of a run-down hotel. Forty-four percent of the voters, pollsters told us, did not recognize Burdick by name, a surprise since Quentin or his father had been on statewide ballots for a quarter of a century. But it was correctable, starting with my old standby, the billboard. Within weeks the candidate's imposing figure, fifty times life-size, dominated the highways: "Burdick Will Make a *Strong* U.S. Senator." I selected that well-traveled line because North Dakota had a tradition of forceful solons, and it indirectly exploited his opponent Governor Davis's image of weakness. Our foot soldiers loved the billboards and added to their number by putting up "extras" on barns and buildings throughout the state. The four-word banner was equally effective, and BEAT BENSON WITH BURDICK instantly became the campaign's leitmotif. This was a reference to Eisenhower's Secretary of Agriculture Ezra Taft Benson, who was extremely unpopular with farmers in North Dakota. We had established the conditions of the campaign and would never deviate from them.

I quickly saw why Burdick was unknown to almost half the electorate—he was uncomfortable with people he didn't know. He had none of the small talk and easy banter that most politicians use with strangers. Quentin was shy in the extreme.

I was filming him around the state to establish visually his bona fides with the people. We were traveling with a cameraman and twenty-two-year-old Scott Anderson, a member of the state legislature and executive director of the state party. We stopped at the Missouri River at the site of the Bureau of Reclamation's Garrison Diversion Project, which would divert water from the river to irrigate a huge chunk of the state's dry acreage. After hours of filming, we stopped to eat in a café-market in Garrison. It was Saturday, and the place was crowded. Burdick, head down, headed straight for a booth in the rear, where he buried himself in the Bismarck *Tribune*. We ate and left, exchanging nary a word with anyone but the waitress. I was boiling, but silent—until we reached the sidewalk. At my signal, Scott and the cameraman had gone ahead to the car. I thrust my jaw in the candidate's face and began: "I never have seen such a disgraceful performance by a candidate in my life. You had a hundred hands to shake in there, and you didn't touch one of them. If Bill Langer or your dad had been here, they would have had everybody in there believing that they were there just to see them. But you slunk in and out like a terrified rabbit, scared that somebody might say hello. Now, if you don't go back and shake every damned hand in the place, I'm going straight to the Bismarck airport to catch a flight to Washington, and I'm never coming back. Furthermore, I'm going to tell LBJ and everyone not to waste a cent on a candidate who won't campaign."

He said nothing but, with a rueful half-smile, turned and went back into the café. I waited a goodly time until he came out with a satisfied smile on his face. We were quiet as we drove back to Bismarck, and Scott later had the grace not to question me. I had read the riot act to candidates before, but never that brutally. Weeks later, Burdick and I were on Fargo's main street. He gave me that half-grin and said, "Watch me." I followed him into stores and cafés to witness him shaking hands with the aplomb of a Hubert Humphrey.

"Pressing the flesh" was *sine qua non* of the political process, and for some it was wearing. By initiating contact, a person opened himself to a familiarity that easily could be abused. I saw that veteran campaigners, such as Senator Henry Jackson, could be quick to take umbrage at some stupid remark. George McGovern told me that the happiest moment of his ill-starred 1972 campaign for president was telling off a heckler. And I remember the expression of unholy glee on Nelson Rockefeller's face when he gave the finger to a booing audience.

But Burdick needed to shake every hand he could find. The Republicans had an excellent candidate in Davis, a silver-haired charmer who could boast of an excellent record as governor. Arthur Edson, one of the two national reporters the Associated Press had sent out to cover the campaign, told me that Davis was "one of the most attractive campaigners I've ever encountered." He dismissed Burdick as a "cloddish hayshaker." Barry Goldwater, chairman of the National Republican Senatorial Committee, knew what was at stake: "If we Republicans lose this special election just prior to the Democratic convention, it will influence the whole campaign this year. If we can't win in a key pivotal state like this, we may lose the presidential election."

The race was a top GOP priority, and the party sent in a five-man team of professionals to mastermind the Davis campaign. It was headed by the "Gray Fox of Republican Politics," Victor A. Johnston, chief of their senatorial campaign unit and a native North Dakotan. He was aided by Jack Mills, their top campaign honcho, and Mike Gill, Mamie Eisenhower's nephew and an experienced pro. The Grand Old Party had sent in its best, no doubt about it.

Vic and I were friendly old rivals, and I knew his tactics. His specialty was painting Democrats with a Red-tinted brush and, as Joe McCarthy's one-time right-hand man, he had plenty of practice. But he had a kind of honesty about it. "I never use hearsay or innuendo," he once told me. "If it's not on the record, I won't touch it. And I won't use anything personal. What they drink and who they screw is their business."

Since Burdick had been associated with many a Henry Wallace-type prairie radical and presumably a real, live Communist or two, we braced ourselves for what the Johnston team was brewing. We figured they had the raw material because it had surfaced in the 1956 campaign. It was just a question of how and when they would use it.

I was determined not to give them any ammunition. My prediction that the race would cost $100,000 was pretty accurate, and most of it had to come from outside the state. Most of the funds would come from organized labor, but reporting that money would give Vic Johnston the opportunity to trumpet that Burdick was a stooge for the "Eastern labor bosses," usually a winning issue for Republicans in the farm belt.

The device to avoid reporting the money was a little-known District of Columbia statute that legalized a "front" committee that made its contributions to only one candidate. Accordingly, I set up an account for the "D.C. Committee for Civil Rights" at the Riggs National Bank, with two of my neighbors as the signing officials of the body. Into that account went the contributions from organized labor and other organizations that we did not want identified in North Dakota. That money immediately was transferred to the campaign—unreported.

The outside money was buying the first professional media campaign in North Dakota. I had gone all-out on television and radio, producing a thirty-minute documentary on Burdick around the state, a fifteen-minute documentary on his life story, and sixteen sixty-second spots on every possible issue on voters' minds. My newspaper "jewel" was a four-page picture tabloid supplement to be inserted in every daily newspaper ten days before the election.

It hardly was excessive. The Republicans had been on the air since April and were outspending us by better than two to one. And all their national stars—Nixon, Rockefeller, Goldwater and Halleck—were campaigning throughout the state as if it were their own bailiwick. In the larger picture, North Dakota (and its three electoral votes) wasn't much; but for the moment it was the only game being played, and both sides were fighting fiercely for every vote.

The press loves a good fight, and they were flocking to cover it. The national reporting team of Arthur Edson and Relman "Pat" Morin was filing stories for the Associated Press every day. Stanley Wyman of *Life* seemed to be everywhere, shooting pictures with his Leica. Reporters from the *New York Times*, the *Wall Street Journal*, and various national publications roamed the countryside attempting to lay bare political sentiment on the prairie. The little "Flickertail State" was receiving its "fifteen minutes of fame"—and loving it.

No group loved it more than the volunteers who were flooding makeshift Democratic headquarters across the state to work the telephone banks, canvass voters, and address campaign pamphlets. Some of them had labored in losing obscurity for so long that just having Stan Wyman take their picture was reward enough. Without such people, political campaigns would continue to function but without the heart and soul that make them joyous enterprises.

The Democratic campaign that spring was unveiling a promising new face—William L. Guy, a young farmer from Amenia who had won a seat in the state legislature after three losses. Scott Anderson, his legislative seatmate, had sensed his potential and encouraged him into the race for governor. Now running unopposed for the Democratic nomination, he was spending forty-five days on the stump, principally for Burdick. Bill turned out to be an asset we had not anticipated. His Norwegian good looks and firm speaking voice projected well on television and helped him draw large crowds.

Creative ideas were not an exclusive province of the pros. Burdick's sixteen-year-old daughter Jennifer had the idea of making an event out of her father's fifty-second birthday on June 19, which also was Father's Day and nine days before the election. Her idea mushroomed into an extravaganza. I checked with Ted Sorensen and found out that Senator Kennedy, flying overnight from Durango, Colorado, could make it. Not to be outdone in farm country, Senator Stuart Symington of Missouri, an outside contender for the Democratic presidential nomination, said he would be there, too. LBJ, who had been in North Dakota earlier, was tied up and sent John A. Burns, the Hawaii congressional delegate, to represent him. Four thousand people showed up at the Fargo fairgrounds, the same number that crowded the Bismarck ballpark a few days later to hear Minnesota neighbor Senator Hubert Humphrey raise the rafters for Burdick. Our campaign was going into the stretch with all cylinders firing.

In the short weeks before the election, the "smear" that we had anticipated was surfacing. We obtained a copy. Headlined "Quentin Burdick and his Communist Associates," it was the same old stuff, nothing new or anything that even called for a rebuttal. The layout was more striking and the text more vitriolic than we expected, but basically it was drearily dull. Most significantly, it was unsigned.

There was an obvious opening here for us. The mailing or distribution of anonymous material in federal election campaigns is illegal by statute. I called Eddie Higgins, the politically astute chief of staff to Rhode Island's nonagenarian Democratic senator, Theodore Francis Green, chair of the Subcommittee on Privileges and Elections. "Collect depositions from persons who have received this junk in the mail or in person," he said. "Then send them to us with a formal complaint. We will move on it right away."

Eddie was as good as his word. Monday morning before Election Day, Green announced that two subcommittee investigators were flying to North Dakota to look into the use of anonymous "smear" literature against Burdick. The story was headlined in the North Dakota edition of the Minneapolis *Tribune,* and the media throughout the state followed suit. The story cast a shadow over the Republican campaign, and the phone calls that poured into our headquarters told us we had struck a chunk of pay dirt. After the campaign, Vic Johnston told me that the "smear sheet" was unsigned because state G.O.P. officials refused to put their imprimatur upon it.

On the day before the election, it was one of my standard gimmicks to cloak my candidate in patriot's garb by delivering a five-minute speech entitled "The Longest Line." It went something like this: "Tomorrow you will stand in the longest line in American history—the line that leads to the ballot box. George Washington, Thomas Jefferson, Davy Crockett and Meriwether Lewis, Albert Einstein, and Joe Louis—all the diverse and unique people who have made our country the world's greatest—have stood in that line. But not one of their votes counted any more than that of the poorest sharecropper or the lowliest city-dweller. Our genius is: one person, one vote."

It went on in that vein, climaxing with a nonpartisan appeal to vote. Sure, it was corn, but an effective antidote to the charge that Republicans were offering in those years that Democrats were sort of un-American. On the occasions when I had filmed "The Longest Line," it was with rippling flags and patriotic music. It brought tears to the eye.

I had Quentin narrate an audiotape. He gave it a competent reading, but his flat midwestern voice lacked any dramatic quality. Fred Waring and His Pennsylvanians would provide the missing element. I had pirated them before—notably in the Neuberger campaign—and with perverse pleasure, because Waring was such a dedicated Republican. Behind Burdick's voice we dubbed the Waring rendition of "America the Beautiful" and "The Battle Hymn of the Republic" into a stirring blend of voice and song. Al Hamilton, the dubber, said, "It sort of makes my hair stand on end, if I say so myself."

Coming into the last weekend, all kinds of late money was materializing, as it so often does. People get fired up near the end and write checks, and the campaign manager has to be prepared to spend it effectively. Late developments can affect the difference in tight races, but they are seldom visible to the outside eye. My *modus operandi* was to pour the money into expanding the television and radio schedule. Because of network programming, adding to video coverage was limited, but radio's capacity to absorb late money was infinite. North Dakota's airwaves were flooded that weekend with Burdick's get-out-the-vote exhortation. Driving around, I heard it twice and got teary despite myself. It was that effective. (Not long before he died in 1992, Burdick and I were reminiscing about the campaign. "If any single thing won for me," he remembered, "it was 'The Longest Line.' I had more comments on it than anything else in the campaign.")

Burdick's day-before-election schedule was jammed, but he had only one thing on his mind at the seven o'clock breakfast. "What," he demanded of me, "are we going to do with that half-hour of statewide television tonight?" It had been on my mind and I had a definite plan, but I wasn't prepared to talk about it at that ungodly hour. We were going to meet that afternoon and do it then. His nervousness was warranted. The television program was not to be taken lightly. Originating live from the National Broadcasting Company affiliate, WDAY, which blanketed eastern North Dakota, it also was being fed to stations throughout western North Dakota. The time was absolutely prime—eight o'clock in the evening, the peak viewing hour. A bummer could blow the entire campaign.

That afternoon, I explained my plan. In a living-room setting, Quentin would informally discuss the campaign with his children, of whom he had seen little in recent months. Bill Guy, the gubernatorial candidate and by now a polished performer, would be there to keep the conversation moving—

not a difficult task, since the Burdick girls were lively talkers. I had a gimmick to keep the program from drifting into banality. Not one of the Bur-
dicks had seen the fifteen-minute documentary on Quentin's life that had
run twice on statewide television. It was a good film with some wonderful
old footage, including his Minnesota football exploits. Guy would show it
on a movie projector, just as one would present a home movie. Then Quentin
would be left with enough time to sum up his campaign with the spiel he
had been using on the stump.

We arrived at WDAY before seven, which gave us a bit more than an
hour to get comfortable with the set and the cameras. There was no real
rehearsal; it might blunt the informal spontaneity that would make the performance seem homegrown. The red light came on, and the program was
on the air. Praise be, everyone outdid themselves, and it went off better than
if it had been scripted and rehearsed a month in advance.

I was watching in the studio along with Mark Andrews, the Republican
national committeeman who had been assigned to "shadow" Burdick. Afterward, he grudgingly said, "It was corny bullshit, but pretty good." Then I was
surrounded by a jubilant candidate and his family. "Come out to our house,"
they urged. Suddenly, I was tired and talked out, and hitting my bed at the
Gardner Hotel seemed like the best idea in the world. I declined and walked
back to the hotel.

Crossing the lobby, I encountered Vic Johnston. "Where are you going?"
he asked. "To bed," I said wearily. "The hell you are," he boomed. "We've
got a party going on the F-M Roof, and I'm going to serve you up on a spit
as the *pièce de résistance!*" Remarkably, my blood surged. The idea of booz-
ing and doing verbal battle with the top-dog Republicans seemed like a per-
versely fitting way to climax this campaign. Vic and I drove across the Red
River to Moorhead, Minnesota, and the F-M Hotel's Roof, which turned
out to be a swinging cocktail lounge overlooking Fargo's lights. There, around
a large round table, sat the GOP high command: National Committeeman
Andrews, State Chairman Arley Bjella, Lt. Governor C. P. Dahl, banker Bill
Stern, Jack Mills, Mike Gill, and more. They were well along in the drinking department and boisterously informed me that my candidate was going
to receive a royal ass-kicking on the morrow. For awhile I sat there, smiling,
and parroted a line I had learned from my first campaign: "The results will
speak for themselves."

They got to me by my third drink, and I heard myself saying, "Would you like to put your money where your mouth is?" Yes, they sure would, and I ended up with seven bets at $100 apiece. I awoke at four A.M. in my own room in a boozy sweat. What had I done? I couldn't afford to lose $700, and I cursed myself for allowing them to goad me into doing such a dumb thing.

Coming down Fargo's main street election morning, I ran into Bill Stern, the only one of my Republican drinking companions who had not bet me. President of the Dakota National Bank and a founder of Northwest Airlines, Bill was a GOP bigwig here, but I had known him in Seattle as Warren Magnuson's closest confidant, and we had winked conspiratorially about his role out West. He was headed for a brunch with his GOP associates, after which they would play a round of golf, have a few drinks in the bar, and then go to Republican headquarters to enjoy the early returns and make a betting pool on the exact time when Burdick would concede. I continued on to the Fargo Labor Temple, where banks of telephones and a fleet of cars were ready for a major get-out-the-vote effort. Every precinct had been canvassed, and now it would be up to the foot soldiers to get targeted voters to the polls.

After the polls closed, there was a rush to Burdick's house, on a bluff over the Red River. A bar was open, and huge platters of cold cuts were laid out. Thirsty and famished, the campaign's principals and foot soldiers were gorging themselves while waiting for the first returns. A retired woodsmith had presented the candidate with an ornately carved nameplate that read "Senator Burdick." I was superstitious enough that I would upbraid anyone for calling a candidate by the title of an office he was running for *before* he was actually elected. I am still embarrassed by what happened next. I went outside and threw the nameplate into the Red River. I still can see the stricken look on the carver's face. My unease may have had its roots in the story of Charles Evans Hughes, who went to bed on Election Night in 1916 believing he had defeated Woodrow Wilson. When a reporter called the next morning and asked for Hughes, he was haughtily informed that "the president" was asleep and could not be disturbed. "When he wakes up," the reporter replied, "tell him he isn't the president. California went for Wilson by three thousand votes."

The early returns were not good. Davis was piling up the usual Republican majorities in the cities, and each new tally fattened his lead. The boisterous mood at Burdick's shifted to apprehensive and then to grim as Davis's lead topped 10,000 votes at ten o'clock. Quentin's face sagged into exhaustion. P. W. "Bill" Lanier Jr., a Fargo lawyer who had worked to organize Dakota Democrats, told Burdick's children to get him to bed, and we left for Lanier's house to continue the vigil.

By midnight, Davis's margin was almost 12,000, but then the returns from the west and the country started to come in. Slowly but steadily, the Davis lead was shrinking and by four in the morning, when the paper-ballot counters called it quits, it was only 3,000. We were all shouting now and must have disturbed the neighbors.

The counting was resumed at eight o'clock on Wednesday morning, and all of us—Democratic and Republican operatives—weaved bleary-eyed into the Gardner Hotel coffee shop. Northeastern North Dakota was the first to report with complete returns, and the Burdick trend suddenly went into reverse with the Davis margin climbing to 4,200 votes. I did a projection with a veteran analyst of the state's voting pattern. With what remained, there was no way that such a margin could be overcome. We had made one hell of a race, but we were going to be nipped in the stretch. I talked to Quentin at home, and he appeared resigned to it. When LBJ and the AFL-CIO's Al Barkan called, I told them the bad news and they muttered condolences. I was left alone with Vic and his jubilant Republicans, seven of them counting my money.

At the Fargo *Forum*, the state's largest newspaper, the incoming tallies were being counted. John Paulson, the editor, banished us from the city room, and I was exiled into the circulation department with Vic and his cohorts. Paulson periodically sent over reporters to give us the latest count. Davis's lead—down to 3,000—was holding firm.

Just before four that afternoon, there was a stir in the city room. Something had happened—but what? Arthur Edson, the Associated Press's national reporter who had dismissed Burdick as a "cloddish hayshaker," saw me staring, scribbled something on a slip of paper and handed it to me. "Your bum just went ahead," he muttered in disbelief. I was dumbfounded. I looked at the slip, which read something like:

Sioux County: Burdick 896, Davis 23

Rolette County: Burdick 720, Davis 18

My god, the Indian vote had delivered. In the closing rush, I had forgotten about it. Back in March, a wizened Sioux woman from the Standing Rock Reservation had come into Democratic headquarters in Bismarck. She and I had drunk coffee in the Patterson Hotel coffee shop as she asked me for gas money to organize the reservation vote. She had been a longtime friend of Quentin's dad Usher. I gave her $50. Later, she said that she also could organize the Rolette Reservation, where she had cousins. I gave her another $50 and then forgot about it. Now it appeared that the $100 had been the best political money I ever spent.

Amazingly, it was all over. I commandeered a ride to Burdick's house and jubilation. Everyone was there, and the house was rocking. Quentin, his face smeared with the lipstick of his bride-to-be, wore a smile as wide as the Red River. It all had happened inside of an hour. With his lead now surpassing 1,000 votes, Burdick received a call from LBJ, who announced that the ever-gracious William F. Knowland, the GOP minority leader, had agreed to waive official certification. Burdick could be sworn in tomorrow. We took off in Mitch Disney's Cessna 310, with flashes of heat lightning streaking the sky, and raced to Washington.

The next day was a phantasmagoric round of ceremonies, press conferences, phone calls, and visits from fat-cat contributors. The climax was a reception that LBJ gave for his newest senator. I had been through the drill before, but twenty-two-year-old Scott Anderson was moon-eyed in first-time wonderment. Back in April, when I had reported to Johnson on the campaign, I had quite liberally quoted Scott in my analysis. Puzzled, LBJ asked me, "Who is this Scott Anderson?"

"Leader," I began deferentially, "he is the new executive director of the state party. Though he is only twenty-two. . . ." I got no further. Johnson erupted with a bellow. "You mean you've been wastin' my time with what some boy told you? Some goddamn boy not dry behind the ears, some snot-nosed kid, some punk peddling you a pile of chicken-shit and now you're tryin' to tell me it's chicken salad?" He was funny-mad, and I had to stifle a smile. But my dander was up. "Listen, Leader," I replied, "that boy knows more about politics in his state than some people twice and three times his age. He is the real thing, just like you were at his age."

Now I waited to introduce Scott to him. "Leader," I said, "do you remember that boy I told you about in April?" Johnson was uncommonly gracious. He put his big hand on Scott's shoulder and said, "Congratulations. From what I've heard about you, you must be like I was at your age."

10

OUTSIDE ON THE INSIDE

I RETURNED TO WASHINGTON ON NEW YEAR'S DAY 1959, MY THIRTY-seventh birthday. Fidel Castro was marching on Havana from the Sierra Maestre, and television and radio bulletins reported his hourly progress. I kind of felt like Castro. I had been out in the provinces helping win great victories for the Democratic Party and now was returning to the seat of empire to be draped with the garlands of victory. I was expecting to be greeted with fanfare after six months on the road from Maine to Alaska, helping elect a record batch of fifteen new Democrats to the United States Senate.

Atlas did not even shrug. I no longer was new or news. It was a rude fact of life that I found hard to accept. The elections of Neuberger, Church, and Proxmire had been unexpected and dramatic, creating and then preserving the Democrats' one-vote Senate majority. That margin had meant committee chairmanships and cushy staff and policy jobs. As the perceived architect of those victories, I had received unusual praise. I hungrily awaited a new round of tributes.

Instead, the now-fattened majority had made me passé to the Senate Democratic hierarchy. Recalling the early warning of Senator Robert S. Kerr of Oklahoma "not to elect too many Democrats," I half-wondered if Lyndon Johnson and the senior Senate sachems were annoyed because they were faced with such an influx of unknown newcomers. A big majority meant more margin for mischief, a wise old Senate staffer told me. He patiently made me understand why there was little apparent enthusiasm in the leadership councils for these new faces in the upcoming 86th Congress.

Lyndon Johnson, with his one-vote majority in his four years as leader, had won a deserved reputation as a miracle worker for getting through small chunks of the Democratic agenda, such as Social Security liberalization and a modest voting-rights bill. With a big majority, he would be expected to produce major miracles. Every constituent group in the Democratic coalition had an agenda; the AFL-CIO wanted repeal of the right-to-work provision of the Taft-Hartley Act, and the NAACP had a laundry list. Johnson came back from his Texas ranch with a scowl on his face.

One reason for his long face was the abrupt departure of Clements for the upcoming Kentucky gubernatorial campaign. He had been Johnson's right hand as whip and acting majority leader when the Texan had his heart attack. Totally devoted to LBJ but not blind to his foibles, Clements was well regarded by Southern senatorial barons such as Russell and Holland and liberals such as Douglas and Clark. In addition, he knew most of the incoming sixteen new senators. His absence would hurt the Leader.

Before Clements left, I asked him if Johnson was planning to seek the presidency. "I spent a week with him on the ranch in December," he reported, "and I don't believe that he plans to run. He doesn't think the party liberals will ever accept a southerner, nor does he think he can run the Senate and run for president at the same time. Every time I brought it up, he found some new negative."

My sense of relief was palpable. I had spent two years on the fringe of the Johnson circle, during which time I had consorted with most of LBJ's key players. My distaste for Lyndon was such that there was no way that I was going to participate in any presidential effort, but I hated the thought of splitting from Clements, George Reedy, Jim Rowe, Harry McPherson, and the other Johnsonites whom I liked so much. It would have been a tough choice to make.

Ike and his GOP army of occupation had been in nominal control for seven years; but now his time was coming to a close, and the pretenders and fakers from Wall Street and Main Street would be going back to where they belonged. The rightful owner-operators of the federal government were waiting in the wings to resume the management of government to benefit the electorate.

Such was the mindset of many Democrats after the sweep of 1958. That election had been proof that the United States was basically a Democratic nation. The general had been an aberration, maybe even a useful one because his administration had ratified the New Deal and the Fair Deal. Now the interregnum was almost over, and the question dominating conversation in Capitol Hill bars and Georgetown living rooms was who would succeed Eisenhower. Nixon's prospects were cavalierly dismissed.

Democratic Washington was roughly divided into four camps: Jack Kennedy's "Young Slickers," Lyndon Johnson's "Congressional Insiders," Stuart Symington's "Used-to-Be's," and Adlai Stevenson's "Rich Liberals." I knew most of the players in these camps. My six months on the road had taken me to the eight states where presidential primaries would be held in 1960, and I had some on-the-scene working knowledge. In 1959, the primaries were not what they later became, the be-all-and-end-all of the nominating process, but they couldn't be ignored. My reputation in the primary states was my cachet.

Late that January I boarded an Eastern Air Lines flight to New York where I had been invited to a meeting of major Democratic fundraisers organized by Roger Stevens, the financier and producer of Broadway plays such as *West Side Story*. Jack Kennedy sat down next to me. "Glad to run into you," he said. "I want to talk with you about my campaign. Your experience in Wisconsin, Oregon, and West Virginia can be very helpful. What will it take, and how soon can you come aboard with us?"

I wasn't totally surprised. Of all the operatives in the four camps that I had been talking with, Ted Sorensen was the one with whom I had developed a close relationship. I had helped him plan Kennedy's appearances for candidates across the country in the 1958 campaign, and it had been productive. Ted had been completely candid about what Kennedy was looking for—support in 1960 from those he campaigned for—and I had favorably responded to his honesty. In turn, he had indicated that there would be an important spot for me on the Kennedy team.

On the plane Kennedy said that he probably had to sweep all eight primaries to win the nomination at the Los Angeles convention. The Democratic power brokers in the big states were not going to give it to someone with three hexes on him—Catholic, senator, and a playboy reputation. He also asked me probing questions about personalities we both knew in the primary states.

Conversation with Jack Kennedy always was a pleasure. He liked to seek the views of others, and he listened. Most politicians were so absorbed with themselves that they usually were not interested in hearing what the other fellow had to say, unless it was something that directly affected them. Jack Kennedy seemed different. Talking with him was like talking to one of the guys, occasional four-letter words and all. It was hard to believe that one was talking to the possible next leader of the free world.

The plane was taxiing up to the LaGuardia terminal, and he returned to his first question, which I hadn't answered: How much did I need, and when could I start? When I told him that the United Steelworkers of America was paying me $25,000 a year on retainer, he winced. "I pay Ted Reardon [his administrative assistant] $14,000," he said. "Sorensen gets $12,000. It could cause me problems if I paid you that kind of money." I don't remember my exact answer, but it was to the effect that I was not about to take a pay cut. My wife would raise hell if I did.

Kennedy concluded the conversation. "I will have to see what I can work out with my dad. Let Mrs. Lincoln or Sorensen know when you can be available." He got into a waiting limousine and was gone.

My first call was to Earle Clements in Louisville. He had been much like a father in the two years of our intensely close relationship. Except for his family, his whole world was politics, and I had become beneficiary of his encyclopedic knowledge. Despite my pose as an "old political pro" and cynical ex-newspaperman, I was more a naively cocksure wiseacre whom he had to checkrein on occasion. His approval was necessary to me. "Do it," he advised.

The Steelworkers had been generously financing my political activities for almost four years. David J. McDonald, the silver-haired union president, invited me for dinner in his Carlton Hotel suite in Washington. "You're making a bad mistake," he said when I told him of Kennedy's offer and my tentative acceptance. "I like Jack, even though he is a playboy and a lightweight. But he can't win. This country isn't going to elect either a Catholic or a senator, and certainly not both. It is that simple."

McDonald went on to tell me that Big Steel was planning to force the union into a protracted strike when the contracts expired in July. "Blough [CEO of United States Steel] and Cooper [CEO of Bethlehem Steel] think they can break me and destroy all the work-rules we have won since 1938," he said. "It's going to be a long strike. We are going to need you. Stay until it is over. Meanwhile, I have no objection to you doing whatever you can for Jack." We shook hands on it.

I was secretly relieved. If my financial request had been met, it would have become known to others who were making less, and I would be resented. There was much to say for being monetarily independent in a campaign. It was a lot easier to tell the candidate what you really thought when he wasn't paying you.

Kennedy met with a working group on Mondays and Fridays when he was in town. He invited me to join. It consisted of his brother Robert, the Senate rackets committee counsel; his assistant Kenny O'Donnell; Steve Smith, his brother-in-law who had opened campaign headquarters in a nearby office building; Ted Sorensen and his deputy Mike Feldman; Ralph Dungan, a Senate staffer; and a precinct politician just arrived from Springfield, Massachusetts, named Larry O'Brien.

From the outset I felt like the odd man out. Kennedy had introduced me as a resident expert on the key primary states (a questionable premise, as it turned out), and I felt seven sets of skeptical eyes turn on me. It was an understandable reaction. Most of this crew had a bottled-in-the-bond comradeship earned in past Kennedy campaigns. I was a pretender, to be treated as such until I did something worthwhile to prove myself.

Being an outsider was not new to me. I had coped with it in the past and could usually achieve an identity with the group and become "one of the boys." Here I struck out. The meetings were dominated by a humorless intensity that brooked no levity or deviation from the main chance. The ironic Irish humor that I liked in Jack seldom surfaced in these meetings.

Bobby was so grimly all-business that it unsettled me. To me, politics was a freebooting business with humor an essential ingredient, and I had almost made a fetish out of irreverence. But Bobby was not tolerant of *Last Hurrah* characters, and my attempts at wisecracks may have pegged me as one. Hard-nosed assessments of pols and politics in the primary states had no room for sidebar humor.

I liked to drink, and the Carroll Arms Hotel bar across the street from the Senate Office Building was my favorite wateringhole. Housed in the only decent hotel on the Senate side of the Capitol, it was the only saloon on Capitol Hill worthy of the name. Fondly dubbed "the sewer" or the "CA" by its patrons, the Carroll Arms attracted a full range of Hill personalities. Many senators, several of whom lived in the hotel, were regulars, and a few had a reputation for spending more time there than they did on the Senate floor. The rest of the crowd was made up of Senate staffers and secretaries, lobbyists, and visiting firemen. It was a place where one could see everybody.

We entered the CA from the street by going down a steep flight of stairs into a cavern-like room in which screens created small areas of intimate alcoves and cubbyholes. A huge round table near the foot of the stairs was reserved for the regulars, and on any given night a mélange of senators, staffers, and lobbyists was to be found there. The regulars were Democratic senators and their functionaries and labor lobbyists. Winston Prouty, a strange Republican solon from Vermont, and Chuck Colson, an aide to Saltonstall of Massachusetts, sometimes exchanged barbs and gossipy tidbits at the big table. The arch Republicans, such as Capehart of Indiana and Curtis of Nebraska, sat stiffly apart, but when Everett Dirksen of Illinois came in, he usually circled the room and greeted familiar faces, the huskiness of his stage-soft voice resonating pleasantly. Across the room near the bar was a grand piano surrounded by barstools, usually filled by young things from the Senate offices. The pianist-singer was a boyish-looking former seminary student from Buffalo named Mark Russell.

In its day, there was nothing quite like the Carroll Arms. It is a tradition that all legislative bodies are graced with a close-by hangout where spirits are served. Events such as England's Glorious Revolution and the American Revolution were plotted in such places. Every state legislature had one, and I had been in a good number of them, from the Augusta House in Maine to The Tropics in Honolulu and the Baranof Bar in Juneau. A legislature hardly could exist without such establishments.

What made the CA unique was its ecumenicity. Senators did not have Capitol hideaways in those days, and the CA was convenient and convivial. Secretaries, seeking to avoid the blank walls of their efficiency apartments, hung around listening to Russell and hoping someone nice would buy them dinner. Butter-and-egg men from Peoria and Pocatello stared at well-known faces and thought of getting lucky.

The CA was where one learned that senators and congressmen were not Olympian or Augustan figures. Hardly. Some deep in their cups seemed more like a subspecies. One night at the big table a newly elected senator from

New Jersey, Harrison (Pete) Williams cried: "Where are the giants? Where are the Websters and the Clays, the Borahs and the Barkleys? I look around the Senate floor and see a bunch of guys just like myself!"

Alcohol was significant to the culture of Capitol Hill. Liquor was everywhere, largely at the stream of receptions staged by business and farm groups, trade unions, and chambers of commerce. It flowed in offices, bars, and cafés. To those coming from cultures where drink was an occasional thing, liquor's ubiquity could be devastating. Many an innocent from Bangor or Boise had fallen victim and been sent home in semi-disgrace. Washington, D.C., deserved its reputation as the hardest-drinking town in the nation.

I always had taken pride in my ability to hold my liquor. It was a macho thing. From college days on, I had engaged in some prodigious drinking bouts and seldom had been bested. My feat of downing sixteen martinis in one sitting in a Seattle bar and walking home was a record that I believed never would be broken. I could slug whiskey shot-for-shot and never blink an eye. I looked on liquor as a good friend, helpful to my career and to my ability to socialize with anybody. Nobody said anything until one night at the CA Maurice Rosenblatt let me have it with both barrels. "You are like every ex-athlete I've ever known," he rasped. "Your body is turning to squishy fat and your brain is getting addled with alcohol. You are sliding downhill so fast that you'll be out of here before you know what hit you." He intended his words to be shock treatment, and they were—sort of. I joined the YMCA and began playing handball.

But the trouble was in my head, not my body. It often takes a lifetime to understand fully one's ego, and many people never do. In 1959, my comprehension was limited, to say the least. I had an idealized sense of myself that was far removed from reality, and that made realistic self-assessment virtually impossible. Washington, Doris Fleeson had warned me, was brutal on egos, worse even than New York or Hollywood. Mine, which had been blown up like a Macy's parade balloon after the 1958 triumph, had been punctured. I had briefly tasted minor recognition, and I wanted more. It is a common disease, and I had a nasty case of it.

There was, however, solace to be found in New York, my birthplace. The wealthy and influential Democrats of that city believed that it contained the heart and brains, the marrow and cockles, the innermost mind of the party founded right there by Thomas Jefferson and his Tammany Hall friends.

They had the ideas, the intellect, the communications skills, and—not least—the money that it took to win nationwide elections. Hadn't they proven it with one of their own, Franklin D. Roosevelt?

Gotham had many big Democratic players, one of them an extraordinarily wealthy and handsome widow, Mary Lasker. She became my Manhattan "den mother." I had won her favor in 1956 by initiating a Senate amendment that earmarked funds for medical research in the Veterans Administration budget. With her husband, Albert D. Lasker, she had lobbied the National Institutes of Health into existence. Her six-story townhouse at 29 Beekman Place not only was an incredible treasure trove of the French Impressionist art that she and her husband had collected before World War II, but it was also the scene of intimate luncheons and receptions that she held for influential Democrats. As an invitee, I was privileged to break bread with a remarkable aggregation of American figures—financiers such as André Meyer and Robert Benjamin; lawyers-statesmen such as Thomas K. Finletter, Cyrus Vance, and George Backer; emerging politicians such as Ed Costikyan and Ed Koch; and New York *Post* publisher Dorothy Schiff and her editor Jimmy Wechsler.

The *raison d'être* for my presence was as a conquering young general from the provinces called upon by The Establishment to report the latest, not only in the field but at a congressional GHQ—that is, Washington, D.C. Having been in political combat gave me a little swagger with people who hadn't. I can't recall any words of weighty note being said at these gatherings. These were rich, celebrated, and witty people, but the conversation didn't seem to be much above the level of a crowd in a beer tavern in Huron, South Dakota.

But the setting wasn't Huron. I had not been encased in such tasteful opulence since childhood, when Mother and I would visit her wealthy Smith College classmates in their Park Avenue apartments. My Manhattan, after she left Dad in 1934, was one of skylight rooms in dark brownstones, neon-lit cafeterias on streets under the Elevated, apartment hallways that stunk of urine and cabbage, and grimy subway trains. I doubted that Mary Lasker and her guests, for all their humanitarian *noblesse oblige*, had much knowledge of my side of town, only a few blocks away. Mary had told me of being raised in Watertown, Wisconsin, in modest circumstances and coming to New York beautiful, smart, and poor, but I doubt she slept in any skylight rooms.

Being "elevated" to a world that I had read about longingly was an enchantment. To be, if only occasionally, a *mensch* in Manhattan was the penultimate. My blood would race when I got off the plane at LaGuardia. I was in "my town."

A young man with parallel ideas had decided that I could be useful to him. William vanden Heuvel was a Manhattan lawyer of modest means and impeccable lineage who had married Jean Stein, the striking and talented daughter of Dr. Jules Stein, founder-owner of the Music Corporation of America. Bill had a striking resemblance to an earlier descendant of the Dutch poltroons who settled the Hudson River Valley in Nieuw Amsterdam days. With a booming voice and a jaw that jutted like FDR's, he bounded into things with manic energy. He was planning to run against Congressman John V. Lindsay of Manhattan's "silk-stocking" district in 1960, surely his first step on a journey that would take him all the way. Thus, his interest in me.

The vanden Heuvels loved to give dinner parties in their large Fifth Avenue apartment. Jean was a superb hostess who attracted the glitterati to her gatherings. Once I had Dorothy Parker for a dinner partner; another time it was Ilka Chase. I learned that one did not have to be an Algonquin Round Table raconteur at these events. It was easier to listen and enjoy the people around the table, people I had read about in the novels of Louis Auchincloss and F. Scott Fitzgerald. Although I was supposedly mature at thirty-seven, inside was the street kid awed at being among people whose names were in the gossip columns.

New York was a town for girls, and I had two splendid ones to sashay around with. Laura was a blonde Swede from Minnesota who wrote cover stories for *Look* magazine and had numbered Che Guevera and Ruby Rubirosa among her suitors. Our relationship wasn't romantic, but she was usually game to meet me for a drink at the Berkshire Hotel for an evening of bar-hopping from midtown to Greenwich Village.

Anne was a fey blonde English actress who was enjoying minor success on the New York stage and in Hollywood. She had a wealthy suitor in Arizona whom she was planning to marry. I was so pleased to escort her to supper clubs such as El Morocco and the Blue Angel, where she was embraced by Dorothy Kilgallen and Ed Sullivan, that I tolerated being turned away at the doorstep of her brownstone. She was a spunky sport and laughed at me.

I usually stayed in an apartment twenty-odd blocks away in the East 50s that Clay Felker and Burt Glinn shared. Felker was a rising star at Time Inc., and Glinn was a Magnum photographer with whom I had worked on *Life* assignments in the Pacific Northwest. Clay was a ladies' man and seldom slept alone. One morning as I was shaving, his current interest, a showgirl at the Copacabana, came into the bathroom and said, "Clay tells me that you know Adlai Stevenson. He's my hero, and I want to know everything about him." She was naked, and I tried to keep from staring as I stumbled through a verbal essay on Adlai.

To me, Felker, Glinn, Peter Maas, Dick Clurman of *Time*, and their crowd represented the current crop of what Katharine Brush described in *Young Man of Manhattan*, her 1930s bestseller. Ambition oozed out of every pore of these talented trendsetters. They were the antithesis of the neighborhood guys who hung around the candy store and bemoaned life. They were going places, and most of them did.

Exhilarating as this world was, it still was peripheral to the developing struggle for the Democratic presidential nomination, and everyone, save the most insular Gotham Democrats, knew it. New York might control communications and money, but it was a bit player in the nominating process. The hinterlands was where Jack Kennedy was going to have to win it.

JFK knew that my strengths were with organized labor and in the western states. Accordingly, I planned to go to the September convention of the AFL-CIO in San Francisco and then trek around six western states hunting potential delegates. Before leaving, I had two strokes of luck—one good and the other, as it turned out, very bad.

A young Arizona congressman, Stewart L. Udall, was staying with me that summer of 1959. His wife Lee hated Washington summers and took her family home to Tucson. Their suburban Virginia home was sublet, leaving Stew homeless. I took him in. He had become a particular friend. He appreciated my political skills and also taught me something of the inner workings of the legislative process. He was also a leader of an attractive group of young congressmen who hung out together, including Frank Thompson of New Jersey, Lee Metcalf of Montana, "Lud" Ashley of Ohio, Carl Elliott of Alabama, and George McGovern of South Dakota.

Udall was still enamored of Adlai Stevenson. In fact, he had written a *New Republic* cover story entitled "Why I'm for Stevenson in 1960." When I told Kennedy that I had hopes of landing him, he said, "Forget it. There's the *New Republic* piece he can't repudiate and, besides, his wife is a true Mormon. She hates me." Cocksure, I responded, "Bet you twenty bucks I can, Jack." We shook hands on it.

The summer of 1959 was a long and ugly one for Congress. The issue was labor-union reform legislation, brought on by the revelations of the Senate Rackets Committee, with Robert F. Kennedy as counsel. Its back to the wall, the AFL-CIO was throwing its resources into an effort to defeat the most stringent of several bills, this one offered by two obscure congressmen—Republican Robert Griffin of Michigan and Democrat Phil Landrum of Georgia. The legislation was in Senate-House conference, with Kennedy and Udall as co-sponsors.

Kennedy's skills impressed Udall, and he kept saying so. But I wasn't prepared for him impulsively to say one evening, after downing his second martini: "Damn it, I'm ready to sign up with your guy." We seized the moment. I checked and found that Kennedy was still in his office, and we drove to Capitol Hill in the August twilight. I stayed out of the meeting. When we were leaving, Kennedy gave me a wink and slipped me something. It was a twenty-dollar bill. The following April, at the Arizona state Democratic convention, Udall and his cohorts delivered the fifteen-member delegation to JFK, his first nonprimary victory in a conservative state assumed to be Lyndon Johnson's. It was one of Kennedy's most significant wins in the early delegate hunt.

I am being charitable to myself in describing the next incident as bad luck. Sheer stupidity is the more apt characterization. Oregon, a key primary state, was my turf. I was the expert on its Democratic politics and had talked with most of the significant figures about the presidential primary. Although these people represented different elements of a fractious party, they nonetheless were united on one point: Keep Bobby Kennedy out of Oregon.

The recent Senate Rackets Committee hearings, with Bobby as counsel, had centered on Oregon, and Portland's respected Democratic mayor, Terry Schrunk, had been indicted. RFK testified against him in the subsequent trial in which Schrunk was acquitted. The bad blood against Bobby was still boiling, and I was importuned by those I talked with, including such Kennedy supporters as Congresswoman Edith Green of Portland, to let Jack know about it.

Did I stop to think that the relationship between the two brothers, which I had observed close up, should call for a delicate, sensitive approach on my part? No. I blunderbussed my way in a one-on-one dialogue with JFK in which the following took place: "Jack, do you remember the Listerine ads with the headline, 'Even your best friends won't tell you'?"

JFK (puzzled): "Yes, I do."

Me (nervously): "I am in that situation regarding the Oregon primary. Every Oregon Democrat, including your strongest supporters, have told me the same —that Bobby should stay out of the state. They think I should be authorized to give that assurance when I go to Oregon to help organize your statewide committee."

JFK: "I don't fully understand. Why?"

Me (struggling for words): "Well, ah, um, they think that Bobby kind of made a horse's ass out of himself in the Schrunk trial and all."

Kennedy's eyes became pale blue slits, and his voice was as frigid as I had ever heard. "You know more about Oregon than we do, and if we have to accept that judgment, we will. That doesn't mean we like it."

With that I was dismissed. I had blundered, I knew, but how badly I was not to learn until a few months later. In the meantime, I was so absorbed with the fight against Landrum-Griffin and the ongoing steel strike that I had no time to brood over my *faux pas*. Nineteen fifty-nine was turning out to be a year in which everything seemed to be happening at once, and there was no time for reflection. It was just one damned thing tumbling on top of another. Coming next were the primaries and the AFL-CIO convention.

John Salter accompanied me on my western swing. He was more than Senator Scoop Jackson's chief assistant. He was his best friend and more than an equal when it came to politics. As a onetime Catholic seminarian, John had a natural interest in Kennedy, and I had induced him to come aboard. Scoop had grumbled that Kennedy "didn't have a chance" and added "I hope you know what you are doing."

The climate at the AFL-CIO national convention at San Francisco's Civic Center was cold enough to Kennedy to give us pause. Landrum-Griffin had passed Congress a few short weeks before, and many delegates blamed Bobby Kennedy's appearance on Jack Paar's *Tonight Show* as the blow that had defeated labor's frenzied effort to kill the bill. Bobby had urged viewers to write or call their congressmen to pass strong labor reform legislation, and

Congress had been deluged. Labor's margin evaporated overnight, resulting in its most humiliating loss since the Taft-Hartley Act in 1947, only this time it was a supposedly liberal Democratic Congress that did the deed.

When I walked on the convention floor, a familiar Irish brogue was rasping through the huge hall from the dais. "I say that he is a disgrace to the Irish with his slave labor law, the Kennedy-Landrum-Griffin witches' brew. And that goes for his labor-hating little brother and his union-busting daddy, too. They have disgraced their own blood and their heritage."

"For god's sake, who is that?" Salter asked.

"Mike Quill, president of the Transit Workers Union. That's the New York subway workers. He's been a longtime Kennedy hater."

A few feet from us stood Joe Curran, the brawny president of the National Maritime Union. He smiled broadly at me, but it froze when he saw the Kennedy pin in my lapel. "What's that?" he demanded. I explained that while I still was with the Steelworkers, I was also here on Kennedy's behalf.

A tirade followed such as I never had heard. Joe Kennedy, Curran exploded, had tried to put him in jail when Kennedy was chairman of the Federal Maritime Commission in the 1930s, and since then Curran had declared war on all Kennedys—"the lowest scum that crawled the face of the earth." Curran made Quill sound mild. His outburst attracted other listeners, who nodded approvingly. It was the rudest reaction to a political figure that I ever had experienced, and I feared that Curran's anger would turn to violence—against me. Eventually, he cooled down, and I eased away.

Later, I palavered at length with some JFK supporters—including Arthur J. Goldberg, Esther Peterson, and the Electrical Workers' Joe Keenan—and found universal agreement that this convention was not a propitious place to push Kennedy's candidacy. So I was reduced to cultivating my past contacts with labor officials in the primary states, mostly by buying them drinks. The credit cards Evelyn Lincoln had given me to pay for the trip were made out to "J. P. Kennedy, 515 Fifth Avenue, New York," and I signed his name to the drink tabs with swaggering flourish.

The rest of the month-long trip took me to Oregon, Washington, Idaho, Montana, Wyoming, Nevada, and Utah—states in which I had long-standing and warm relationships with most of the Democratic Party leadership. I met with them all, and every one of them asked the question that seemed to be troubling them in this autumn of 1959: What about Kennedy's reputation as a womanizer? It was asked in many ways, some right up front and others more discreetly, but always asked.

I was surprised. True, there were stories circulating around Washington, but now, out in the western "sticks," it had developed into a significant issue. How could I answer it and be believable? I told my questioners that I had traveled thousands of miles with JFK, with every trip featuring a man-killing schedule, and never saw a hint of hanky-panky on his part. Occasionally, I said kiddingly: "If he can manage girls on top of that kind of a schedule, then he's an even better man than I think he is."

Upon my return to Washington, for three straight days I dictated state-by-state reports, plus a separate one on the AFL-CIO convention. Ted Sorensen and I went to lunch at the Methodist Building to discuss my findings. It was apparent to me that something was bothering him. It was not long in coming out. "It has been reported to me," he said through clenched teeth, "that you have been making out-of-line remarks about the senator's personal life. This is serious and can be considered a breach of faith on your part."

I immediately recognized that Utah Democrat Oscar McConkey had misconstrued my remark. When I related it to Sorensen, he was unyielding. The sense of humor that the Kennedys later were to become famous for was not much in evidence among his minions. I knew I had better rein in my freewheeling tongue, or I would become a worse pariah than I already was.

Several days later, John Salter and I had a drink at the Carroll Arms. When we left he said, "See you at Butler in the morning." My puzzled look surprised him, but he said nothing more as he departed. I worked late the next day, and it was well past six when the phone rang. It was Salter. "I'm at the airport," he said. "Meet me at the CA in a half hour."

Usually unflappable, John seemed agitated when he sat down. "Do you know where I've been all day?" he asked. I shook my head.

"Hyannisport," he said. "We met at Butler Aviation at seven this morning and flew up to Ambassador Joe's house in the *Caroline* for an all-day strategy meeting. Bobby sat with me on the flight. The first question I asked him was, 'Where is Joe Miller?' Jesus, he was ugly. 'That son-of-a-bitch called me a horse's ass,' he said. 'Nobody does that to me and gets away with it.' 'Bobby,' I said, 'Joe Miller got me and Scoop into your brother's campaign. I wouldn't be here if it wasn't for him. He's been touting him for two years.' 'No matter,' Bobby said, 'Joe Miller is a loose cannon, and he has no place in our future plans as far as I am concerned.' I've always known the little runt was mean," Salter concluded, "but this is the first time I've seen it up close. It was ugly, and I debated whether or not to tell you. It is best that you know."

Numb as I was over my first big rejection in the political arena, I agreed. It was best to know. Not by nature a brooder or sulker, I nonetheless did my share of it in this situation. Going home to Seattle for the Christmas holidays was a welcome respite. Interest there in JFK had spurted, and I won some tentative commitments from people likely to be selected as convention delegates when Washington state Democrats met in May. This boosted my drooping ego and strengthened my resolve to work through the "Bobby thing" by performing.

When I returned to Washington, Salter got me together with Bobby for drinks at the Carroll Arms. He arrived, unsmiling and tightlipped. We talked about the first primary that Hubert Humphrey would enter—Wisconsin— but nothing I said seemed to strike any positive sparks. Bobby left abruptly with a perfunctory handshake, and Salter decided that the conflict appeared irreconcilable.

Evelyn Lincoln called to say that Senator Kennedy would like me to have breakfast with him at his Georgetown house. As always, Jack came right to the point. "With Jerry Bruno and the others out there on the ground, we seem to be in good shape in Wisconsin," he said. "West Virginia is another story. We have nothing going there. Through the Byrd and Randolph campaigns, you know something of the state. I would like you to manage my campaign there."

My acceptance may have seemed less than unqualified. I explained that I had commitments to Lee Metcalf for the Montana Senate primary in May and to Quentin Burdick for the North Dakota special Senate election in June. The West Virginia primary was slated for mid-May and did not appear to be a significant shootout in the battle for the Democratic presidential nomination. The state had no previous presidential primary history and was ignored by pundits sizing up the obstacles in Kennedy's path. Nobody, including JFK, foresaw that it was destined to be the crucial primary of 1960. His offer to me was almost offhand, as if to say it would give me something to do at a distance from Bobby.

Jack gave me a survey of West Virginia, taken some months before, that showed him leading Hubert Humphrey by a 70–to-30 margin. It was a slim piece of research that I flipped through and noted that it didn't take into account his Catholicism, which had to be an issue in a state as strongly Protestant as West Virginia.

"I have no confidence in those figures holding up," Kennedy said, "if old Hubert and his people bring the Pope into the race. West Virginia is in the Bible Belt, and it's hard to say how much their attitudes have changed since Al Smith in 1928."

I recalled from my brief West Virginia experience in 1958 that a fundamental staple of campaigning for Byrd and Randolph had been church appearances and the teaching of Bible classes; Byrd liked to brag that he had taught the biggest such classes in the state's history. My role in their campaign had been the production of the basic media; I was ignorant of negotiations with local politicians and preachers. In a state as poor as West Virginia, votes were a commodity to be bought and sold just like anything else, a fact of which I was surprisingly innocent. Had I not been, my dialogue with JFK would have been much different.

Shakespeare, in *Julius Caesar*, makes the most telling of observations:

There is a tide, in the affairs of men,
Which, taken at the flood, leads on to fortune.

I drifted aimlessly in the "flood." My West Virginia contacts yielded zilch. Byrd, Randolph, and their staffs had little use for Kennedy and said so. Miles Stanley, president of the state AFL-CIO, and Paul Rusen, the sachem of the Steelworkers Union, were downright hostile to the "real" architect of the just-enacted anti-labor Landrum-Griffin bill. I had been counting on those two to form a nucleus on which a campaign could be built. Without them, I was lost. In short, I struck out with my bat on my shoulder. My ineffectuality probably proved that Bobby was right. I was a vastly overrated fraud.

But Bobby and his crew weren't paying attention to West Virginia. The celebrated Wisconsin primary had turned into a bearcat, with underdog Humphrey—sensing a chance for an upset—coming on strong. The media had focused on Hubert, and he was getting the play that an underrated challenger sometimes receives when he threatens to score an upset. The media were protecting themselves.

West Virginia was not even mentioned when Kennedy invited me to his Georgetown house on a rare day at home a week before the Wisconsin primary. He was snappish. "You worked for Hearst," he said. "What do you do about crap like this?" He handed me the editorial page of the Milwaukee *Sentinel*. The lead editorial read:

McCarthyism? We Don't Think So

Former U.S. Congressman Charles Kirsten was accused of "McCarthyism" when he charged Senator John F. Kennedy with being "soft on Communism."

Wait a minute! All month long the Kennedy campaign song, "High Hopes," has been blaring from street corners across Wisconsin. The singer is Frank Sinatra. And who is Sinatra? He is the same man who recently hired Albert Maltz of the Hollywood "Unfriendly Ten" and a convicted Communist to write the script for his next movie.

This connection leads us to believe that Kirsten may not have been far wrong when he suggested that the senator from Massachusetts, if perhaps unwittingly, was "soft on Communism."

I had read many an illogical editorial, but this one topped them all. "Call Frank Cunniff," I suggested. "He is editorial director of the Hearst Newspapers and also is a liberal Democrat. He will be appalled." Kennedy picked up the phone: "Mrs. Lincoln, get me Frank Cunniff at the Hearst Newspapers in New York."

Minutes later he answered the phone and went into his complaint about the editorial. A puzzled look came over his face. "I'm sorry," he said. "My secretary got the wrong Cunniff. But while I have you on the phone, I'd like to tell you that I never missed 'Terry and the Pirates' when I was a kid, and I read 'Steve Canyon' every day." Mrs. Lincoln had reached Milton Caniff, the comic-strip creator, by mistake. Kennedy, as he usually did, had graceful words to apologize for the error.

His relaxed warmth with me had lulled me into thinking that my problem with Bobby was curable. I was in Bismarck, North Dakota, shortly after Jack had won a narrow victory over Humphrey in the Wisconsin primary when Teno Roncalio called me from Cheyenne. Teno was Wyoming Democratic party chairman and the first state official to declare for JFK. The state's delegates were going to decide on their presidential choice, and Kennedy needed to win them all on the unit rule to compensate for his failure to eliminate Humphrey in Wisconsin. Lyndon Johnson also had thrown half his hat in the ring and was an emerging factor, particularly in western states such as Wyoming, where Kennedy had high hopes.

"I need you," Teno said. "There are some delegates who will listen to you that I can't reach." When I arrived in Cheyenne after a bumpy, seven-stop flight on a DC-3, he assigned me to the three Anselmi brothers from the coal-mining town of Rock Springs. They were key, Teno said, to swinging the delegation to JFK.

Not long after my arrival, Bobby entered the lobby of the Plains Hotel, which was full of local Democrats and agents of every candidate, including unannounced ones such as Stuart Symington. He was accompanied by Byron "Whizzer" White and Joe Dolan, Denver lawyers. Bobby greeted me with what seemed to be genuine warmth and then invited me to join them later in a private meeting with Wyoming's Democratic sachems. I told him that I was going to meet with the Anselmis at the Hitching Post, a restaurant-motel outside of town, and probably wouldn't get back in time.

The Anselmis did not, as it turned out, need much persuading. They simply wanted assurances from a national political professional that a Roman Catholic had a realistic chance to be elected president. The senior Anselmi, who had emigrated from Italy to work in the Wyoming coalfields, remembered the Al Smith debacle of 1928 and was fearful it could happen again.

I was feeling pretty good the next morning at an everybody-come breakfast for Lyndon Johnson when Teno Roncalio pulled me aside. His voice was quivering as he told me what had happened the night before at the meeting with Bobby. Tracy McCraken, Wyoming's richest citizen and longtime Democratic National Committeeman, had said something like this to Bobby: "I was pleased to find out that Joe Miller is helping your brother in the West. Joe is very effective in this part of the country and knows more Democrats by their first names than anyone I've known since Jim Farley. He is a real professional."

Bobby's response, as Teno related it to me, was chilling: "Joe Miller has no place in our campaign after the Los Angeles convention. He is simply someone we have to put up with until then." His voice, Teno said, was ice. I knew Teno was telling the truth but still found it incomprehensible. Was Bobby that big a hypocrite to greet me so warmly and then gratuitously dismiss me like that? I knew that I sometimes evoked strong negative reactions, but this one threw me. Thank heavens I was too damned busy to brood about it.

What was to be my last trip with JFK on the *Caroline*, the campaign's propeller-driven Convair, was an all-night ride from Washington to Spokane in late May for the Washington state Democratic convention. Kennedy's stock had risen sharply after his decisive victory over Humphrey in West Virginia, and there was a flock of uncommitted delegates up for grabs. Johnson, finally in the race, was coming to Spokane with his pal Warren Magnuson, whose chief assistant Irvin A. Hoff was managing LBJ's western campaign. It would be the first JFK-LBJ head-to-head confrontation. Landing at Spokane's Felts Field, our small entourage was whisked off to Bing Crosby's home at Hayden Lake, Idaho, for an early morning breakfast.

JFK appeared to have it all over LBJ at the convention. Salter and I kept a steady stream of delegates flowing into his suite at the Davenport Hotel, yet too many still were holding out for Stevenson for us to consider the trip an unqualified success. With Scoop Jackson a putative candidate for vice president, we pushed the line that a vote for Kennedy was a vote for Scoop. It turned a few delegates, but most uncommitteds said they would wait and see until Los Angeles. Despite the presence of Maggie and Irv Hoff, LBJ had little support.

If Spokane had not been exactly boffo, it had far surpassed JFK's trip to the Colorado Democratic convention at Durango. He had gone there at the insistence of Byron White and Joe Dolan, but it was a dry haul and he knew it. As they departed, he turned to White and said: "Byron, if I get one-half delegate out of this, I'll kiss your ass in the lobby of the Brown Palace Hotel at high noon." You have to like a candidate like that.

With Johnson in the race and Los Angeles short days away, it was inevitable that there would be delegates with their hands out for transportation, lodging, and whatever else they could negotiate. I was equipped with travel vouchers and credit cards to use as the situation arose, and arise it did. A time or two I was too late. One night in a Seattle bar, an Irish-American delegate berated me. He already had taken travel expenses from an LBJ agent and was morose about it. "Me old mum in County Clare would whirl in her grave if she knew I wasn't going to vote for a Kennedy," he moaned. "It's your damned fault for not getting to me sooner." When I suggested that he return the money and plane tickets and let me take care of it, he shook his head. "I have a reputation," he said. "Once bought, I stay bought."

From Spokane I backtracked to North Dakota and the last weeks of Quentin Burdick's Senate campaign, with side trips to delegate-selection conventions in Minnesota, South Dakota, and Montana. Delegate-hunting now was hard-scrabbling, one-on-one infantry warfare. It took an infinite capacity to listen to local political minutiae and a cast-iron liver to be really good at it. My *métier* was media, which was a pushbutton, bombs-away kind of battle. Get all the ammunition in the television can and on the radio tape, and you may fire when ready, Gridley. It beat the hell out of footslogging through the mud for a stray delegate or two.

Burdick's upset victory in North Dakota on June 28, with its byproduct clinch of that state's delegation for JFK, was a big boost for my uneasy ego. The West Virginia primary had proven to be winnable after all, and the prevailing wisdom was that money was the reason why. On July 7, I headed for Los Angeles, filled with confidence that I was destined to do something spectacular for Kennedy and win back whatever I had lost because of Bobby's enmity.

John F. Kennedy and Miller on a swing through Hawaii during the 1959 political campaign that introduced statehood.

In May 1950, President Truman dedicated Grand Coulee Dam in Coulee City, Washington. Tepid support for the Columbia Valley Authority (CVA) came from Mon C. Wallgren (back to camera), a former Washington State governor; Secretary of the Interior Oscar Chapman; Rep. Henry M. "Scoop" Jackson (D-WA); and Sen. Warren G. Magnuson (D-WA). Rep. Hugh B. Mitchell (D-WA) (right) was the only true CVAer in the crowd. The twenty-eight-year-old Miller, at the time executive secretary of the League for a CVA, is holding the sign in front.

Miller's early career was as a journalist, and he wrote for the Portland *Oregonian* in the early 1950s. He is shown here with A. Robert Smith, longtime Washington correspondent for the *Oregonian* and other Pacific Northwest newspapers.

Joe Miller at the Democratic National Convention in Atlantic City in 1964. Bobby Kennedy was cheered, but LBJ was nominated.

Richard Lewis Neuberger (*right*) was one of Miller's first political clients and became a beloved friend. He is shown here on the Alcan Highway in about 1950.

Miller (*right*) is shown in the Capitol Rotunda in about 1970 with his friend U.S. Rep. Wendell Wyatt (R-OR). They often disagreed over politics; but, Miller writes, "I never had a better friend than Wendell."

Joe Miller (*right*), with Bob McElroy (*center*), staff director of the U.S. House Merchant Marine and Fisheries Committee, and Herb Brand of the Seafarers Union. With the subsidy money that the committee authorized—based on the supposed patriotic premise that the Merchant Marine was "America's Fourth Line of Defense"—maritime labor (and management) entertained lavishly and contributed generously to any politician who would support the subsidies. Herblock, the *Washington Post* cartoonist, portrayed the maritime unions as pirates raiding the good ship U.S.S. *Congress*.

Erna Miller and Scoop Jackson attended a Norwegian-American Society dinner honoring the new Chief Justice, their fellow Norwegian Earl Warren. According to Miller, Scoop hated to date women taller than he was, but he made an exception in Erna's case.

Miller spent a good deal of time at Democratic fund-raisers such as this one in Washington, D.C., 1970. He poses here with (*from left*) Jesse M. Calhoon, a maritime union president; Sen. Edmund S. Muskie (D-ME); Rep. Charles Diggs (D-MI), chair of the Democratic Black Caucus; and Jane Muskie. At the time Ed Muskie was the frontrunner for the Democratic nomination to take on President Richard M. Nixon.

To Joe Miller
with Best Wishes

10

In 1977, Vice President Fritz Mondale asked Miller's help in getting his college-age son a summer job as a sailor. He got the job and did well. Miller did the same for a number of scions of senators and congressmen.

Joe and Erna Miller are shown here on one of their frequent trips to New York City. Erna was the long-time personal secretary to Henry M. "Scoop" Jackson, her hometown neighbor in Everett, Washington.

Miller kicked up his heels with an Ohio congressman to the music of trumpeter and U.S. Rep. Bob Leggett (D-CA), a member of the Congressional High Notes. Leggett lost his seat, Miller reports, when he dared Ben Bradlee, editor of the *Washington Post*, to print the story of how he was keeping a mistress at a suburban Virginia lake across from hearth and wife. "You don't have the guts to print it," he said. Bradlee did—eight columns on the Sunday front page—and Leggett was gone.

Joe and Erna Miller married in 1963 and lived a few blocks from Capitol Hill.

George McGovern (*left*) and Joe Miller posed for this photo after having a few drinks at their friend Gaylord Nelson's home.

Miller (*left*) hiking on Maryland's Eastern Shore with Jesse Calhoon, president of the Marine Engineers Beneficial Association.

Joe Miller (*right*) with Thomas E. "Doc" Morgan (D-PA), chairman of the House Foreign Affairs Committee. Throughout a forty-year career in Congress, Morgan maintained a full-time general practice in his hometown in Washington, Pennsylvania.

11

THE CAMPAIGN AND AFTERMATH

RETURNING TO WASHINGTON IN LATE JUNE, TWO WEEKS BEFORE the Democratic National Convention in Los Angeles, a pile of invitations awaited me. The convention may choose the next leader of the free world, but it also was going to be the grandest and gaudiest party of my experience. Bill vanden Heuvel called to invite me to a Saturday night affair at his in-laws, Dr. and Mrs. Jules Stein, at Misty Mountain, their palatial estate overlooking Beverly Hills. Since Stein was the founder-owner of the Music Corporation of America, I didn't doubt it when Bill said that "all Hollywood would be there."

Roger Stevens weighed in with an invitation to Gore Vidal's party at Mike Romanoff's restaurant. "All Hollywood would be there," he said. Similar calls came from noted Washington hostesses Perle Mesta and Gwen Cafritz. The calls were made in lieu of formal invitations for fear that word would get out and the Democratic hoi polloi would try to crash the parties. As one of the lowly hoi polloi, I had attempted that at previous conventions with some success. Now I was going to enter through the front door.

I left for Los Angeles several days in advance with no firm idea of what actual role I would play. My status with the Kennedys was ambiguous at best. I checked in at JFK headquarters at the Biltmore Hotel and was given vague instructions to ride herd on the Washington, Idaho, and North Dakota delegations. Bobby was friendly, cool, and brief, leaving no doubt that I was a peripheral player.

JFK appeared to have a lock on the nomination; he had won all eight primaries and had captured such big-state delegations as Ohio and Illinois. It took 671 delegate-votes to nominate, and he was in counting reach of that number. Yet, there was still strong sentiment for Adlai Stevenson, and late-entry Lyndon Johnson was threatening Kennedy's support in such segregationist bastions as Alabama and South Carolina. With many of his delegates only committed to a first-ballot vote, JFK had to make it on the first ballot or face the erosion that had doomed many a front-runner as the balloting dragged on. A few old-timers remembered the record 103 ballots it had taken to nominate John W. Davis in 1924 and the disaster that had ensued afterward.

The Washington state delegation was indicative of the underlying unease that still confronted the front-runner, despite his vote count. Salter and I had only one-third of the delegation in camp, and some of those were shaky. Several delegates—upscale professionals from the Puget Sound megalopolis— were beholden to no one and had come to L.A. to shop for The Best Man. Kennedy's youth, his Catholicism, and his father made them skeptical.

Governor Al Rosellini, an Italian Catholic elected in a Scandinavian Protestant state, was no help. Facing a tough re-election campaign himself, he was fearful of another Catholic at the head of the ticket and was gandy-dancing us all over the lot. Jerry Hoeck and I had a shouting match with him in his Mayfair Hotel suite, and I was fearful that Jerry might slug him.

Scoop Jackson was our hole card. Encouraged by Bobby Kennedy, he was running hard for vice president. A committee had been formed, had raised money, and had a headquarters in the Statler Hotel filled with volunteers and campaign paraphernalia, banners and buttons galore. Jackson was the only one "running," and his agents—myself among them—were tirelessly touting the attractiveness of a western Scandinavian Lutheran balancing a Boston Irish Catholic. Many delegates were kindly disposed to Jackson, and Thomas Ludlow Ashley of Ohio organized fifty-some of his fellow congressmen to work their delegations on his behalf. We all knew that the choice would be made by one man, the nominee, but Scoop seemed to be a worthy cause.

The first thing Nordy Hoffmann, the Steelworkers Union's political director, did when we arrived five days in advance was to visit the large shop where the Biltmore Hotel's telephone operators worked. Nordy closeted himself

alone with the head-op while I flashed my most winning smiles at the women on the switchboards. He emerged with a satisfied grin and a wink. "We'll have a direct line up here," he said, as we navigated a freight elevator back to his four-bedroom suite. "That's the first thing you always do—take care of the girls on the telephones. When you call, always say you are calling from Nordy's suite, and you'll get right through. The head girl remembered me from the Steelworkers' convention here in 1956. We'll get priority service." He was right. All week our calls sailed through while the other lines were hopelessly jammed.

Convention floor passes and seats in preferred galleries and admission to the VIP bars and lounges were our next priority. David J. McDonald, the Steelworkers' president, had a retinue of hangers-on who he liked to impress by dispensing largesse. If he didn't have passes to hand out, he could be downright ugly, Nordy said. Getting them in advance was my job.

Glory be, Democratic National Chairman Paul Butler understood my problem, and he slipped me into the stockroom where the passes were under lock and key. Take what you need, he said, but hide it so that the hangers-on won't see. I stuffed so much into my shirt and suit that I looked like an overfed penguin waddling back to Nordy's suite. I made it without incident. At the age of thirty-eight, I wondered about having to resort to this kind of schoolboy trick.

I was getting little sleep, and liquor and cigarette consumption increased proportionately with lack of shut-eye. On Saturday night, I headed to Misty Mountain and the Steins' party, the *primus inter pares* affair of the week. All Hollywood was indeed there, and I found myself in conversation with Mrs. Stein, who had danced with my cousin Llellwyn in the Zeigfield Follies. As we talked in the foyer, Gary Cooper and his wife Rocky came down a circular staircase and joined the conversation. As luck would have it, Cooper remembered my Uncle Mort from amateur theatricals in Red Lodge, Montana, and was telling a funny story about him when the butler opened the front door and ushered in Lyndon and Lady Bird Johnson.

Lyndon never was comfortable outside his own environment, and it showed in this instance. The Steins were not quite sure who he was, and there was an awkward, hanging moment. I couldn't resist the opportunity. I introduced LBJ and Lady Bird to the hosts and the Coopers as if I had known everyone forever. Lyndon rewarded me with the most baleful eye he could muster. He hated being upstaged, particularly by an underling whom he disliked.

I also talked to Eddie Albert and Desi Arnaz, who were interested in Hawaiian politics. It was more of the same at the other affairs: Gore Vidal's grand luncheon at Romanoff's, the party for Joe Kennedy at Dave Chasen's restaurant, and the receptions given by Perle Mesta and Gwen Cafritz. Back in Nordy's suite, I couldn't resist bragging about rubbing shoulders with Hollywood's elite. But then Nordy took me aside and said in a low voice: "You could have taken your old buddy with you to at least one of those fancy parties. I've been stuck here for almost a week and would have welcomed the chance to get out." I was shamefaced. Nordy was the main reason I was free to operate on the political circuit, and I hadn't even thought of including him. Had I become that selfish and self-centered? What was wrong with me? Some soul-searching was in order down the pike, but not now.

I had a room at the Beverly Wilshire, far out in Beverly Hills, that my wife was occupying, but I seldom saw it. She was there for pleasure and I to further my political career—not a good mix. Politics is notorious for producing neglected wives, and the idea that the convention was an opportunity for a late honeymoon away from the kids was turning out to be absurd. This and lack of sleep had my usually placid nerves stretched.

On the day that nominations were being made, Adlai Stevenson's supporters massed outside the Sports Arena, their mission to stampede the convention for their man. It was an unruly mob scene. Norman Mailer, who was covering the convention for *Esquire*, described the demonstrators as seeming "to have more than a fair proportion of tall, emaciated young men with thin, wry beards . . . accompanied by a contingent of ascetic, face-washed young Beat ladies in sweaters and dungarees, not to mention all the Holden Caulfields one could see from here to the horizon."

The LAPD had doubled its force for this day, and every entrance was being guarded with extra vigilance. The Stevensonites, determined to enter the arena, had staged exploratory forays, and police nerves were edgy. Ed Muskie and I had left the convention floor for a soft drink at a VIP lounge outside the main entrance. On the way back, a *Wall Street Journal* reporter, Bob Novak, stopped him, and I went ahead through a side entrance that my credentials allowed me to use. A rangy man in a suit muscled me back and snapped, "Get the hell back." He pushed me into the door.

That did it. Without a word I threw a punch that landed solidly on his jaw. He retaliated, and suddenly there was a melee. The next thing I knew, three L.A. cops had me spread-eagled and suspended in the air. I saw Nordy and Governor Bert Combs of Kentucky running toward me. Thankfully, the police were pretty decent with Nordy and Combs there to vouch for me. We shook hands all around, and blamed it on the demonstrators. I took a cab to the Beverly Wilshire and slept for twelve hours.

I didn't miss anything. There was little real action taking place on the convention floor. The acoustics were abominable, and it was impossible to see or hear what was going on at the podium. Frank Church, the boy orator of Idaho, was halfway through his keynote speech before most of us on the floor knew he was speaking. A shadowy figure on the large television screen hanging above the podium was flailing his arms, and occasionally an audible phrase would reach the floor. "My god, that's Frank," an Idaho delegate muttered near the end.

The keynote speech was considered a prize because of the television exposure, and it had worked in the past to propel obscure politicians into prominence. I had helped Church win the spot over two notable orators, Governor Gaylord Nelson of Wisconsin and Congressman Hale Boggs of Louisiana. After the speech, Nelson came over to me on the floor. "So that's your great orator out of the West?" he sneered. "Hell, I've made better speeches in Wisconsin barrooms when I can barely stand up."

In the midst of all the milling and swaying, Scoop Jackson was trying to run for vice president, an office that really can't be run for. First, there is no process or mechanism for running, and, second, no one gives a damn except the person who is running and his supporters. Nevertheless, a respectable number of Scoop's congressional colleagues had signed onto his "nominating committee," and a group of us prowled the convention floor, hotel hallways, and state delegation meetings daily looking for names to swell the total. Bobby Kennedy had told Jackson that he favored his nomination, with the caveat that widespread backing was needed to select Scoop over Stuart Symington, the choice of Harry Truman and most party elders. I was confidant that he would pick Scoop if we could corral enough support. When I ran into a red-eyed JFK in a Biltmore service elevator, I gave him a brief rundown on the Jackson effort. "Good, good," he said. "Keep it up."

The Jackson candidacy was our main card in attempting to swing the undecided Washington delegates to Kennedy. How, we argued, could he pick Scoop if his state's delegation wasn't for him? Delegates listened but didn't exactly leap into our arms. Feuds and slights from long ago surfaced as if they had just happened yesterday. Warren Magnuson's relationship with LBJ held back several, and I argued with Maggie that Scoop's shot at the post should transcend his friendship with Johnson.

The evening of the presidential balloting, I was standing at the head of the Washington delegation as the votes for JFK mounted. The only suspense in the hall was which state would cast the 671st vote to give the nomination to Kennedy. If New Jersey's Governor Robert Meyner gave up his futile favorite-son candidacy, it might be Washington or Wisconsin.

As we waited for New Jersey, I was surprised when Magnuson walked up to me. "All right," he said. "I voted for Kennedy. Now let's see if he comes through for Scoop." With that, he spun and went back to his seat. And Wyoming got the honor of putting Kennedy over the top.

The following afternoon, I was in a crowded Statler Hotel bedroom with Jackson awaiting the call from JFK. It looked good. Kennedy aides had asked Scoop to seek the blessing of Democratic sachems such as Chicago Mayor Richard Daley and Pennsylvania Governor David Lawrence. We had rushed him into one-on-one meetings with the appropriate party elders and now sprawled around the bedroom awaiting The Call. Outside in the suite's big living room, a swarm of newspeople and hangers-on filled every inch of space. They all smelled a winner.

The call came shortly before four that afternoon. Scoop, seated in an oversized wing chair, took it as planned. As he listened, an amazed expression came over his broad Norwegian face. He put his hand over the phone and whispered to us, "It's Johnson."

We went into instant shock. The Senate Majority Leader's name never had surfaced in any discussion. That morning's *Los Angeles Times* had featured a front-page headline: "It's Symington or Jackson for VP." Johnson was not even mentioned in the story. Far-out dark horses like Governors Herschel Loveless of Iowa and George Docking of Kansas supposedly still were under consideration. But Johnson? Nothing sounded crazier.

Scoop's end of the brief conversation was limited to one "I understand" and a couple of "I see's" until he said, "No, I don't think I would want to do that, Jack." When he hung up, Salter did not offer regrets, but—ever the practical politician—said, "What did you say no to?"

"He asked me to be chairman of the Democratic National Committee."

"Get him back on the phone, for god's sake. It's better than nothing. We haven't been breaking our backs for months only to end up with the empties. Get him back and say yes."

When he did, Kennedy asked Jackson to announce it in the Statler ballroom, crowded with newsmen and television cameras. Accompanying Scoop to the ballroom through a hallway, I was accosted by Joe Rauh and Walter Reuther, president of the United Auto Workers (UAW). "Is it Scoop?" Rauh asked. "No, it's LBJ," I answered. If ever two faces reflected total disbelief, it was those two at that moment.

The rest was anticlimactic, as such things usually are. A scramble to line up bona fide liberals to second Johnson's nomination followed. I wrote two labored and forgettable two-minute panegyrics to be delivered by Steelworkers President David J. McDonald and Arizona Congressman Stewart L. Udall. Instead of going out to the Sports Arena for LBJ's big moment, a group of us drifted to the Statler bar, where we drank without joy or effect. Everybody's tank was sputtering on empty.

The day after was more of the same. At the traditional post-convention meeting of the Democratic National Committee, Scoop took over from Paul Butler, the ascetic Indianan who had done so much to build the party at the grassroots level, only to incur the wrath of its elders. Stepping down, Butler vanished into obscurity without so much as a handclap.

The members of the Jackson team were a bedraggled lot of sad sacks when the banners came down in the L.A. Sports Arena and the crowds evaporated. Johnny Salter summed us up: "There isn't enough energy in this crowd to push a peanut ten feet."

We all went off to Las Vegas to recharge our batteries. We couldn't afford not to. Jack Conlin, Nevada Senator Howard Cannon's chief honcho, had the tab picked up for all of us. That was standard operating procedure for Vegas. If one had any vestige of political clout, the hard-eyed guys were happy to say "our pleasure" and tear up the check. And we were more than willing to let them.

Vegas was poolside sun all day and shows every night. One evening, as we watched the Parisian apache dancers cavort in Les Folies Bergère, someone quipped: "Weren't those guys part of the Stevenson demonstration in L.A. last week?"

Vegas was followed by Reno, Lake Tahoe, Carmel, and San Francisco, then back to Washington for the August-long post-convention session of Congress that Sam Rayburn and LBJ had called to showcase Johnson's talents on the expectation that he would win the Democratic nomination. Day after day, the session droned on pointlessly, passing unimportant bills and deep-sixing the legislation that Kennedy had promised as the cornerstone of his blueprint for the future: federal aid to education, medical protection for older people, revitalization of the cities, and the like. Stuck on his Senate back-bench with meaningless votes to cast, JFK fumed in frustration as Nixon ranged the country, attracting surprisingly large crowds in Democratic bastions of the Deep South. No one reflected the boredom more than the candidate himself. Kennedy spoke with an ugly rasp; his strained voice had not yet recovered from the battering it had taken in winning the nomination. The couple of times that I saw him during that period he was downright snarly.

Nothing was going right. I had moved into Democratic National Committee headquarters at 1001 Connecticut Avenue in downtown Washington. Bobby Kennedy, Larry O'Brien, and a score of JFK primary veterans had arrived at the same time. The office space was barely enough to accommodate the fifty-odd regular staffers of the DNC, and there were daily struggles for desks, typewriters, and telephones. Every day more people showed up, and conditions got worse. Friction and feuding erupted as people literally fell over each other in the cramped and sweaty space.

I had the good luck of acquiring a remarkable secretary, donated to the campaign from Senator Cannon's staff. Barbara Cavanaugh Thornton didn't type very well and couldn't take dictation worth a damn, but she had an Irish personality that could melt Bobby Kennedy at his meanest moments. I nicknamed her "Stanky," for Eddie Stanky, the New York Giants second baseman and three-time National League All-Star. Somebody once said of him: "He can't hit. He can't run. He can't throw. All he does is beat you." That was Barbara. Give her a near-impossible assignment, and she got it done. She even talked Jacqueline Kennedy into recording radio spots for our congressional candidates in Spanish, French, and Italian.

My role was to coordinate the congressional campaigns with the Kennedy-Johnson effort. While it gave me what seemed to be a wide-ranging involvement in all 435 congressional districts, my presence was at the pleasure of the candidates. During the August session, I saw enough senators and congressmen to realize that those who thought the Kennedy-Johnson ticket would help them would cooperate and those who didn't wouldn't.

The indifference of some congressional Democrats came as a shock. "What's Jack Kennedy ever done for me?" one House committee chairman grumbled. "Why in hell should I help him? He can't give me anything that I don't have anyway."

That attitude wasn't widespread, but it did make for a minor but disturbing attitude on Capitol Hill. I was still naive enough to think that an all-for-one, one-for-all ethic would prevail after the convention. Instead, I listened to outbursts of resentment about the manner in which JFK had won the nomination, fulminations against his father, and the influence of his money.

So, Stanky and I produced advertising designed to promote a team concept for the campaign. Out of our little shop came a flood of sample television and radio scripts, newspaper display advertising mats, and related materials. We shipped it across the country, hoping it would inspire the locals to use it and pay the freight. It was good journeymen stuff, but nothing special. At least it kept us thinking we were making a tangible contribution.

The growing frustration, punctuated by Nixon's continuing lead in the Gallup polls, was registered in our drinking patterns. At night, a polytypical lot of us congregated at the Carroll Arms Hotel bar and bitched. None of us had been in a presidential campaign before, and we were perplexed by our inability to get off the ground. Precious days were being wasted, and the grumbling at DNC headquarters rose to a crescendo.

Scoop Jackson's role as DNC chairman was ambiguous. JFK had assured him of a meaningful role, but what it was nobody seemed to know. Bobby seemed to be in charge of everything, and Jackson's presence hardly was felt. His uncertain status was not helped by his Norwegian negativism. The early reports that he passed on to the Kennedy brothers were discouraging, made even less palatable by what Bobby called Jackson's "I-told-you-so" style. He acquired a nickname: "prophet of gloom."

There was real reason for Scoop's pessimism. I didn't realize it until I went to the Midwest Democratic Conference in Oklahoma City in late August.

It was a listless and sparsely attended affair, in contrast to earlier such meetings where Democratic prairie populists had lifted the rafters with their passion. At the opening banquet, LBJ spoke to a couple hundred of the faithful huddled up front in the huge hall. Behind them were 1,500 glasses of tomato juice and place settings, a sight as depressing as the empty auditorium at Omaha that Harry S Truman had spoken to in 1948. I ran into George Reedy, LBJ's press secretary, going into the pre-banquet reception. A friend had invited me to a press party that John Wayne was throwing at the Oklahoma Press Club to introduce his new movie, *The Alamo*. I urged Reedy to go with me. "Love to," George said, "but can you imagine Lyndon when he finds out that I have deserted him for John Wayne?"

I hung around the reception for some time, making talk with party wheelhorses from the midlands. They had the same thing to report: a galling resurgence of the anti-popery sentiment that had doomed Al Smith in 1928. The revival of anti-Catholic fears came as a shock. Along with many others, I had naively assumed that the West Virginia primary in May—a surprise victory for Kennedy in a largely Protestant state—had put that sort of thing behind us for good. My own kin had given me enough clues, but I was too dense to read them. My mother in Seattle had pointedly said that she intended to vote against Nixon, a view echoed by my mother-in-law and aunts. All of them raised as midwestern Protestants, they were seeking to rationalize their votes for a Catholic.

I had arrived in Oklahoma City to learn that Norman Vincent Peale had rescued Scoop. Peale, author of *The Power of Positive Thinking*, was the nation's best-known Protestant preacher. For weeks, rumors had circulated that he had fermented opposition to Kennedy's candidacy on purely religious grounds. Now he had made it public. The unseen beast had appeared in material form.

Peale's Armageddon-like aggressiveness to spotlight the *real* issue of 1960 gave Jackson the target he was looking for. When Scoop arrived in Oklahoma City, he was seething with a sense of fair-play indignation that registered superbly on *Meet the Press* and other talk shows that he did from his hotel suite. For the first time, I felt good about his chairmanship. His outrage that such bigotry still existed, made more powerful by his respectful restraint, came across beautifully on the little tube.

A newspaper friend of mine had contributed mightily to Scoop's performance. At the Wichita *Daily Eagle*, he had collected all the anti-Catholic, anti-Kennedy materials that the paper had received since the convention and had driven down from Wichita to give Scoop the whole package. Some of the publications were crude screeds that could have been written by Gerald L. K. Smith and other hate-mongers. The others were thought-provoking and raised questions that clearly might have perplexed open-minded people. They could not be answered simply by claiming bigotry or wrapping the candidate in the battle flags of PT 109. They had to be answered in depth.

I thought of Paul Blanshard, whose book *American Freedom and Catholic Power* had won widespread acceptance in liberal circles. I had met Blanshard through a man I considered to be one of the West's leading intellectual liberals, Dean Boyd A. Martin of the University of Idaho. Martin had widely distributed Blanshard's anti-Catholic tracts and had freely expressed his bias against the Roman Catholic Church as an institution. Yet, he and his cohorts were passionate Kennedy-style Democrats. How would they resolve their dilemma?

Those questions plagued me as I winged back to Washington. When I gave Ted Sorensen a rundown, he answered briskly: "We are going to square up to the issue next week in Houston. The Greater Houston Ministerial Association has invited the senator to appear for questioning, and we have accepted. He is going to take on all the tough questions." Looking back, I always thought the campaign was won as much by that September 12 appearance as it was by the televised debates with Nixon. As Theodore H. White put it in *The Making of the President 1960*: "He [JFK] had for the first time more fully and explicitly than any other thinker of his faith defined the personal doctrine of a modern Catholic in a democratic society." Over the next two months, the film of the Houston meeting was played over and over by Kennedy volunteers in both Protestant and Catholic areas. His eloquent performance finally answered the honest questions that many Protestant and Jewish Democrats had on their minds about JFK's allegiance to the church in Rome.

Then, in mid-October, just when the religious issue seemed to be dying down, the Catholic bishops of Puerto Rico instructed their parishioners to vote against the woman mayor of San Juan because she had flouted some doctrine of the church. With one stroke, they relit the issue, and the media jumped on it. I was traversing the midlands and intermountain West at the time, and the story led the television news and ran page one for as long as a week in virtually every newspaper in the region. It was devastating.

I closed out the campaign with George McGovern, who was trailing the Republican incumbent senator Karl Mundt in South Dakota. In Denver, Scoop had given me some "late money" to spend as I saw fit, and there was a chance that a late television blitz might enable George to catch the lackluster Mundt. When I met with McGovern in Rapid City, he was philosophical about what he thought would happen. "The three top names in the Democratic column are Kennedy, McGovern, and Fitzgerald," he wearily said. "That's too big a load for a Protestant state like this to swallow." No matter that his father was one of South Dakota's best-known Wesleyan Methodist ministers. The Irish name was enough to doom him in 1960. Nevertheless, we spent the money in a mad dash around the state doing live telethons, usually arriving at a station minutes before George was due on camera. It was a vainglorious effort, but the most fun of the whole damned campaign.

Returning to Washington, D.C., on a midnight flight from Omaha to cast my absentee ballot by Election Day, I perused my pocket calendar and learned that I had only spent ninety-six nights in my own bed all year. That statistic depressed me as the United Air Lines puddle-jumper bounced through the murky night. More depressing was the realization that, for the first time in a decade, I hadn't given the campaign the best I had to offer. I wasn't emotionally ready to admit that I had failed abysmally on the West Virginia primary and had been only marginally helpful in rounding up delegates. It was easier to blame Bobby.

I lazed around the house Election Day, watching the raccoons gambol in Rock Creek Park through the front window, and then went down to Scoop's suite in the Mayflower Hotel to catch the first returns. The Democratic sachems—Jim Farley, fundraisers Matt McCloskey and Jack Kelly, and New York Mayor Bob Wagner—already were on the scene, along with the faceless people, of which I was one. It was a cocky "it's in the bag" crowd, and not even an early computer-fueled projection for Nixon by CBS could shake their optimism. Given the way JFK had closed out the campaign, with roaring crowds, there was no way he could lose. Faces only started to get tense when the western returns came flooding in for Nixon, and Kennedy hung suspended, 30 short of the 269 electoral votes it took to win. It was still in doubt when I went home to bed in the early-morning hours. When my daughters awoke me to report that Nixon had conceded, I mumbled "good" and returned to deep sleep.

Two days later, Stewart Udall and George McGovern arrived at my Broad Branch Road house for an indefinite stay—Stew, who had won his House race in Arizona, campaigning for secretary of the Interior, and George, who had predictably lost to Mundt by around 10,000 votes, running for secretary of Agriculture. It was a pleasure to have two contenders in the house.

I knew McGovern pretty well but not well enough to know how he would take the painful defeat. The first night, rehashing the campaign in my bar overlooking Rock Creek Park, George suddenly zeroed in on me. "Joe," he said, "do you remember all that crap you were peddling to me across South Dakota about how sometimes it was good to lose and that losing this time might be the best thing that ever happened to me?"

Yeah, I remembered that I was trying to soften the blow by telling him how much losing had helped Lincoln, Cleveland, and FDR.

"Well," he went on, "I've been trying to rationalize what you told me, but I still hurt all over. Losing to a tub of shit like Karl Mundt is more than any human being should have to bear."

We erupted in laughter, and then and there I decided that this McGovern guy had what it took. He was laughing the hardest.

Some nights later, the three of us in tableau at the same bar, Udall received a phone call. Listening intently, his dark, stubbled face suddenly creased into a gleeful smile. He put his hand over the phone and whispered, "The FBI is investigating me." We silently cheered the announcement. Being investigated meant he was in the final stage of the nomination process. The president-elect confirmed his appointment a few days later.

McGovern did not fare as well. Orville Freeman, Minnesota's governor, didn't want Agriculture until Murray Lincoln, a farm insurance executive, convinced him that he could do great things there. McGovern, the second choice, was relegated to Food for Peace director, which actually was a pretty good consolation prize for an ambitious farm-state politician. George didn't cry too hard in his gin over losing Ag. This job would give him ample involvement with South Dakota.

The morning before Inauguration Day was sunny. Starting at eight o'clock with a champagne breakfast, I went from one party to another until three that afternoon. Then I came home to change into my tuxedo for the evening round. The sky had glowered all day, and big flakes were cascading down. We emerged into a blizzard and barely made it up the hill on Albemarle Street. Then I got a break. LBJ's limousine came around Linnean with a police escort, and I burrowed in behind and followed him down Connecticut to the Shoreham Hotel. Rosalie and I were going to the same function, a reception for the nation's governors.

Afterward, no one—save Lyndon, possibly—was going anywhere. The snow was falling so hard that nothing was moving outside. The Shoreham lobby was jammed with big-name Democrats, corporation presidents, and union bigwigs. Warren Magnuson, who lived at the Shoreham, had scheduled a small party just off the lobby for Washington state's re-elected governor, Albert Rosellini. It became the place to be. Maggie, always the good host, ordered up more liquor and food.

At nine o'clock, someone noted that the snow had stopped and traffic was moving. Frank Sinatra had organized a star-filled gala as his contribution to JFK's inaugural, and word was that it was starting late. I had box seats, and it seemed a shame to miss it. We sailed out in record time and arrived at the D.C. armory to hear Sinatra introduce the first act.

As glittering as Sinatra's constellation of stars was, the best part of the show was the presidential box over the stage—Jack and Jacqueline spotlighted in regal splendor, with Joe and Rose beaming proudly next to them and all the other Kennedys strung out like shining satellites. We knew we were looking at the new American royal family. It was close to four in the morning when an exuberant crowd grudgingly went out into the snow under a diamond-cold moon.

I had promised my two daughters that I would take them to see Kennedy inaugurated. They were shaking me at nine that morning to hold me to my word. Totally numb, I got up and we headed for the Capitol. We sat directly in front of the stand on Pennsylvania Avenue as Chief Justice Earl Warren swore Kennedy in and, later, just fifty feet from the Inaugural Stand as the parade swept down Pennsylvania Avenue. The girls had met Kennedy on a few occasions, and I imagine that seeing him anointed in that awesome ceremony was thrilling for them. I know it was for me. He was a guy of my generation, with whom I had traded locker-room talk. Now he was the Leader of the Free World and no longer Jack.

I no longer was what I putatively had been, "the Democrats' answer to Madison Avenue," as the *Washington Post* had so generously put it. My contribution to Kennedy's victory had been negligible, and I knew that I was only as good as my last campaign and that new "boy wonders" were emerging all the time. When newsmen who used to seek me out with a big hello now only gave me vague nods, I knew something had happened, and it wasn't good. The big brass ring had come around, and my hands had slipped off it.

The Inaugural Ball at the Sheraton Park Hotel, with Al Hirt's trumpet blowing the "Battle Hymn of the Republic," was still going strong when we called it a night. On the morrow I would take up my new trade of lobbying, going to a downtown office for the first time. I didn't relish the prospect, but whatever job I would have been offered in the new administration—probably a post in the cabinet subsecretariat somewhere—would not have paid enough. And I suspect the job offer would have been a grudging one. I was damned if I was going to be in the position of being a supplicant.

My friends had urged the lobbying game on me. "Make some money," they said. "Cash in while you have the connections. You owe it to yourself and your family." Still, I was reluctant. It seemed like out-and-out whoring to use honestly earned relationships to gain an advantage for someone who was paying you. I probably was as hesitant and lackadaisical a lobbyist as there was in town.

12

A LOBBYIST IS A LOBBYIST
IS A LOBBYIST

PUBLIC RELATIONS CONSULTANT, GOVERNMENT AFFAIRS COUNSELOR, legislative advocate, lawyer—call it what you will, the fact remains: a lobbyist is a lobbyist is a lobbyist. This play on Gertrude Stein's celebrated aphorism weighed on my mind as Maurice Rosenblatt, Charley Brown, and I opened the doors of our new offices at 1028 Connecticut Avenue in the heart of downtown Washington on January 22, 1961. I was doing what I had promised myself never to do. I was going to use the contacts and connections I had made in five furious years of political campaigning to open doors and influence decisions on behalf of whoever would hire me.

Stripped to its essentials, that is what my new game was all about. I had no illusions about being a legislative expert or a bill craftsman. I was a political campaign functionary with some expertise in the election process. Since Washington was a totally political town with its paladins of power depending on the ballot, it wasn't a bad skill to trade on.

I told myself that lobbying would be an interim thing to fill in the time between campaigns. I was going to be like the French girl from the provinces who only worked in the Paris bordello to get her grubstake so that she could go home and live a respectable bourgeois life. The idea of making a long-time career out of influence-peddling was anathema to me. Being a high-priced lobbyist and driving around town in a limousine like Clark Clifford or Tommy Corcoran was not in my nature. Newspapering and campaigning had bred in me a kind of proletarian professionalism. I was a working stiff, a union man, with no craving for the fancy office suites, exclusive clubs, and other appurtenances of power and prestige that seemed to be the hallmarks of the successful Washington lobbyist. I liked driving a twelve-year-old Volkswagen, shopping at Safeway, and buying clothes off the rack. Handball at the YMCA was my game, not squash at the Metropolitan Club. I made my own phone calls and fixed my own coffee. I was a reverse snob.

When I expressed my misgivings to a business-lobbyist friend, he laughed and said: "Just wait until you make a hundred thousand for getting an innocuous amendment or little clause added to an obscure bill. You'll get hooked. It's like hitting the jackpot. You get addicted." He was right.

In 1961, Washington was not crawling with lobbyists as it is today. There was a rather elite corps of well-established advocates of the nation's traditional interest groups: the U.S. Chamber of Commerce, National Association of Manufacturers, American Medical Association, and Farm Bureau Federation on the right and the AFL-CIO, NAACP, National Council of Churches, and Catholic Welfare Conference on the moderate left. All the major economic interests had their own lobbies, usually sheltered in marble-façaded edifices close to the Capitol and the White House. An indelible mark of prestige was to have either building framed in one's office window to impress visitors.

There were also the downtown law firms whose principal *raison d'être* seemed to be influencing Congress, the departments, and regulatory agencies of government on behalf of their clients. Through fundraising for various Senate candidates, I had become familiar with most of them. Many were former functionaries from the New Deal and the Fair Deal who had come to Washington with idealistic stars in their eyes. Along the way, the stars had been transmuted into dollar signs, and these lawyers had done well working for the interests they had once regulated and curbed. Many were big names— cabinet officers and the like—and I was somewhat in awe of their celebrity. Could little me be breaking bread with The Secretary, The Ambassador, and Tommy the Cork? Earle Clements demystified them for me. "They are chasing the almighty dollar, same as anybody else," he said. "Don't ever forget it."

My partners and I didn't recognize it at the time, but we were in the vanguard of a new wave of lobbyists flooding into the national capital. The incoming Kennedy administration promised to be noticeably different from the middle-aged, comfortable, and somewhat prosaic Eisenhower and Truman regimes, and Kennedy campaign figures from the outback were pouring into town to capitalize on their new status.

One of them was an old sidekick of mine from Korean War price-control days—Hyman B. Raskin, a white-maned operator from Mayor Daley's Chicago organization. With his usual candor, Hy told me about his session with the incoming president. "Jack asked me if I wanted an appointment, ambassador or something. I said, hell no, I want to make money. He laughed and said, 'You've come to the right place.' And now I'm making more money than my wife can spend." Maurice Rosenblatt, who had been on the Washington lobbying scene since 1945, explained that it had been that way since the founding of the republic: "Every new administration from Jefferson on has arrived here with a new army of players: friends of the president, idealists who are going to reshape the world, patronage job-seekers, camp followers, hangers-on, and people like Hy who figure it is their time to make a buck. This army is a natural byproduct of democracy, also known as the spoils system, and not even the most draconian reforms will kill it."

As a quondam student of American history, I liked the idea of historical context. Our forebears were Andy Jackson's frontiersmen—"To the victor belong the spoils," James Polk's "war hawks" dragging the nation into the Mexican War, Lincoln's newly minted Republicans looking for the money opportunities that were to come from the Civil War, Grant's Grand Army veterans out to get theirs, McKinley with Mark Hanna and the first Ohio "gang," Harding and the real Ohio gang that came to town to loot the U.S. Treasury. No wonder there was opprobrium attached to the label of lobbyist. I wasn't broadcasting to my friends in Seattle what I was doing.

Indelible in my memory is a jubilant election night in Seattle when our candidate for governor had won. One campaign hanger-on, a grossly fat fellow, got somewhat drunk and very excited. Eyeballs bulging grotesquely and sweat pouring down his porcine face, he proclaimed to one and all: "Tomorrow I'm going to be first in line to get mine!" How many times had my friends and I mimicked that line as the mantra of all that we detested in politics, the idea that it was a crass calling of people out to get theirs. I had experienced big-time politics up close for five years, but I still clung to the notion that my principles had an essential nobility about them and that the real purpose of it all was the betterment of humanity. If that sounds hopelessly naive, I plead guilty.

My partners were far wiser to the ways of Washington and, equally significant, to the motivations of people. Maurice Rosenblatt had filled a *mélange* of lobbying roles, from the American Committee for a Free Palestine to the nonscheduled commercial airline operators. He had created two enduring political entities: the National Committee for an Effective Congress, headed by Encyclopedia Brittanica publisher and former senator Bill Benton, and the Council for a Livable World, chaired by Leo Szilard, a lead scientist in the Manhattan Project who, horrified by the atomic bomb, wanted it outlawed. Maurice was a fascinating blend of practical political idealism and shrewd commercialism, and I was to learn much from him.

Charley Brown was a country-shrewd political humorist who had served two terms in Congress as a Democrat from a Republican district in Missouri's Ozarks. Starting as a circus barker and stock auctioneer, Charley had gone into advertising, promoting country music and its performers. By 1956, he had done well enough to indulge his first love, politics. He took on a supposedly unbeatable incumbent, Dewey Short, dubbed the "Ozark admiral" for his perfervid support of the U.S. Navy. Charley's victory in an Eisenhower year was one of the minor political headlines of the year. His four years in Congress had established him as a colorful and quotable figure. In 1960, busy promoting the presidential aspirations of his fellow Missourian, Stuart Symington, Charley had himself been upset. Now he was ready to join Maurice and me in the new business of capitalizing on connections.

The three of us came to the partnership with our own stables of clients and a loose arrangement to share new ones. We also shared office rent and secretarial help. Thus, we were free to operate on our own but with the protection of "partners" who could serve as backup if needed. Our offices were situated in the shabby old LaSalle Building at the southwest corner of Connecticut Avenue and L Street in the heart of downtown Washington. Everything seemed just a few steps away: the National Democratic Club, Duke Zeibert's and Harvey's restaurants, the Colony Club and the Mayflower, and the Statler and Carlton hotel bars.

Downtown Washington was a cozy and intimate place in those days.

K, L, and M streets, the thoroughfares dissecting Connecticut Avenue, were lined with two-story, mostly nineteenth-century buildings, many of them mansions that had been converted into high-style specialty stores or lawyers' offices. My favorite was the one on 19th Street that housed the law firm of Arnold, Fortas and Porter. It was a privilege to be invited there at the cocktail hour to hear Judge Thurman Arnold and Paul Porter tell stories. Abe Fortas was more taciturn, but we knew that, had he desired, he had some yarns to spin, such as his role in Lyndon B. Johnson's 87-vote margin in Texas' 1948 primary for the U.S. Senate. It was a warm and intimate world but one destined not to last. Soon the old buildings and mansions started to come down, to be replaced by coldly functional twelve-story buildings of aluminum, glass, and faux marble. Only an old statute that limited the height of buildings (not to exceed the U.S. Capitol) kept downtown from turning into a mini-Manhattan.

With the new buildings came an army of new lobbyists. Every economic group and subgroup in the nation seemed to have decided they needed their own representation in Washington. We were the beneficiaries of that explosion. We came into our partnership with a plentitude of clients. Besides the United Steelworkers, my flagship client, I had the Western Forest Industries Association of Portland, Oregon, comprising the West's leading independent lumber and plywood producers; Big Rivers, a consortium of southeastern rural electric cooperatives seeking their own federally backed generation and transmission facilities; the Oregon and California Land Grant Counties Association, eighteen Oregon counties that derived substantial income from their share of the receipts from timber sales on railroad land grants that the government had revested after a series of land scandals; and a few Pacific Northwest companies seeking federal concessions or subsidies. Maurice and Charley had similar client combinations, and we all were suddenly making more money than we ever had in our lives.

Alas, the partnership was short-lived. Maurice had a client named Connie B. Gay, a radio mogul of sorts who had developed a music-and-news format for a string of Dixie-based rural radio stations, including WGAY in suburban Washington. He and his wife also were players in the Virginia Democratic Party. Connie wanted to be appointed governor of the Virgin Islands. So did someone named Ralph Paiewonsky, a St. Thomas rum manufacturer and liquor dealer.

Between the November election and the January inauguration, Maurice had been a regular visitor to my house. Stewart Udall was staying with us at the time, and Maurice talked with him about the Virgin Islands, which were under Interior's jurisdiction. I remember Udall asking: "Maurice, why don't you go down there as my consultant and give me a full report on the political picture?" And Maurice had gone, taking along investment banker John B. Nuveen. He gave me a copy of his report to Udall—a masterfully written, harrowing tale of Caribbean political intrigue and chicanery. Maurice's main villain was Ralph Paiewonsky.

I read the report with fascination, but a warning bell went off. Charley Brown had told me that there was a connection between Paiewonsky and Joe Kennedy, the president's father. Harold Leventhal confirmed it. An old friend from the Office of Price Stabilization days, Leventhal invited me to lunch at the Hay-Adams Hotel. He got right to the point: "Paiewonsky is my client, and he is Joe Kennedy's candidate for governor. It is in your best interest to see that Rosenblatt's report does not become public. Udall is going to name Paiewonsky soon, and Clint Anderson, chair of the Senate Interior Committee, has promised quick hearings. The report only would be an unnecessary embarrassment."

It was too late. Maurice's findings already had been leaked to Anderson's Interior Committee staff, who had promptly leaked it to muckraking columnists Drew Pearson and Jack Anderson. Udall's announcement of Paiewonsky's appointment was immediately followed by an Anderson-Pearson column labeling "Pai" as a "notorious rum-runner." Senator Clint Anderson, a crustily independent New Mexico Democrat, said that his committee would examine the allegations. The columns continued, and the confirmation hearings over an obscure and unimportant appointment found their way to the *Washington Post*'s front page. Paiewonsky finally was confirmed, but it cost the Kennedy administration a few chips.

Early one summer morning, Charley Brown took me to Scholl's Cafeteria for coffee. "We've got to break up this partnership," he said. "The Kennedys are running this town, and we can't afford to be associated with what happened to Paiewonsky. I hate to do it, but we've got to get out." I reluctantly was forced to agree. Fortunately, I was offered an out that would not bruise Maurice's feelings. President Kennedy had asked John Salter, my mentor and campaign sidekick, to head a lobbying effort that would revamp the nation's foreign-aid program. The new foreign policy initiative would be asking Congress to give up its most precious prerogative—the right to authorize and appropriate funds each year. Kennedy believed that the perpetually troubled foreign-aid program could be rescued through gaining the authority to operate for five years at a time. It was going to be a tough sell, and Salter needed all the help he could get. The new organization was named the Agency for International Development, or AID, and critics quipped that it would need it.

Salter recruited me to help organize a citizens' committee to spearhead the lobbying effort. The "citizens" were the likes of George Meany, president of the AFL-CIO, publishers Henry R. Luce and Oveta Culp Hobby, Eisenhower's secretary of Health, Education and Welfare, a slough of Fortune 500 CEOs, and strays such as humorist Harry Golden—"the usual suspects," Salter wisecracked. Our front man was a white-haired windbag who had been CEO of TransWorld Airways. Happily, he was content to be left in New York and was only called to Washington for ceremonial meetings at the White House. Putting the names on our Citizens Committee for International Development letterhead turned out to be largely window-dressing, but gave us the entrée to call on their Washington lawyers or lobbyists for help. Most of them gave us little more than lip service, though there was one exception: an irrepressible, owlish former newsman from the Fairbanks Whitney Corporation named Debs Myers. He had been around Washington since early New Deal days and knew everybody, mostly on a first-name basis. The kings were naked, as far as Debs was concerned, and his irreverence loosened us up.

Our offices in the LaSalle Building were not a lavish setup, even though we had the money for more. I had learned early on that virtually no one in authority came to see a lobbyist, so there was no need to impress with an ornate office. Our operation was utilitarian—telephones and typewriters on scarred desks. If we had to have a meeting or conference, the Fish Room at the White House was available. That impressed the "suits."

Ever since Harry Truman proposed U.S. technical assistance for friendly nations in 1947, foreign aid had been a tough sell in Congress, and that body was showing no inclination to ease its funding authority for an untried new president. Spend the money at home instead of pouring it down foreign ratholes was an insistent refrain from Capitol Hill.

The Kennedy strategists came up with a telling answer. Eighty-three percent of foreign-aid money went to U.S. companies for goods and services. When broken down by congressional districts, it made a good sales pitch to tell a congressman that "X dollars of this money is being spent on these companies in your own district." The first vote in the House of Representatives was on the five-year authorization, and we won that fairly handily. But all too many members said: "I'll go with you on this one, but don't count on me for the other," the actual appropriation of money.

We made a major-league effort, with the administration throwing in its first-line troops—Vice President Johnson and Larry O'Brien twisting arms and the cabinet, including Secretary of State Dean Rusk, pitching in. Foreign-policy establishment, business, and labor lobbyists swarmed Capitol Hill, yet we lost—quite ignominiously as it turned out—on an amendment offered by a one-term California Democrat, Dalip S. Saund. The bill passed by a fair margin, and suddenly we were as dead as Kelsey. Oh, we claimed a half-a-loaf victory and vowed to come back the next year for the other half, but, as Debs Myers brutally observed, that was just "loser talk." The foreign-aid program was alive but without the new look that Kennedy had envisioned.

It was a crushing loss, but the fight had been exhilarating. If this was what lobbying was about, then it was as stimulating as a good political campaign, with the bonus of being able to go home every night knowing that you were working for a good cause.

The downside of my new occupation turned out to be a very nice client who had retained me at $30,000 a year and expenses, a generous sum in 1961. He owned an engineering firm with some impressive achievements to its credit. He wanted federal government contracts, and the Interior Department had a number coming up. Stewart Udall was my friend, and I was expected to use my influence with him. If a few contracts came my guy's way, then he would contribute generously to the Democratic National Committee or whomever Udall designated. It was one of the oldest ploys in politics, practiced by political machines of every stripe. I wasn't naive. I knew what I was supposed to do and thought I could do it.

It turned out that I couldn't. It was just too crass. I had participated in any number of illegal maneuvers to get corporation and trade-union treasury money into campaigns, but I had rationalized that it was all for a noble end—getting my guy elected. Besides, the other side was doing it, so why shouldn't I? There was no such exculpation for contract-hustling. After a couple of months thrashing around in that uncomfortable territory, I told the client that I wasn't cut out for the role and offered to refund what he had paid me. He was gracious, refused the money, and we remained casual friends. I learned a good lesson on the cheap—this sort of thing just wasn't what I wanted to do.

If this sounds holier-than-thou, and it does, it may have been a defense mechanism on my part. A fat fellow on the AFL-CIO staff, a professional liberal for whom the term "political correctness" later was invented, disliked me intensely because I had eased him out of two Senate campaigns. With my entry into the lobbyists' ranks, he was peddling the line that I was sure to become the "five percenter" of the Kennedy administration, a phrase that denoted the influence-peddlers of Truman days. I ignored him, but his insinuation got under my skin. I was damned if I was going to give him any excuse to say I told you so.

A correlative situation arose with a client I was sharing with Maurice—the National Coal Policy Association. Its president was big bluff Joe Moody, long-time spokesman for the nation's bituminous coal operators. He had one mission on Capitol Hill, to block nuclear-energy development, and he needed help with Democrats—hence, Maurice and myself. Unbeknownst to me, the Washington Public Power Supply System (WPPSS, later to become infamous as "Whoops" when its bonds failed) had an ambitious scheme in mind: to convert the atomic reactor at Hanford, Washington, which had produced the plutonium for atomic bombs, to the commercial manufacture of electricity. WPPSS, the major marketer for the Pacific Northwest's public power systems, had political influence and an impressive lineup of congressmen to steer the proposal through the legislative labyrinths of Capitol Hill. They were led by Washington State's two Democratic senators, Warren G. Magnuson and Henry M. Jackson, who had brought me to the political dance in the first place.

Defeating the Hanford reactor became Joe Moody's grand passion. I was unable to share it with him. While Scoop and Maggie and their staffs expressed bemused tolerance at my coal role, I felt uncomfortable, particularly since I was also working on a major project to increase hydroelectric production on the Columbia-Snake River systems. My roles conflicted, and

I was spending sleepless hours agonizing about it. Voluntarily giving up that much money was almost sacrilegious to a child of the Great Depression, but I felt great relief at leaving the coal operators. It was important that I felt good about who I was representing and what they were advocating.

I was also learning to be cautious—not an adjective my friends would have used to describe me. One well-known operator around Washington, a former congressman, invited me to his Georgetown townhouse to meet with some clients of his from the Virgin Islands, where Ralph Paiewonsky, Joe Kennedy's candidate, was about to become governor. They wanted a permit to build an oil refinery slated for St. Thomas, and the Interior Department was the licensing agency. I was there because of my relationship with Udall. After a couple of drinks, the leader of the group invited me into a side room.

"We know," he said, "how these matters work in Washington. Our friend, the congressman, has briefed us. You will need the tools to do the job, and we will provide you with those tools."

With that, he opened an attaché case sitting on a desk. Stacks of "dead presidents" stared at me. My mouth started to salivate and my heart thumped, but a warning buzzer sounded, too. I knew the former congressman superficially through some campaign fundraising efforts, a nice guy to have a drink with, but that was all. The guys from the V.I. didn't quite click with me, especially the one who had shown me the money. I pleaded a dinner engagement and got out of there.

Two days later, I met with John A. Carver, an old Idaho friend who was Interior's assistant secretary with jurisdiction over the Virgin Islands. Without naming anyone, I told him what had happened. "You did the right thing," he said. "I know the guys you met with, and they ain't exactly kosher. Besides, Leon Hess has made a much better offer to build the refinery, and it looks as if he will get it."

Another good lesson: Beware of setups in which cash is the medium of exchange. I was no stranger to the long green—one dealt with a lot of it on the campaign trail—but when it came to lobbying, cash seemed tantamount to bribery. I won't pretend to virginity. There were a few times that I slipped a key congressman an envelope and muttered that it was a campaign contribution. Such transactions were rationalized—on both sides—with the justification that there were expenses in campaigns that could only be met with cash, which actually was true. Even so, it made me uncomfortable.

But on the whole I ended my first full-time year at the trade with a shift in my attitude toward lobbying as a life pursuit. Not only was it a fascinating game with complexities and subtleties that I had not imagined, but it was also legitimate. The federal government had become such an incredible octopus that it was bound to be baffling sometimes, even to sophisticated entrepreneurs from the hinterlands. Functionaries who understood the workings of government and politics had an invaluable role to play, principally as middlemen or brokers who could talk straight to both parties.

One thing that struck me that year was the large gap in the way businessmen, politicians, and bureaucrats often seemed to view each other as characters out of a novel, an old movie, or a political screed. Sometimes my eyes would roll as I listened to these egregious misrepresentations. Protestations that "it really wasn't this way any more" were hardly heard. Educating both sides that the other was honest and decent seemed to be a major function of the lobbying process, and I found myself at home in that role.

My insight was of the preeminence of the personal relationship. Although dealings between government and an individual or group were governed by mountains of statutes and regulations, human beings still carried them out. If they liked you, then the chances of an interpretation in your favor was increased—nothing illegal, mind you, but the regulations had their ambiguities and sometimes could be defined in more than one way. In such instances, it was a plus to have the bureaucrat thinking kindly of you.

13

NO VESTAL VIRGIN
IN THE WHOREHOUSE

IF THE PRECEDING CHAPTER IMPLIES THAT I WAS A VESTAL VIRGIN dragged unwillingly into a cathouse of whores trying to seduce Congress, I have misrepresented myself. My blooding in that arena had come in the 1959 nationwide steel strike, the concurring battle in Congress over the Landrum-Griffin bill, and earlier legislative efforts to curb the dumping of foreign steel at below-production costs. In my mind, the difference was that working for working people did not constitute lobbying, as it was perceived in the special-interest sense. Lobbying to bring advantages to trade unions I saw as "doing the Lord's work." Literally.

In January 1959, David J. McDonald, the well-coiffed president of the United Steelworkers of America, had let me know that a steel strike was coming. We were having dinner in his Carlton Hotel suite when I informed him that Jack Kennedy had asked me to be a deputy campaign manager in his coming run for the presidency. "I am going to really need you this year," he said. "Our contracts are not up until June 30, yet the Big Steel companies already have drawn a hard line in the sand. On the work-rules issue, this union will stand together to a man for as long as it takes. This fight is going to get into Congress, which is why I need you. Do anything you want to do for Jack. I don't care. But stick with us until it is over."

Naturally, I did. The strike began quietly in July. At strike headquarters at the Roosevelt Hotel in New York, McDonald and Arthur J. Goldberg, the union's counsel, gave me my first assignment—a proposed Senate Joint

Resolution calling for establishment of an impartial public fact-finding committee to investigate the conflict and make recommendations for settlement.

"We can't lose on this one," Goldberg said. "This strike clearly has been precipitated by Big Steel in a blatant attempt to break the union. Any impartial fact-finding committee is going to have to reach this conclusion. That's why this resolution is so important to us. All of our friends in the Senate *must* cosponsor it."

Jack Kennedy had agreed to be the resolution's principal sponsor, Goldberg continued, and he handed me the statement he had written for him to use on the Senate floor. It sounded like a Wobbly pronouncement. The language was sulphurous: "Profit-crazed steel barons" were trying to "grind their steel-studded boots into the workers' faces." My reaction showed on my face. "I don't know, Arthur. It isn't exactly Kennedy's style."

Goldberg, my genial neighbor with whom I rode downtown every morning, suddenly turned into Captain Queeg. He strode over and thrust his face into mine. "Don't change a word, not a comma," he barked. "If there is any attempt to change anything, I am to know immediately—regardless of the time."

I took Goldberg's statement to Kennedy at 363 Old Senate Office Building. He read it, his brow furrowed with frowns, and asked, "Did you write this?"

"No," I said. "Goldberg did, and his pride of authorship is such that he doesn't even want a comma changed."

Kennedy smiled wryly. "You know that it isn't my style."

"I told him that," I said. "But he didn't listen. So I am just here as a messenger. He is totally *meshugenah* about no changes."

Kennedy called Ted Sorensen in, explained Goldberg's intransigence, and gave him the statement. I went back to my office. A couple of hours later, Sorensen brought me his revision. As bad as Goldberg's "cruel steel barons" prose was, Sorensen's was worse. It was filled with enough pabulum for a mother-love resolution. Per instructions, I dictated his revision to Molly Lynch, Goldberg's secretary, and waited for the explosion. It came almost immediately. "Hold everything," Goldberg raged. "I'm coming on the next flight." I don't know what transpired between Kennedy and Goldberg, but soon I was informed that the Kennedy resolution was now the Symington resolution. The senator from Missouri had agreed to introduce it with Arthur's statement unchanged by a comma or a curlicue. That behind us, I settled down to loading up the resolution with co-sponsors. I went after the easy ones first, figuring that a show of numerical strength would help influence the fence-sitters and stragglers.

Philip A. Hart, just elected from labor-strong Michigan, was one of my "easy ones." Not only had organized labor made a massive effort for him, but I had written and produced some of his media and had gotten to know him well. He would surely be an automatic signer. "I'd rather not," he told me. "When I was in the Michigan state senate I fell into the cosponsoring trap and, as a result, I found my name on things that I didn't know anything about. When I came down here I resolved not to do it again."

I masked my disappointment. "I understand, Phil," and rose to leave.

He grimaced. "Oh, boy, I'm going to be hearing from Chuck Younglove [Michigan Steelworkers Union director] and all the others."

"Not on my say-so. Even though we hate it, your position is perfectly understandable." An hour later my phone rang. "Dammit," Hart said. "You were so nice about it that I've been feeling guilty. Put my name on."

It was a good lesson. Bombast and threats—the tools of some old-style labor lobbyists—didn't carry water with the new legislators on the Hill. Besides, it really wasn't my style. I had been "educated" the year before when the Kennedy-Ives labor bill was on the Senate floor. It had been an innocuous bill, and John L. McClellan of Arkansas, no friend of labor, planned to toughen it with a "labor bill of rights" amendment drafted by the National Association of Manufacturers. The AFL-CIO was in high gear to defeat McClellan.

One of my lobbying assignments was Senator John Sparkman of Alabama, Adlai Stevenson's running mate in 1952. Andy Biemiller, the AFL-CIO legislative director, told me that Sparkman was one of labor's few friends in the South. The senator greeted me cordially and spoke of his long friendships with Alabama labor officials, particularly Barney Weeks, who had called him from Birmingham. When I recited the evils of the McClellan amendment, he nodded in seeming agreement. I left, warmed by his friendliness and confident of his vote.

I was in the gallery when Sparkman, talking with other members in the rear of the Senate chamber, passed on the first roll call for the vote. Then, with the voting time running out and McClellan losing by a good margin, he approached the clerk's desk and voted aye, with McClellan. I charged into Earle Clements's office, wild with anger. "That cracker bastard double-crossed me" was one of my more coherent outbursts. "I'm going to tell him off like he's never been told off," I bellowed.

Clements, chuckling, took me into his inner sanctum and poured me a generous glass of Very Old Fitzgerald. "Now, calm down," he said indulgently. "When John indicated that he was going to support your position, I'm sure that he expected to. That was before the contractors put the heat on him. He has a lot of friends in that crowd, especially in his hometown of Huntsville. Like most of us who get caught on that spit, he waited to the last minute before voting. Then, when he saw that your side had won, he gave his meaningless vote to the contractors. I'm pretty sure that he wouldn't have voted against you had it counted. Now, you can tell him off and make yourself feel better, but I will guarantee you that you will never talk to John Sparkman again." It was another great lesson. I smiled and spoke cordially to Sparkman the next time I saw him. It paid off. Every time I called his office for an appointment, I got it, and I never lost his vote again.

The steel strike meandered on into autumn. I collected sixty-four senators as co-sponsors on the Symington resolution, but Lyndon Johnson was disinclined to bring it to the floor and there was no great pressure on him to do so. The steel companies, in anticipation of a long strike, had built up large stockpiles. With a sluggish economy left over from the 1958 recession, there were no pressing demands for the resumption of steel production.

It was a strange strike. Picket lines were token—and quiet, mercifully without violence. There were no soup kitchens for strikers, who seemed to be doing quite well with strike payments and supplemental unemployment benefits. When I asked some pickets outside a struck plant how they were doing, the collective response was: It sure as hell beats working in a hot mill during the summer. No one seemed eager to go back to work, especially if one comma of the work rules was changed.

With the Symington resolution languishing in LBJ's back pocket, we were momentarily stymied on Capitol Hill. Nordy Hoffmann, the union's legislative director, had a new assignment for me—joining the team negotiating a contract with the Kaiser Steel Company. He had shrewdly observed my friendship with the union's Kaiser negotiators, Charles J. Smith and Joe Angelo, and my rapport with Kaiser's main men, Edgar J. Kaiser and Eugene Trefethen.

It was good duty. The negotiations were conducted in well-appointed hotel suites—the William Penn in Pittsburgh, the Carlton Towers in New York City, and the Carlton in Washington. We always ate at the best restaurants, and the smooth lawyers, at sword's point all day over some obscure contractual clause, were full of bonhomie at night as they sipped their 1948 Chateau Lafitte Rothschild.

I was in a quiet daze. My past notions—fed by images of the Homestead Massacre of 1892, the great sit-down strikes of the 1930s, and Little Steel's Memorial Day Massacre of 1937—were being knocked into a cocked hat. Had I not talked with those cheerful guys on the picket lines, my feelings of guilt would have been unbearable. As it was, I thoroughly enjoyed myself.

The Steelworker strategy was obvious: sign a contract with Kaiser, and the rest of Little Steel would crack. Big Steel then would be isolated and forced to give up its drive to eliminate the work rules. That is exactly what happened. When Kaiser signed a work-rules-preserving contract in October, the jig was up for Big Steel. Jones and Laughlin and Republic Steel quickly followed, and it was only a matter of time before Big Steel surrendered. Some legal folderol, a management maneuver that the union won in the Supreme Court, followed. It only delayed the inevitable. Big Steel, its last hole cards gone, capitulated in early December and agreed to keep the work rules.

David McDonald staged the signing of the new contract in the grand ballroom of Washington's Shoreham Hotel. The union delegation—faces beaming with victory—arrived first, basking in the whirring of television cameras. Suddenly there was a hush. At the head of the stairs leading down into the ballroom appeared the lords of Big Steel, led by Roger Blough and Conrad Cooper. Silently, they filed down the stairs. I tried to remember where I had seen faces so frozen and tightlipped. A Steelworker staffer named Cass Alvin reminded me: the German generals signing the peace treaty in 1945.

I was operating in a three-ring circus in that incredible year of 1959. Concurrently with the steel strike, an all-out effort was being made by business forces—led by the National Association of Manufacturers and the U.S. Chamber of Commerce—to pass a measure that would further regulate labor unions, particularly in their internal operations. The legislation, sponsored by conservative Democratic Congressman Phil Landrum of Georgia and Republican Robert Griffin of Michigan, was fervently opposed by the AFL-CIO and its member unions.

It was ironic that organized labor should find itself in a defensive position. The 1958 elections had been its greatest triumph at the polls since 1936. Fourteen new labor-backed Democratic senators and forty-four more Democratic House members should have been ample insurance against any serious effort by business and its congressional allies to weaken labor's position. But the persuasive power of public opinion—mightily created by the new medium of television—had been upsetting that apple cart. Its genesis centered on the committee created in late 1956 by the Democratic Senate to investigate corruption, particularly in the Teamsters Union. The committee, chaired by a crusty conservative from Arkansas, John L. McClellan, had held televised hearings in 1957–1958 that had shocked the public. Cases of corrupt financial dealing by the Teamsters general president, Dave Beck, and its Midwest vice president, James R. Hoffa, had viewers glued to the screen. Labor's standing with the public plummeted. The main beneficiaries of the latest video extravaganza were labor's friends, the Brothers Kennedy—Jack as the McClellan committee's deftest questioner and Bobby as the committee's crusading counsel. They became public figures overnight.

Senator Kennedy, trying to prevent any rupture with his labor allies, crafted a mild, permissive bill that would have curbed the more egregious excesses revealed by the hearings. He was joined by a moderate Republican from New York, Irving Ives. Their bill, dubbed Kennedy-Ives, eventually reached the Senate floor. There McClellan was waiting with a lengthy amendment, called a "labor's bill of rights." The AFL-CIO pulled out the stops to defeat it and succeeded; the amendment was no friend of labor.

Kennedy-Ives died in the 85th Congress, but the labor corruption issue still was very much alive when the 86th Congress convened in January 1959. When a new bill came to the Senate floor in May, a better-prepped McClellan made his second try. The AFL-CIO was so confident of the outcome that Andrew J. Biemiller, its legislative chief, told Hubert Humphrey that he could leave before the vote for Minneapolis, where he was to be the grand marshal of a civic parade. The voting turned out to be closer than anyone had expected, finally hinging on the vote of a freshman Democrat from Connecticut, Thomas Dodd. To the AFL-CIO's shock, Dodd voted for McClellan, and the hated "bill of rights" was now part of the Senate bill. Dodd later explained the reason for his vote to a *New York Times* reporter.

"Those labor so-and-sos backed Chet [Chester] Bowles against me at the nominating convention," he said. "I've been waiting since then to get even."

Its back to the wall, the AFL-CIO pulled out all the stops as the fight moved to the House. It rented the entire Congressional Hotel, adjacent to the House office buildings, and filled its rooms with trade-union leaders from all fifty states. From a first-floor suite, their efforts were directed by Andy Biemiller, the rotund, erudite former congressman from Milwaukee. With Nordy Hoffmann in New York directing the Steelworkers' strike effort, I subbed for him on Andy's strategy committee. My cachet was Stew Udall, a leading member of the House-Senate conference committee attempting to craft a compromise. Every night, Stew, who stayed with me that summer, gave me his dispassionate analysis of how he thought things were going, which I duly passed on to Biemiller.

Every contestable congressman was fought over with a ferocity that was unmatched in my experience. We sweated, courted, and cajoled every vote, and the Capitol Hill bars were doing standing-room-only business every night. One of my targets was a freshman Democrat from a Nebraska farm district with virtually no union members. Don McGinley and I became friends when our paths had crossed on the campaign trail in 1958. Don told me he would vote with us. I was honored by his expression of confidence, as he had nothing to gain politically in Ogallala, Nebraska, by this vote and much to lose. As a matter of fact, it eventually caught up with him and cost him reelection, for which I forever felt guilty. Shamefully, at the time the New York street hustler in me felt a jolt of pleasure at conning this gullible country boy into his vote. Later, I tried to exorcise the ugliness by "confessing" to McGinley. He smiled, patted my arm and said, "I'm really not that much of a rube."

The night before the final vote, Biemiller took his confidants—Cyrus T. Anderson of the Railway Brotherhoods, Harold Buoy of the Boilermakers Union (later its president), and me—to one of Washington's fanciest French restaurants, the La Salle du Bois, for a pre-victory dinner. Andy was in a euphoric mood. He had his final head counts, and they showed a 25–30 margin. Encoded on three-by-five cards, Andy gleefully read aloud individual state counts as he shuffled through the cards like a blackjack dealer.

The next morning I was awakened by a call from Senator Kennedy, asking me to be at the House television studio for a filmed dialogue on the Landrum-Griffin issue that he was going to do with George McGovern, at the time a young South Dakota congressman aspiring to the Senate. On the way to the studio, Kennedy and I encountered Joseph D. Keenan, a Kennedy partisan and secretary-treasurer of the International Brotherhood of Electrical Workers. His normally genial Irish face was clouded. "What's the matter, Joe?" Kennedy asked.

"The teller vote," Keenan rasped. "We got murdered on the teller vote." The teller vote, an old legislative device borrowed from the British Parliament, was a kind of preliminary vote before the roll-call vote on final passage. It usually approximated the final vote, so it was often a harbinger of what was coming.

Stunned, I raced to the Congressional Hotel and into Andy's office, where a huddle of labor lobbyists were trying to regroup for the roll-call vote. Jack O'Brien of the Machinists Union snarled: "Your phony friend Bobby Kennedy did it to us. He killed us by going on the Jack Paar show and telling everyone to contact their congressman to vote against labor corruption. They did, and we lost votes by the dozens. That rotten bastard." The vote was 221 to 208, a debacle and disgrace for organized labor.

I was feeling my way around my new lobbying turf, somewhat like the New York street kid I once was, venturing furtively and fearfully into an unknown neighborhood where gangs might be waiting to jump me. When the phone rang in my new office, it was comforting to hear the familiar Kentucky twang of my mentor, Earle C. Clements. "I've got a new client for you, my boy," he boomed. "Meet me at the Statler men's bar at six. And tell your sweet little lady that you won't be home for dinner. These boys want to have a good look before they make a deal with you."

The mahogany-paneled bar was thick with tobacco smoke as I found Clements and my prospective new clients seated in a booth. He introduced me to J. R. Miller, manager of the Green River Rural Electric Cooperative of Owensboro, Kentucky; his assistant, Guy Harris; and John R. Hardin, manager of the Henderson-Union Rural Electric Cooperative in Henderson, Kentucky. They all professed to remember me from last year's campaign for governor. I faked the same memory, and we were on a pseudo-friendly first-name basis when the next round of drinks arrived. It was a typical faux-fraternal meeting of politicians, each looking for something from the other. By now, I was used to this sort of encounter.

They were public power men, and that made them somewhat special to me. I still retained a naive perception that such figures were somehow ennobled by their roles as "protectors of the people's power." Public power people were seekers of the Holy Grail, I thought, and that was all that I needed to know.

As the conversation and the bourbon flowed, that illusion underwent swift puncturing. My perception of Southern white males mainly came from the pages of Faulkner, Welty, and Thomas Wolfe; one of hard-drinking romantic gallants who would have ridden with Jeb Stuart had they been born in that time. Of the three, J. R. (for James Rufus) Miller fit that billing. It didn't take me long to realize that J. R. was as true a son of the South as I had ever met. A rangy six-footer with an athletic mien, his sharply chiseled dark face was crowned with a thick mass of oily, curly black hair. His quickly darting black eyes missed nothing, and I knew that he was sizing me up. Clements obviously had convinced him that I was key to his ambition to build his own generating plant and transmission lines with low-cost U.S. loans, to serve his western Kentucky customers.

On scratch paper, Miller drew me a map of his plan. The two co-ops distributed power to rural customers in six counties, power purchased at wholesale rates from Kentucky Utilities (KU), a private company. There was the rub. KU's benign old CEO, who had sold the power cheap, had died, and the rates were going way up. To get out from under, J. R. wanted to produce and distribute his own power. His route was to be the creation of a "Big Rivers G and T," shorthand for a power generation and transmission cooperative that would free the co-ops from dependence on KU or Louisville Gas and Electric. J. R. had written assurances of an ample supply of low-cost coal to supply the generating plant. Now he needed a $25 million loan from the U.S. Rural Electrification Administration to build the plant as well as contracts from the Tennessee Valley Authority and the U.S. Southeastern Power Administration for secondary and peaking power. All this and approval by the Kentucky Public Service Commission. It was a complicated but fascinating project.

The time was ripe. Public power, having reached its apogee in the New and Fair Deal era, had been fighting a defensive battle during President Eisenhower's administration. Now it was readying itself for a comeback, and J. R. wanted to be there when it happened. I saw "Big Rivers" as the breakthrough project that would politicize the rural electric cooperative movement as a new arm of the Democratic Party.

It didn't take me long to find our point man in the Interior Department. Morgan Dubrow was the newly appointed deputy assistant secretary for water and power and perfect for the role. He was an original New Dealer, a former TVA engineer, and a native of rural South Carolina who had spent two decades as the Bonneville Power Administration's representative in Washington, D.C. He also was a Southern gentleman of the old school, but one who liked his liquor and was not averse to the attractions of the ladies of the night — a Faulknerian figure, if ever there was one.

I put Morgan and J. R. together one memorable night in the summer of 1961. The locale was J. R.'s suite at the venerable Washington Hotel, across the street from the White House. J. R. had brought a contingent with him. His connecting suites were amply supplied with liquor and food, and, between sips and bites, we settled into an evening of Kentucky storytelling.

As the night wore on, the pall of smoke grew to a haze, and the decibel level was near the screech stage. With a knock at the door, however, the hubbub quickly tuned down. The four attractive young women who entered the suite could have passed for suburban housewives or government secretaries. A trim but aging blonde woman, who introduced herself as Susan, seemed to be in charge. There was humor and character in her face, which might make her someone worth talking to, I thought.

J.R. opened by asking, "Would you beautiful ladies care for a little toddy for the body?" He was greeted by a chorus of laughing yeses. Guy Harris mixed the drinks, and the oldest game in the world began. I had a pretty good eye for those who made their living in what they called "the life," yet I would not have spotted those four women. Even the one who said she was a stripper at the nearby Blue Mirror could have passed for a graduate-school student. I was briefly tempted to invite one of them into an available bedroom but decided to talk to Susan instead. Something about her interested me. The newspaper reporter in me sensed that there might be a pretty good story there.

We sat in an alcove, and it didn't take too many questions to get her started. Susan, of course, was not her real name. "Honey, I've had so many names in my life that I can't even remember what my real name was. I've been every heroine from Mary Magdalene to Joan of Arc," she roared. From the shards and fragments she offered me, I gathered that she had been in "the life" since her teens and had become very good at it. She had developed an impressive list of girls she supplied to convention managers, politicians, labor and corporate chieftains, lawyers, and the fight crowd.

Susan called me at my office one afternoon. She said that she wanted to talk some more and hoped that she wasn't interrupting any business, and we had a long and warm talk. Her calls became a periodic thing, and Terry, my secretary, would say with a smile: "Your friend is on the line." Our talks consisted mostly of my telling her about who I was doing business with on Capitol Hill, and I looked forward to the late-afternoon calls. I still did not know her real name or where she lived. Working late one evening, I found out. Susan called. When I told her that I was free, she replied succinctly, "I will pick you up at Connecticut and L in twenty-five minutes. A blue Oldsmobile sedan."

My eagerness to see her again was mixed with a certain apprehension. God knows what I was getting myself into. She was, after all, a "criminal" with a long police record. In my five-plus years in Washington I had made some serious enemies, most notably Bobby Baker, Lyndon Johnson's right-hand man in the Senate, and the fear of being "set up" always existed. Yet, I was there, waiting.

Susan and her roommate Alice lived in a spacious two-bedroom apartment in a modern high-rise just off I-95 in the seemingly endless northern Virginia suburbs. Alice was a stunner, a tall and willowy brunette with long, tapering legs and the warmest of smiles. She greeted me with a hug, and we settled down to generous drinks and, not long after, to Alice's story. I was an avid listener at supper. I never discussed my own domestic problems with anyone, and I had no intention of breaking that rule. Hell, I didn't understand myself, so why should I expect my spouse or anyone else to understand such a mixed-up piece of baggage?

At thirty-nine, I was not yet into introspection, and I had no realization of what a fragile, starved ego I had and how dependent it was on externals. A simple warm smile from a stranger could cheer me as much as a look of disdain could cast me down. Like most males, I liked to think of myself as a "tough guy," one impervious to the slings and arrows of others. I would not have admitted to weakness or doubt. I had had my share of casual encounters that were meaningless and quickly forgotten. What had made this one so different? It took me some time to figure it out. Susan had restored my confidence in myself. She had recognized me as a wounded creature, despite my sheen of success and bravado. And because I had shown her respect and friendliness, she had given me the best of herself. "Besides," she added when I told her this, "you really laugh at my jokes."

Susan didn't call for several days. Then, one twilight when I was alone in the office, she called. "You brought us luck," she laughed. "We've been busy every night making big spenders happy. The rent is paid for six months. Come out soon for supper and bring your friend Morgan. Alice really likes him because he is such a true-born Southern gentleman." So that is what we did—Morgan and I, several times in the next year or so. Our only contribution to the party was liquor and food, and the subject of money never came up.

Time, divorce, and remarriage tailed off the relationship, and Susan was among the first to applaud my good fortune at finding a wife so suited for me as Erna. When I tried to say thanks for our relationship, she said, "I hated to see a good guy so unhappy." The comment surprised me. I didn't understand that my despair was that obvious. It was something I didn't even admit to myself.

Susan did not surface again until the Bobby Baker scandal erupted in Washington in 1964. She called to tell me that she was under investigation. Did I have any ideas or know anything? She sounded apprehensive but not scared. "I've had bigger boys than them put me on the grill," she laughed. I did have an idea. The *Life* magazine reporters tracking the story — Russ Sackett and Bill Lambert — were old colleagues of mine, and I knew they could be trusted. Would she be interested in talking to them if they took her under their wing? She would, and I made the arrangements. It apparently worked out. Susan kept her name and picture out of the papers, and my *Life* friends told me she had been invaluable. I didn't ask for details.

In the meantime, the Big Rivers Generation and Transmission Corporation was charging toward reality, propelled by the nonstop prodding and manic maneuvers of J. R. Miller. One snowy February night, for example, my wife Rosalie and I were at Washington's National Theater, celebrating our twentieth wedding anniversary. An usher found me and said, "You have an emergency call, sir." It was J. R. "We've got a crisis with Dave Francis," he growled. "The Aero Commander is on its way to pick you up at Butler Aviation. It'll be there in an hour. I'll explain everything to you when you get here. Sorry to louse up your anniversary, but it couldn't be avoided." He hung up.

Later that night in Frankfort, he told me that Francis, chair of the Kentucky Public Service Commission, was balking at issuing the license Big Rivers needed to proceed. Early the next morning we met with Governor Bert T. Combs, who I hadn't seen since the 1959 campaign. "How's old Cabbagehead?" he grinned, remembering my boyhood nickname. I was flattered. He got right down to business. "What's the problem, J. R.?"

"Dave Francis, governor," J. R. said. "I thought we had a deal with him to get our certificate right out, and now he's gandy-dancing all over the place. And he ain't returning our phone calls. I think KU has him."

Combs whistled softly and picked up the phone to his secretary. "Tell Dave Francis I'd like to see him here right now." He turned. "I'll handle Francis, J. R."

Outside, J. R. gave a whoop and grabbed me. "You did it, podner," he chortled. "It's all going to be downhill from here. That certificate is more than half the battle."

"Did what?" I protested. "I didn't do a damned thing but say hello. What are you talking about?"

"All you had to do was be there," J. R. explained. "Combs thinks your television and advertising stuff elected him, and Clements has him convinced that you are in with the Kennedys, so that Interior and the REA will act fast on our loan application after we are certified by the Kentucky PSC. So I had to have you there."

He drove me to the Frankfort-Lexington airport and put me on a plane to Washington. Hours later, I was home, shaking my head over the ways of Kentucky politics. As they like to say, "The landscape is the grandest, and politics the damnedest in Kentucky."

J. R. was right. After he got the Kentucky PSC license, events moved quickly. The $25 million loan to build the plant was approved by the Rural Electrification Administration. Now the task was to make deals with the Interior Department's Southeastern Power Administration and the Tennessee Valley Authority to gain secondary power from the TVA's Barkley and Kentucky dams. That entailed endless meetings and countless weekends. I was getting comfortable with places like Elberton, Georgia; Owensboro and Henderson, Kentucky; Jackson and Vicksburg, Mississippi; New Orleans; and even Las Vegas, Nevada.

Then, suddenly, it was over. The Big Rivers plant on Kentucky's Green River went up in a hurry, which led to ceremonial weekends dedicating the plant and breaking ground for new factories. Politicians made the same speeches hailing the dawn of a new industrial era in western Kentucky. The congeries of hoary clichés were swilled down with large swallows of whiskey and digested with chunks of greasy fried catfish. I boozily professed eternal friendship with good old boys I hardly knew, and they professed it back. None of us believed a word of what we were saying. We were just observing old Southern customs.

Did the low-cost power from Big Rivers benefit the common folk of western Kentucky? Most of it seemed to go to companies all too willing to locate their plants where bargain-basement power was available, the same as they did in the Pacific Northwest when Grand Coulee and the other big federal dams started churning out billions of kilowatts for sale. When I saw the silk-suited businessmen from Atlanta and New York at the plant dedications, I couldn't help but wonder: Was this really power for the people?

And J. R.? He became Democratic state chairman and led his party to a string of victories that brought it control of the statehouse and the congressional delegation. He then topped off his new political career by winning the mayoralty of Owensboro. As mayor, he built a new road to his ranch at nearby Maceo. That turned out to be beyond the pale, even for J. R.-jaded partisans. When bumper stickers protesting the road appeared everywhere, he prudently decided not to run again. The sticker read: "They shot the wrong J. R."

14

THE SPOTTED OWL
AND OTHER VARMINTS

"THE JAPANESE ARE OUTBIDDING US FOR RAW MATERIALS RIGHT in our own backyard," cried the excited young man from Oregon with the brush-cut hair. "They could cause an economic Pearl Harbor in our industry if something isn't done." He wasn't talking about automobiles, television sets, or transistor radios. They would come much later and create bigger headlines than his issue. His issue was timber, which Japanese buyers had begun buying in boxcar amounts at public auction from the federally owned forests of the Pacific Northwest. Japan had exhausted its own forests in World War II and now, experiencing its first prosperity since the war, had developed an insatiable appetite for timber.

It was March 1961, and the excited young man was Joseph W. McCracken, the chief factotum for an association of small-business lumbermen. His members, up in arms over Japanese competition, had sent him to Washington, D.C., to find out what the newly installed Kennedy administration was going to do about their problem. He also was recruiting me as a lobbyist.

I knew his organization, the Western Forest Industries Association (WFIA), headquartered in Portland. During the 1950s, I had traveled to Oregon to help WFIA fight off attempts by Big Timber to restrict the volume of federal timber available for open bidding at public auction. The David-versus-Goliath game was my bag, and I was a natural to become the association's first lobbyist, a role I was to play for thirty-two years.

Actually, log exports to Japan were relatively small at the time, just 210 million board feet in 1960. By 1988, exports would balloon to 4.2 billion board feet, but—thanks to our unremitting efforts—it was not wood from publicly owned forests. Weyerhaeuser and other companies with large timberland reserves were making big bucks selling to the Japanese for more than they would have made domestically. Consequently, those companies did not contest WFIA's early efforts at blunting the Japanese buying foray.

Congressional hearings convinced Agriculture Secretary Orville Freeman that something had to be done to protect independent operators. He found an obscure statute that authorized small business set-aside sales when U.S. property—timberland, for example—was sold. The Freeman initiative eased the problem, and in 1968 Senator Wayne Morse of Oregon got Congress to agree to a log-export ban on all federal lands in the West.

The forest-products industry in the Pacific Northwest is divided between the "haves," who own their own timberland, and the "have-nots," who buy theirs at public auction from the state and federal governments. Most of the timber from public auctions comes from the nineteen national forests in Oregon and Washington, which produce 40 percent of the wood sold nationally by the Forest Service and yield more than half its total income. Each year, Congress determines how much timber will be cut from each national forest. The two subcommittees that approved those amounts were my principal theater of operations for WFIA.

For a long time, it was a piece of cake. With Northwest congressmen dominating the subcommittees, it was easy to increase the amount of timber put up for sale over what the Forest Service had requested; that agency would then justify the add-on under its sustained-yield guidelines. Sustained yield was the mantra—never would more timber be cut than would be grown back in a forest in a year's time. It was the article of faith to which almost every forester swore. Sometimes I wondered whether this doctrine was being stretched to satisfy an aggressive congressman, but WFIA wasn't paying me for heretical thoughts.

Early on, I learned that federal bureaucrats generally were willing to cooperate with congressional increases in timber harvesting; the increased revenues to the U.S. treasury strengthened their positions. The two-and-one-half million acres of western Oregon timberland—known as the Oregon & California (O&C) Revested Lands—served as my first case in point. The O&C lands were unique in that they had been revested by the federal government in 1916 from the Southern Pacific Railroad (formerly the Oregon & California Railroad) when it violated the terms of the law that had created it in 1868. After decades of controversy, in 1937 the lands—administered by the Bureau of Land Management, not the Forest Service—were opened for timber cutting on a sustained-yield basis.

I had been friends with John A. Carver, the assistant Interior secretary in charge of those lands, from Idaho days. When I broached the idea of increasing the cut on the O&C, he was more than one step ahead of me. He already had determined that the lands were under-producing and that timber sales could be substantially increased without violating the sacred sustained-yield limitations. My new clients were delighted, and I basked in their acclaim for something I had nothing to do with. I also learned a significant secret of the lobbying trade: how important inside or advance knowledge was to my new livelihood. Carver was going to increase O&C sales regardless, and my knowing it in advance enabled me to play the hero. I tried not to ham it up too obviously. Carver had trusted me, and my newspaper training had imbued in me the doctrine that one never violated a confidence.

The WFIA had been formed in 1945, when the demand for housing exploded and returning veterans were offered easy, low-interest home loans. Those homes would need all the studs the Northwest could produce. Sidney Leiken, a Connecticut native, had come to Oregon in 1937 to plant trees with FDR's Civilian Conservation Corps. He had liked Oregon and decided to stay, going to work as a laborer in a lumber mill. By war's end, he was managing the mill, with a growing family and a seat in the state legislature in the offing. Sid and others like him realized they needed an organization to protect their interests or else they would be picked off, one by one, by Big Timber. Thus, the Western Forest Industries Association, the "Peck's bad boy" of the industry, came into being.

WFIA members—some of whom had been my classmates at the University of Oregon—were a rough-hewn lot who loved the thrill of the bidding game at the public timber auctions held by the Forest Service. Bid right on a sale and make a bundle; bid wrong and take a bath. These guys were throwing the dice and living on the margin every day.

The feds, starting with the Truman administration, were playing right along. For them, cutting more trees was a trifecta: a plentiful supply of low-cost lumber to build the Levittowns that were springing up across the nation, more funds for the U.S. Treasury, and a competitive industry in which the little guys could battle the Weyerhaeusers on a level playing field. The impact of wholesale clear-cutting on the environment was not taken very seriously. It actually was good for the land, people argued, to replace old trees, many of which were dead and dying, with vibrant young seedlings. The Forest Service and the region's forestry schools encouraged this thinking, and just a handful of people—notably David Brower of the Sierra Club—questioned the dogma.

I began hearing dissident voices as early as 1959. My closest political pals were Congressmen Stewart Udall of Arizona and George McGovern of South Dakota, Governor Gaylord Nelson of Wisconsin, and my home-state senator Scoop Jackson. I had a conveniently located house and a well-stocked bar, and we congregated there regularly.

Udall was fascinated by Rachel Carson, who lived nearby and was writing a book on the damage that pesticides and chemicals were doing to the land and wildlife (*Silent Spring*, published in 1960, was an instant best seller). Nelson, in his first act as governor in 1959, had created a conservation program on Wisconsin's state lands, to be paid for by an increase in cigarette taxes. He was surprised by the support he received from conservatives who didn't want their surroundings desecrated, one of the first indications that environment with a capital E was the rare kind of issue that crossed ideological lines. Jackson, ever sensitive to good-government issues with vote-getting potential, chaired the Interior committee that could take up the ecological cudgels—if the political climate was right.

Yet, the environmental politicos were still a corporal's guard. Nelson, who came to the Senate in 1963, noted that there had been only six senators then with a working knowledge of environmental issues. One was Edmund S. Muskie of Maine, who chaired a public-works subcommittee where he was able to develop the popular issues of clean air and water. Muskie's then-best friend in the Senate, Eugene J. McCarthy of Minnesota, quipped: "Ed, you've found issues better than motherhood."

My environmental connections did not bother my lumber clients one whit. Joe McCracken, a Princeton-educated Montanan, professed his fealty to the health of the land and, as if to prove it, spent his vacations hiking in the Northwest forests. When a mining operation was proposed for Idaho's White Clouds, one of his favorite hiking areas, his screams of rage were as loud as Dave Brower's.

The main reason for the forest-products industry's indifference to environmentalists was the imposing presence of the U.S. Forest Service. With its Smokey Bear logo and Gifford Pinchot as its godfather, that agency rivaled the FBI in the public eye as the exemplar of federal institutions. If the Forest Service said it was right, it was right—no questions asked. And the nation's prestigious forestry schools—from Yale to Berkeley—were there to back them up. Only Arnold Bolle, dean of Montana's forestry school, occasionally offered a negative note on the agency's clear-cutting practices on inland forests. But not much attention was paid. The Pacific Northwest was an immense piece of real estate with its dark-green forests stretching across mountain ridges from the Continental Divide to the Pacific. There was enough for everybody.

At the time, I was developing a strong relationship with the Forest Service people. Being good stewards of the 187 million acres on more than 150 national forests was the ethic that dominated their work. The beau ideal was Arthur Greeley, associate chief. Art radiated a bedrock integrity that made his word inviolate to even the most skeptical lumberman or environmentalist. When he spoke, they—and Congress—listened because he had no axes to grind.

Greeley prepared the Forest Service budget every year, and he always requested funding for comprehensive and balanced management of the forests—for reforestation, watershed management, hydrology, control of stream siltation, and the timber sales program. Only the sales program would survive intact in Congress. Art would be philosophical but profoundly unhappy, because he knew the forests were deteriorating.

I had a brilliant idea. My old friend from Oregon political wars, Lloyd Tupling, had just become the Sierra Club's Washington lobbyist, the first paid representative for the environmental movement on Capitol Hill. He and I agreed that the ecologists and lumbermen had a mutual interest in preserving the health of the forests. What better project could there be than our joining together to lobby Congress for the restoration of the slashed funding? My enthusiasm for the project knew no bounds. Tup liked the idea, but his enthusiasm was more restrained. He knew human nature better than I did.

When I broached the idea to Joe McCracken, he looked at me with disbelief but said I could try it out on WFIA's leadership. Never in my life have
I been so completely rejected. The mind-set was fierce and unyielding, and
I was accused of asking them to "get in bed with the devil." Tup reported
the same reaction from his crowd. Over a few drinks in a Capitol Hill saloon,
we had a rueful laugh and dropped the issue. To this day I regret that we did
not push the project harder. Mutual stewardship of the forests is an idea whose
time will come. I only hope I live to see it.

The forest-products industry did well with Congress on the bread-and-
butter stuff, which was principally the amount of timber put up for sale every
year. Beyond that, it was another matter. The industry's strongest supporters in Congress knew how thin its support was, but the industry didn't. A
seemingly innocuous bill, the National Timber Supply Act, burst their bub-
ble in 1970. The legislation would have funneled the funds from timber sales
on the national forests into a separate account, with the money used to refur-
bish those forests. It was patterned on the 1956 highway bill, which had placed
increased gasoline taxes into a special fund to build the interstate highway
system. It was hard to imagine that it might cause a firestorm.

Into the act came the Sierra Club, the only cohesively active environmental lobby at the time. The group had just concluded its successful fight
to "save" the Grand Canyon, and it was looking for new issues to keep its
members excited. According to the Sierra Club propagandists, the bill was
a "power grab" by the forest-products industry to take over the national forests.
Mail, telegrams, and phone calls from their members poured into Capitol
Hill as Congress prepared to take up the bill in early 1970, and defections
from the pro-timber-bill ranks were starting to occur.

A Michigan congressman named John Dingell was an old friend of mine.
He also was one of the first to embrace environmental issues. He called me
and said, "Get up here. I've got an idea that may save your butt on the timber supply bill." When I walked into his office minutes later, he was sitting
there with John P. Saylor, a Republican congressman from Pennsylvania and
the leading environmentalist on the conservative side. Dingell wasted no
time in pleasantries. "John and I have an amendment to your bill," he said.
"It will earmark 10 percent of the total receipts for environmental stuff—
reforestation, watershed management, stream protection. If you can get the
industry to back it, we will vote with you."

Bank-night bingo! I raced downtown to the National Forest Products Association (NFPA) headquarters and was ushered in to see Jim Turnbull, the president. I gave him the Dingell-Saylor proposition. He frowned. "Why should we do that?" he asked. "We've got the votes. We don't have to give up anything."

Turnbull was an experienced timber executive but a tyro when it came to the sometimes strange ways of Capitol Hill. I explained that none of our commitments was carved in granite and that the initial Sierra Club barrage had scored several big hits. He waved me off. "I don't hear it from my people," he said in dismissal.

I reported my failure to Dingell. "Oh, are we going to whip your fanny," he chortled. "Kid, you are going to lose this one in a big way."

Prowling the House office buildings, I became convinced he was right. Too many congressmen that NFPA had listed as rock-solid votes were hemming and hawing, clutching and grabbing. "I was all for you," one told me, "but look at this." He pointed to a stack of mail on his desk: "All against the bill—and all from my district." He was lost, and we wouldn't get him back. The industry's strongest supporters—led by Tom Foley of Washington State—now spoke with one voice. "Take the bill down," they chorused. "It will be clobbered."

Turnbull and the NFPA executives were unmoved. Since I represented a fringe group, the WFIA, they did not tolerate or trust me that much anyway. "We're going to hold their feet to the fire," they huffed. "We're going to make those bastards be counted."

The bill was brought to the House floor on the afternoon of February 26, 1970. The industry wives, all dressed in their finery for the celebration afterward, were seated in the family gallery of the House. I sat behind them, one of the few times I ever allowed myself this luxury instead of working the halls below to hustle last-minute votes.

It was a sorry spectacle. The issue was whether the House should adopt the rule to consider the bill, and from the start it went badly for our side. As the debate progressed, Dingell could not resist leering and winking at me periodically. Some of the wives turned and glared at me. The vote was 226 to 150 against allowing the bill to the floor. It was the most humiliatingly abject beating I had ever witnessed in a legislative body.

"And we did it without breaking sweat," Lloyd Tupling chuckled over the drinks he bought me afterward at the National Democratic Club bar. The defeat didn't surprise me. When it came to public opinion and politics, the industry was a paper tiger. Two years before, WFIA had placed an initiative on the Washington state ballot that would have barred export sales of timber from the state forestlands. It led in the polls by a two-to-one margin—until three weeks before the election when the exporters unleashed a media blitz on the theme: "Don't let the timber barons rob our schoolchildren." (The funds from these timber sales went into school funds, and the Japanese paid the highest dollar for the logs.) The measure lost by a near two-to-one margin.

The timber-supply debacle was such an embarrassment that the NFPA did not emerge from its lair to fight another major congressional battle until 1976. A federal district court ruling had barred clear-cutting on the Monongahela National Forest in West Virginia. The order, upheld by the Fourth Circuit Court of Appeals, threatened to end clear-cutting on all national forests unless Congress acted. John Maguire, the Forest Service chief, and a few senators—Hubert Humphrey of Minnesota, Jennings Randolph of West Virginia, Dale Bumpers of Arkansas—saw an opportunity in the exigency to reshape the agency. The legislative product that emerged was named the National Forest Management Act (NFMA) of 1976, and its result was to reorder the priorities on the nation's timberlands in favor of the ecology, particularly fish and wildlife.

Those of us in the industry had no inkling that it would end up that way when we charged up to Capitol Hill in the spring of 1976 to lobby for the Monongahela bill. Solving the clear-cutting crisis was the paramount issue for us, and the rest of the bill—new directives for the Forest Service—was "enviro garbage," a price we had to pay for muting their opposition. After all, we had suffered passage of two environmental bills—the National Environmental Policy Act (NEPA) in 1969 and the Endangered Species Act (ESA) in 1973—without serious damage to the timber program. If NFMA added to NEPA and ESA, so what? No one had even heard of the northern spotted owl.

Monongahela's progress was tedious, with endless hearings marked by long, technical discussions. The Senate bill-drafting was accomplished in open sessions with two committees participating—Interior and Agriculture. With industry and environmental lobbyists hovering over every clause and comma and with both sides equally represented on the committees, NFMA inched glacially forward. The chairman, Scoop Jackson, developed a technique for breaking seemingly endless impasses by saying, "We seem to have reached general agreement on this point. Let us leave it to staff to draft the language." The adversaries usually were relieved.

As the bill neared final passage—Congress approved it on September 28, 1976—environmentalists showed up to lobby against it. "You rolled us when we weren't looking," Brock Evans of the Sierra Club complained to me. I just grinned. We were getting even for the timber supply debacle of 1970; and my role as intermediary between the industry and key senators Mark Hatfield of Oregon, Scoop Jackson of Washington, and especially Dale Bumpers of Arkansas to bring the bill to the floor had helped.

Right after passage, the NFPA held an impromptu victory party at a nearby club. When I walked in, everyone raised their glasses and sang "For he's a jolly good fellow." I basked in their momentary esteem, since I had generally been regarded as an *outré* industry renegade by most of those doing the singing.

After that celebratory moment, I met Gaylord Nelson at our favorite wateringhole, The Monocle on Capitol Hill. I told him about my moment of glory. He laughed. "The industry had a victory party? That's funny. I've just come from the environmentalists' victory party. They think we passed one hell of a bill—for them."

As it turned out, he was right, yet for a long time it appeared as if the industry had won. With an omnivorous demand for wood increasing yearly, Congress kept upping the sales volume, particularly in Oregon and Washington. In 1986, it ordered the agency to sell 700 million board feet more than proposed; in 1988, a billion board feet more. Congress was still playing within the existing rules. The Forest Service's sustained-yield figure for the region was 5.2 billion board feet per year. Congress never exceeded that and only once approached it.

But the Forest Service was undergoing a metamorphosis. Thanks to the NFMA, it now had on its staff three times as many wildlife and fishery biologists and ten times as many ecologists as before. This timber-oriented institution now was looking at its land for other values to preserve, and fish and wildlife ranked high on the new agenda. How the northern spotted owl became the metaphor or synecdoche for an unparalleled controversy is perhaps the most unusual story in the long history of conflict between developers and preservers on our remarkable continent. I still shake my head in disbelief that it ever happened.

The spotted owl story began in 1968, when Eric Forsman, a forestry student working summers for the Forest Service in the Willamette National Forest, heard a strange hoot. He hooted back, a conversation took place, and, *mirabile dictu*, the owl fluttered out of the dark forest to take a closer look at his new pal. It was a northern spotted owl, a species so rare that it had been seen only two dozen times in the entire history of the region.

Forsman had found his owl in an old-growth section of the Willamette, just the type of area that the Forest Service was focusing on for future timber cuts in its Northwest forests. In the years that followed, he and other Oregon State University biologists determined that the owl needed the old growth to survive. But how much acreage per bird? And could the creature be defined as an endangered or threatened species under the new Endangered Species Act?

Environmental groups were quick to see that drab twenty-ounce critter as their potential bluebird of happiness, bird of paradise, and Maltese Falcon. The owl was unique in that it responded to calls from humans, thus overcoming the problem defenders of rare wildlife faced—they couldn't prove a threatened species was really rare because they couldn't find it. "The owl was made for our cause," crowed Andy Kerr of the Oregon Natural Resources Council, and it was hard to dispute his boast.

The battle over the northern spotted owl and how much unlogged habitat it needed to survive was to go on for seventeen years. When it finally ended, the environmentalists had won an unprecedented victory and national passions had been aroused, virtually all of them in favor of the owl. "I knew for sure that we had won when the owl made the cover of *Time*," said Andy Stahl of the Sierra Club. He was right. When the national network news showed scenes of clear-cutting in Northwest forests, I watched lumbermen's wives wince.

The result was a revolution in forestry management. No longer would growing trees for lumbering be the primary purpose of the national forests; the federal cut in the Northwest had plummeted from around five billion board feet to less than a billion. The Clinton administration's plan—adopted in 1993 as Option Nine—emphasized watershed protection, salmon preservation, and other hitherto ignored aspects of land management.

The public, even in the Northwest, seemed to approve; polls showed the owl favored over clear-cutting. And the big surprise? The Northwest's economy boomed with an influx of high-tech plants and retirees relocating from California and other high-price, high-tax places. A page-one headline in the October 11, 1994, *New York Times* said it all: "Oregon, Foiling Forecasters, Thrives as It Protects Owls." Even the industry, whose spokesmen had predicted a "new Appalachia in the Northwest," was thriving. Oregon remained the nation's leading lumber state, cutting its yearly five billion board feet largely from private tree farms. Innovation and efficiency became new buzzwords; and Tom Maloney, a wood materials scientist at Washington State University, noted that the industry was getting 15 million tons of product out of material it had burned for waste thirty years before. Substitutes for dimension or framing lumber came out of the same forests in products called waferboard and fiberboard, made from chips cut from once-worthless trees such as alder. The industry's response to the owl was akin to the auto industry's response to OPEC's oil-price increases: it got smart.

This revolution in the woods was aided considerably by an invisible division in the industry, a split that had existed since World War II. My crowd, those who depended on federal timber to operate, was fighting the change as if their lives were at stake. The big landowning companies ostensibly were on their side and pitched in big bucks for a new lobby called the American Forest Resource Alliance. It looked like the industry was unified against the threat.

I was suspicious from the start. Too many times I had heard Charley Bingham of Weyerhaeuser decry the existence of "too many companies and too much production." Lumber prices, he contended, were being held down by oversupply. Bill Swindells, CEO of Willamette Industries, was equally vociferous in saying that federal production needed to be cut back for the good of the industry.

The *Washington Post* detailed the split on August 4, 1991, in a lengthy article appropriately titled "The Owl's Golden Egg—Environmentalism Could Boost Lumber Profits and Prices." Its main point was this: curtailed production was yielding higher prices and greater profits to companies that had their own wood supply. Any CEO of such a company who was ambivalent about the environmentalists' success was hardly being true to his own stockholders, however much he might be paying into the American Forest Resource Alliance. And what about the smaller operators? Remarkably, most survived and continued to make money. The huge decline in federal log supply was compensated for by purchases from private timberlands and other sources, even exports from as far away as New Zealand. A warning note: Some industry analysts believe that too many young trees are being cut and that the region will ultimately pay a price for depending on these immature stands.

The forest has always been a mystery to humankind, the land equivalent of endless oceans. Trees are essential to survival, providing habitat for food, materials for housing and locomotion, and a place to hide from enemies. Humans had worked to unravel the perplexities of the forests, and when I became WFIA's lobbyist I thought the mysteries of the forest had been revealed and we had found all the answers. The "cut-and-get-out" ethic that had decimated the forests of the Upper Midwest had become a symbol of long-ago profligacy, when Americans thought their resources were limitless. In the wake of that disaster had come the forestry schools, and for almost a century foresters had been trained in the latest scientific methods to make the nation's forests even better. Our proud boast was that the nation now had more trees standing than were there when the *Mayflower* landed at Plymouth Rock. With new super-genetic hybrid strains coming out of the laboratories, the nation's forests had no place to go but up.

This was the canon: the forest's basic value was in its wood, which was best produced by neat "row farming" methods. Other aspects, such as wildlife, were incidental to the forest's health. Only a few dissidents, contemptuously dismissed as "tree-huggers," complained. Who would take issue with Smokey Bear? The myth of the "omniscient forester" prevailed. But then a few foresters began to question the canon. One was Jerry Franklin of the University of Washington. Observing what happened to the forests decimated by the Mt. St. Helens eruption of 1980, Franklin became convinced that leaving dead trees standing and rotting logs on the ground was what Nature had in mind for the perpetuation of life in the forests. Clearing it all out to plant trees of a single species in even rows was a flawed idea. Trees are more complex than corn or cotton, he reasoned, and named his way of thinking the New Forestry.

Franklin's hypothesis was later examined in President Bill Clinton's plan to renew the health of the Pacific Northwest's federal timberlands. The chief of the Forest Service under Clinton, a craggy biologist named Jack Ward Thomas, made it clear that no one has all the answers. "Our world has turned out to be more complicated than we originally thought," he said. "Understanding what we now call ecosystem management is like trying to eat Jell-O with chopsticks."

Wendell Wyatt had been the industry's most forceful supporter during his decade in Congress from 1964 to 1975 representing Oregon's First District. A Portland lawyer with lumber clients, he is one of the most candid and honest people I know. In 1985, when the owl issue first was hot with the media, I asked him if he thought the controversy was good or bad for Oregon. He looked around, as if to make sure no one was listening. "If you tell my clients what I'm about to say, I will haunt you forever," he said. "Yes, I think the owl issue has been good for Oregon. It has forced us to rethink how we are managing our land. I have always thought that we were doing a good job, but now it has become obvious that we can do better. In the long run, this will benefit the industry because it will learn to get more out of less." A myriad of questions remains to be answered in this unending saga of man and the forest.

15

MIKE'S "FISH BOWL"

SOMETIME IN THE SUMMER OF 1962, THE PHONE RANG IN MY CLUT-
tered Connecticut Avenue office. My secretary was out, so I answered. "Joe,
this is Darrell Jones, calling from Milwaukie, Oregon. Do you remember me?"

I nudged my memory and saw a moonfaced fellow built like an NFL center. "Yes, you're a Clackamas County commissioner, and you're involved with
the Oregon and California Land Grant Counties Association," I said.

A gurgle of appreciation. "Joe McCracken said you would remember. Yes,
I am president of the association, and we have a big problem. There is a powerful congressman from Ohio who is trying to put us out of business, and we
are told that he is a friend of yours."

My ears twitched. "You must mean Mike Kirwan, Darrell, but it doesn't
make sense to me. Mike prides himself on being the best friend the West ever
had in Congress. I can't believe he would do anything to jeopardize that."

Jones explained that Oregon's maverick senator, Wayne Lyman Morse,
had infuriated Kirwan by using the Senate's arcane rules to kill the Ohioan's
pet project, a $10 million "national aquarium" on the Potomac River. By
Kirwan's standards, Morse had betrayed his support for western issues, and
revenge was the only recourse. It could be exacted by slashing funding for
Oregon, including funding for the Oregon & California land grant—2.5 million acres of the choicest timberlands in the nation.

The small lumbermen were totally dependent on federal O&C and Forest Service timber to stay in business. Consequently, the bidding wars were

fiercely fought, which jacked up the prices paid to the feds and to the eighteen western Oregon counties in which O&C lands were located. Fifty percent of the yearly gross receipts was paid directly to these counties, divided up according to the percentage of O&C lands within their borders. Another 25 percent of the receipts went to the intensified management of the lands, making the sale of more timber feasible. The remaining 25 percent went into the U.S. Treasury. The generous payments were occasioned because the counties had experienced years without tax revenue early in the twentieth century, when ownership of the land grant had been fought out in federal court. Congress had settled on the 50–25–25 formula in 1937.

Oregon was vulnerable. In 1962, its small congressional delegation was at its weakest, with no one on the Senate and House appropriations committees for the first time in decades. Those committees funded the big developments that Oregon depended on—the huge Columbia River dams, flood control, navigation, reclamation, forest development, salmon hatcheries, coastal port improvements. Without someone on the inside to speak for Oregon's interests, the state was dependent on the kindness of others—like Mike Kirwan, the longtime chairman of the subcommittee that appropriated the funds for virtually all of Oregon's federal projects. Fifty-two percent of Oregon's land mass was within his financial jurisdiction.

How could the superbly intelligent Morse have been so stupid to incur Kirwan's wrath over such an insignificant issue? I wasn't going to find out from Morse. He and I hadn't spoken since 1959 as a result of his ugly feud with Dick Neuberger. Morse had challenged me to take sides, and I refused to declare. Nasty words spewed out of him. From then on, every time he saw me with another senator, Morse later delivered a screed on my general rottenness. These philippics were played back to me, usually in bemused fashion, and I learned to ignore them—and him. As Jack Kennedy said, "Poor Wayne. How can he be so brilliant and so childishly irrational at the same time? He can't stand it if you don't go with him when he's convinced that he is right. He is colorblind. Can't see the grays."

For reasons I never fathomed, Kirwan had taken a shine to me. I guess it was because I loved to listen to his colorful and fanciful stories about his past. The House had a group of big-city Irish congressmen, whom I dubbed the "Irish Dukes"—Bill Green of Philadelphia, John Fogarty of Rhode Island, Tip O'Neill of Massachusetts, Jack Shelley of San Francisco, and a few others. Kirwan was *primus inter pares* among them, and he wielded them like a shillelagh to get what he wanted. It was a bravura performance from a man who had left school at the age of nine to work in the anthracite coalfields of Pennsylvania and had fought his way out to win election to Congress from Youngstown, Ohio, in 1937. He was an American original.

I took Mike to lunch at his favorite hangout, the National Democratic Club. After we had downed a second bourbon-and-branch, he looked at me with his shrewd Irish eyes and said: "There's something on your mind, Miller. Out with it."

I gulped a little. "You're right, Mike. There is. It's—well, it's Oregon."

He stopped me there. "Oryee-gun," he snorted. "That miserable excuse for a state. Miller, when I get through with it, it won't even be that. I'm going to slice that cancerous sinkhole off the country and shove it out into the Pacific Ocean where it will sink like that lost continent and never be seen again. That's what I'm going to do to Ory-gone, and I mean gone."

I roared with laughter, probably the best thing I could have done. I adopted a bit of his Irish brogue in my comeback: "Jaysus, Mike, you can't do that to Oregon. Its eastern part is loaded with Irish sheepherders from Clare and Kerry. You can't sink those boyos, good Democrats, all of them."

More bourbons arrived, and we drank them. Mike was in the mood. The booze mellowed him, and he seemed to relent on his desire to treat Oregon in such draconian fashion. "There is a way," he confided, "that can save that stinking armpit." I was all ears and even sobered up a bit. "There is going to be a testimonial for me in Youngstown in October, and my friend Governor Pat Brown of California is going to be the main speaker. I want Wayne Morse there to eat crow and humble pie before God and everybody. And to kiss my fanny, too. If you can do that, Miller, I may spare Oryee-gun." He favored me with a benign smile. I signed the check, and we made an unsteady exit.

Bill Berg was Morse's chief of staff, and he and I had remained friends in spite of Morse's enmity for me. I called and related Mike's terms. The relief in Bill's voice was palpable. "He will be there and eat that crow as if it was the best steak he ever had." To seal the reconciliation, I suggested that we write a tribute to Kirwan's role in funding western development, to be titled "The Best Friend the West Ever Had," and put it in the *Congressional Record*. Done. The threat to Oregon's yearly appropriations was over.

Now I faced a dilemma. The Kirwan problem bad been solved with a long lunch, which I had charged to my main Oregon client, the Western Forest Industries Association. When Darrell Jones had asked me on the phone about financial arrangements, I had mumbled something about talking about it later. Money matters of this nature embarrassed me, and I found it nearly impossible to place a price on something that had been fun.

My erstwhile partners had no such qualms when I turned to them for advice. Charley Brown listened to my full account and then made a judgment. "You saved those counties the loss of god knows how many millions of dollars. I know Mike. He would have slashed Oregon. Your fee should be at least $50,000—not a penny less." Maurice Rosenblatt concurred. "It's a bargain for them," he argued. "That's how it is," Charley said. "We've spent a long time in politics and government learning how it works. Our know-how is valuable to a lot of people. We can't be giving it away."

I was still wrestling the problem when Darrell called to invite me to the O&C Counties Association's annual meeting in December. Would I be interested in representing the association on a permanent basis? he asked. Yes, I said. "We used to pay Senator Cordon $650 a month," Jones said. "Would that be acceptable to you?" I agreed, and my dilemma was solved. I represented the O&C Association for many more years, and it was the most satisfying professional and personal relationship of my life. Not only did it keep me tied to my Oregon roots, but my friends among the commissioners are among the best people I have known in a long lifetime. American county government, as Alexis de Tocqueville observed in 1835, is the form of governance that is most responsive to the people. Friends such as Ray Doerner and Mike Gleason reflected that affinity. They were real.

My rapport with Kirwan yielded an unexpected benefit, one that would be important to me in the years to come. One evening, I was taking Julia Butler Hansen, a freshman congresswoman, to the National Democratic Club. She had been a legend in the Washington state legislature, where she had been speaker *pro tem* and chair of the powerful Roads and Bridges Committee. She could have come to Congress years earlier had she not been loath to give up the clout that had forced governors to yield to her wishes. Finally, in 1960, she had responded to entreaties, including one from presidential candidate John F. Kennedy, and had run. Now she was out to gain the power in Congress that she had had in the legislature. To do so, she knew that she had to get where the money was—the Appropriations committee.

That bastion of masculinity—termed the "College of Cardinals" in the House—never had been sullied by the swish of a woman member's skirts, and Chairman Clarence Cannon, a crusty old Missouri misogynist, was determined to keep it that way. He scoffed at Julia's "outrageous" aspirations. Divvying up the nation's budget was men's work, he said. Women might be competent enough to put together a household budget, but no more.

When Julia and I left the Cannon Building that night, there was Mike Kirwan, sitting on a ledge, sunning himself in the late-summer haze. "Introduce me," Julia commanded. I did and, sensing an opportunity, invited him to join us for drinks. He accepted, with a courtly bow to Julia. Mike was about to get the full Julia treatment, known as the "Madam Queen massage" in the Washington legislature. My role for the evening, I knew, would be to prompt Kirwan to tell Julia one or another of his endless collection of stories. I also knew that she would respond as if they were coming out of the mouth of Mark Twain or Artemus Ward. After a couple of hours of banter in the Democratic Club bar, I suggested dinner.

"Will you stand Paul Young's, Miller?" queried Kirwan. Of course. Paul Young's, across from the Mayflower Hotel, had become the eating establishment of the Kennedy Administration. Tourists did not wander in off the street and get tables. Young knew me; his son had been squiring my younger daughter to high school parties. I called and asked him for a center table, knowing how much Mike enjoyed the limelight. Not only were we in the center, but I swear a soft spotlight was focused on our heads. Or so it seemed.

There we sat, Mike beaming at his new consort and awaiting the procession of those seeking his favor. He received them all—the likes of Hubert Humphrey, Everett Dirksen, Larry O'Brien, and Wilbur Mills. O'Brien feigned kneeling to kiss the papal ring. I felt like I was a chamberlain to royalty.

Kirwan took on Julia's cause with the zeal of a convert. Finally, Cannon capitulated, after Kirwan said that he would take her on his Interior Appropriations subcommittee, exactly where she wanted to be. Four years later, she was chair of that body, a record ascent in the history of House Appropriations.

With gavel in a hand made strong from pumping well water, Julia knew how to wield power. In the state legislature, her technique had been adapted from old-school politics. At the start of each session, she had given each member a list of the bills she wanted and then kept score. Only near the end did she dole out the funds for roads and bridges in each member's district, and woe to anyone who opposed her bills. Few did. And because she was genial and open about her *modus operandi*, she suffered little criticism for her strong-arm tactics. As a fixture in the state capitol's watering holes at night and on the job all day, she was accessible to everybody. Even those who opposed her found it hard not to like her. As chair of Interior Appropriations, she applied the same technique with similar success. "No different from Olympia," she said with a satisfied smile.

Her years as chair were good ones for me and the Pacific Northwest lumbermen and the O&C counties I represented. With strong support from Wendell Wyatt, her Republican colleague on the subcommittee, she made sure there was plenty of federal timber available to keep the mills running. Even more important, as it turned out, she and Wyatt foresaw the need for a more environmentally based approach to forest management and initiated programs for reforestation, hydrology, and watershed management. The over-cutting of forests did continue during her time as chair, our *mea culpa* being that we were following the guidelines of the Forest Service and the forestry schools.

It probably would be a cliché to say that Julia Butler Hansen was the last of a breed—history has a way of showing up such overused phrases—but I am pretty certain that we shall not see her likes again. She and Mike Kirwan came from a species of politicians who have all but died out. Their way of doing business may have been crude, but everyone knew where they stood. And, perhaps surprisingly, the public interest never seemed to suffer unduly.

16

PIRATES OF PORK

"KILL H.R. 163." JESSE CALHOON'S VOICE WAS SOUTHERN SOFT BUT steely. The president of the Marine Engineers Beneficial Association (MEBA) was giving me my first real assignment since I had become the little union's lobbyist in the fall of 1967. Now it was July 1968, and—looking out at New York harbor from Calhoon's nineteenth-floor office—I welcomed his command and, with it, the chance to strut my stuff on Capitol Hill.

I had been out of the labor movement since December 1963, when Lyndon Johnson, ten days into his presidency, told Steelworkers Union President David J. McDonald to fire me as the union's political operative. I had survived with Oregon lumber clients, but, oh, how I missed the labor movement. Theirs was the only legislative agenda that I really gave a damn about. The businessmen I represented were good guys, but I had no passion for their programs. They were mostly about making money, and I did not see that as life's principal goal. I needed a cause, and I believed the labor movement had the only mainstream one in town.

H.R. 163 turned out to be an obscure bill that would permit U.S. ship owners to insert foreign-built "midbodies" in their ships, which would double their carrying capacity. To Calhoon, it represented a serious breach of the U.S. statutes that prohibited foreign construction of any federally subsidized U.S. ships. That reason turned out to be merely a cover, although Calhoon didn't tell me so at the time. H.R. 163's principal promoter, Paul Hall, was president of the Seafarers Union and the recognized current grand sachem of maritime labor. Hall, a volubly articulate sailor who had risen from the "black gang" in the ship's hold, had earned George Meany's confidence by performing some tough tasks for the AFL-CIO president. That gave him clout, and the other maritime chiefs treated him with caution. Consequently, his H.R. 163 had been unchallenged until Calhoon summoned me.

Hall's principal lobbyists, the indefatigable Phil Carlip and Bill Moody, had done an excellent job of greasing the skids for the bill well before I got into the action. My meeting with the chairman of the House Merchant Marine and Fisheries Committee, Eddie Garmatz, a Democratic machine politician of the old Baltimore school, told me what I had suspected.

"Damn," he expostulated after I conveyed Calhoon's desire to stop H.R. 163, "you're too late." The Seafarers and Joe Kahn, a New York shipowner, he said, had gotten there first. "Where in the hell have you guys been?" he asked. "I've been collecting proxies and pledges for three weeks, and I'm ready to get it out of committee next week. I would have just as soon been with you and Calhoon, but what can I do now?" There was no point in my protesting or attempting to discuss the bill's merits. It just would have embarrassed Garmatz, a decent man who operated under ancient political rules now going out of style. In his world, a deal was a deal; he had made one, and he would stick with it. I had dealt with enough big-city machine congressmen to know their rules. Who was for it and who was against it was what mattered, not what the issue was.

H.R. 163 came out of committee with a commanding margin, and my attempts to get it pigeonholed by the House Rules Committee were futile, despite a spirited effort by Rules' ranking Democrat Richard Bolling of Missouri. The bill immediately was sent to the floor, where it was overwhelmingly approved without much debate. Now the apparently one-sided contest shifted to the Senate and its Commerce Committee—familiar turf to me. Chairman Warren G. Magnuson had been my original political mentor, and frequent exposure had put me on first-name status with most of the committee members, including the Republicans.

My confidence quickly burst. Magnuson's top staffers, Jerry Grinstein and Stanley Barer, bluntly informed me that the Seafarers and Seatrain, Joe Kahn's cargo shipping company, had been there way ahead of me and that twice as much "grease" had been applied to the skids as had been expended in the House. "You don't have a prayer" was the way Grinstein assessed it.

After our whipping in the House, Calhoon had assigned his trusted lieutenant Leon Shapiro to work with me. Leon was a fellow New Yorker of my vintage, and we understood each other by old-neighborhood osmosis. He was new to the byzantine ways of Capitol Hill and its often duplicitous machinations, but he was a quick study. In the probable event that we would lose, I was glad he would be there to document the impossibility of our assignment.

But we were not without hope. It was getting well into July, the traditional August recess was coming, and the September-October congressional wrap-up would be truncated because a tough election—with Richard M. Nixon and Hubert H. Humphrey at the top of their tickets—was on the horizon. Most incumbents of both parties were hard-scrabbling on the hustings at every opportunity. This was all to the good, because time was what we were playing for. If we could keep the bill bottled up in the Commerce Committee until the August recess, we had an outside chance. There were two ways to do that, I explained to Shapiro. "Good," he said. "We'll do them both."

The first was to apply some discreet heat to Magnuson. If there was one thing I knew about him, it was his abhorrence of controversy, especially when it was between groups that always had supported him. He had been a perfervid backer of build-American statutes, particularly as they applied to shipbuilding; thus, his support of H.R. 163 was out of character. But he needed to be reminded of that by Puget Sound shipbuilders. Leon had contacts, and the shipbuilders registered their displeasure directly to Magnuson. The bill stayed in committee, despite the frantic efforts of Moody and Carlip to get it out before the recess.

Our second card was the hole one, and it was not an easy one to find. Unlike the House, the Senate is a great place to kill a bill if you can find a senator or two willing to take the heat for doing your bidding. The device was a mischievous legislative procedure called a "hold." Simply by applying a "hold" to a piece of legislation, a senator could anonymously freeze a bill in place. He did not need a reason; a "hold" could be applied by fiat, and the bill was "held" until he removed it.

Our problem was to find a committee member willing to challenge a popular chairman. Finally, we got a break and snared an unlikely ally. Norris Cotton, an affable New Hampshire conservative who was the committee's ranking Republican, was facing an uncertain election campaign that fall against a popular Democratic governor having the full support of organized labor, and he wanted at least one labor endorsement to show he was a friend of working people. When Leon and I held out MEBA's backing in return for a hold, he bought it. And Cotton didn't need or want the usual $10,000 contribution that accompanied the endorsement. For the record, Cotton's refusal of the money is the only time that ever happened to me, and I am still puzzled by it.

Armed with Cotton's premium "hold," we now searched for a Democrat on the committee to give him bipartisan cover. I knew one who always was willing to accept cash "campaign contributions," regardless of whether he was running that year or not. I went to see him alone and made the deal. He and Cotton put time on our side. Magnuson, faced with opposition to H.R. 163 from a core constituency back home, made no move to ask the "holding" senators to remove their objections; if he had, I suspect that H.R. 163 would have sailed through the Senate. Instead, it died with congressional adjournment, and I found myself established as a first-string player in the community of maritime lobbyists.

A week later, in a dark bar opposite New York City's Battery Park, I asked Calhoon the question that had crossed my mind during that frenetic summer: "Jesse, what was the reason that we busted our asses killing H.R. 163? A few congressmen asked me, and my answer was that it was 'anti-American' and 'against our merchant marine.' But it had to be more than that."

"I had no real reason," Calhoon said, a sly smile lighting up his face. "Paul Hall put that bill in without clearing it with me. I just wanted him and his employers to know that he couldn't pass anything through Congress without coming through me. Now he knows it. We had a friendly talk this morning, and he kept saying, 'From now on, we've got to be together on everything.' That's what I was looking for: my place at the table. So the effort was worth it."

My god, I thought, all that scrambling and scheming just to satisfy one man's ego. Couldn't Hall and Calhoon have settled the matter between them so we would have been spared this silly scrimmage? We wasted all that time when we could have been working on something substantive and satisfying. But nobody was paying me to express sense and sensibility. Maritime labor's principal mantra was that all alliances were impermanent; none was based on trust. But why this attitude? Why were they so quick to take offense if they merely thought someone was encroaching on their turf? One of their own explained it to me: "These guys spent World War II aboard Liberty ships jammed into the tightest living space you can imagine. It made them unbelievably paranoid about protecting that little space, and it has carried over into all their future relationships, including the way they treat their wives. Notice how they shy away from touching anyone or being touched themselves. Even the ritual of shaking hands is brief and forced. You can't understand them without knowing this central aspect of their psyches." This capriciousness only added to their standing in labor circles. A man who could close New York harbor on a whim was a creature above ordinary mortals and deserving of the media-star treatment accorded the mafioso of the moment. The maritimers were a throwback to the glory days of the 1930s and 1940s. They swaggered and strutted into meetings and spoke in stentorian tones that belied their actual numerical strength.

The three who spoke strongest were a disparate trio. Paul Hall, the *primus inter pares*, was a nonstop talker who seemed to be forever pontificating. But he was Alabama-sharecropper shrewd and was reputed to be a contender for the AFL-CIO presidency when Meany bowed out. His main rival, Joe Curran, the oak-chested chief of the National Maritime Union, was out of labor's 1930s folklore. With a near-mythological persona emanating from his up-from-the-hold role in the epochal West Coast maritime strike of 1934, Joe had ousted both Communists and racketeers from control of the union and had become a labor icon.

The third was Thomas J. (Teddy) Gleason, likable and lippy and president of the International Longshoremen's Association (ILA). Gleason's hold over his East and Gulf Coast dockers came from his ability to compromise with employers after the table-pounding and fiery rhetoric that was needed to satisfy the union's militant element. He could also fervently denounce the Communists, all the while quietly negotiating with Red-leaning Harry Bridges for One Big Waterfront Union. Teddy also knew how to look the other way when some of his local chieftains persisted in playing the old way when they could.

Gleason's ILA had cleaned up its act enough to be restored to the ranks of respectable unions, but some of the boys couldn't give up the bad old ways. One of them was Anthony Scotto, chief of the Brooklyn locals. College-educated, trim, and eloquent regarding the role of unions in modern society, Scotto seemed to represent a new breed of union leader. When he was convicted of extorting payoffs from waterfront employers, I was nonplussed. And when he was proven to be a bona fide *capo* in the Gambini family of mafiosos, I realized I had been doing business with a figure right out of *The Godfather*.

Jesse Mayo Calhoon aspired to supplant Hall, Curran, and Gleason. He was a year younger than I, a country boy from the Outer Banks of North Carolina, the product of a no-account father and a strong-willed mother who imbued a love of reading in her son. At seventeen, Jesse had been propelled by World War II into the U.S. Coast Guard Academy and a commission as a marine-engineer officer. He liked the travel and stayed in the Merchant Marine after the war, becoming active in the little union that represented the engineers. And he read incessantly, devouring books by the score. Biographies stirred his ambitions.

Calhoon found his patron—Lee Pressman, a brilliant but flawed figure of labor's glory days. Pressman had been the chief counsel to the old CIO, the trusted legal arm of John L. Lewis and Philip Murray. Up from the tenements of the Lower East Side, he had scholarshiped at Cornell and Harvard Law. Felix Frankfurter had sent him to Washington at the outset of FDR's New Deal to work for Henry Wallace at Agriculture, but the emerging CIO had lured him away. There, despite persistent rumors that he belonged to a Communist Party cell, Pressman had flourished as labor's legal star.

Then came the post–World War II reaction against labor, culminating with the 1947 passage of the Taft-Hartley Act. One of the act's clauses required that union officials sign non-Communist affidavits. Pressman refused. Phil Murray, weeding leftists from CIO ranks, was forced to fire him. Other unions, who once had sought his favor, were unavailable when he came looking. Except one—the tiny, fragmented, and leftist Marine Engineers Beneficial Association, so named on its founding in Cleveland in 1875 to disguise its real purpose as a labor union. MEBA offered Pressman a chance to show the rest of labor what they had spurned. Taking over a loosely structured confederation of near-autonomous locals from New York to Seattle, Pressman reformed them into three districts (Atlantic-Gulf Coast, Lakes and Rivers, and Pacific Coast) and embarked on a program that would establish MEBA as a major force in the maritime industry.

It did not take him long to figure out that the nation's shipping companies were ripe for the plucking. Heavily subsidized from the U.S. Treasury and plying trade routes protected by U.S. law, the shipowners had become fat and soft. They were simply no match for a big-leaguer such as Pressman, who had been in the arena with the likes of General Motors and U.S. Steel. Their walls came tumbling down, and over the years MEBA's members found themselves beneficiaries of the highest industrial wages in the world, six-months-per-year vacations, and unparalleled pension and health plans. Future negotiations became almost embarrassing. At one such meeting, Leon Shapiro whispered to me: "What can we ask for? We've got everything we can think of." Pressman always thought of something new.

One thing he wanted was a strong, smart leader to run the union. Ergo, Calhoon. "You should have seen him when Pressman pulled him out of the canebrakes," one old-timer remembered. "His Southern accent was so thick that he could have been talking Swahili, for all we knew. And he dressed like a real rube. Even so, most of us were able to see what Pressman saw: a natural leader with real brains. So we elected him president and never regretted it. He put us on the map."

With Calhoon increasingly in charge, Pressman negotiated his last contract for the union and died days later, in November 1969. Calhoon, helping me write his obituary, was in tears. Pressman's funeral at a Mt. Vernon, New York, synagogue brought out everyone in the maritime industry. "The management guys were there to make sure he was dead," quipped one MEBA irreverent.

Now on his own, Calhoon's ambitions were ready to soar. The time was ripe for new leadership, he believed. The critical mass of labor's leadership had become smug and self-satisfied, paying perfunctory tribute to the glories of the turbulent past but mired in the don't-rock-the-boat torpor of the present. "This bunch hasn't had a new idea in twenty years," Calhoon said. "The old giants—Lewis, Murray, Dubinsky, and Reuther—are gone, and they left pygmies in their place. George Meany is the only one left who is worthy of their shoes, and he is old and tired. The rest are petty bureaucrats and clerks."

Heretical words, and they struck a chord with me. As dedicated as I was to the union idea, my exposure to labor's sachems—the Steelworkers' Dave McDonald, in particular—had created the suspicion that they did not spend day and night bleeding for the working stiff. In retrospect, it was too much to expect. We all were seduced by the manicured suburban world of steak barbecues, Chivas Regal, Cadillacs, and wives who drove the kids to school in station wagons. The maritimers were no exception. Despite their piratical swagger and an occasional display of muscle, they craved respectability and respect.

They got it from their "pals," the shipowners who depended on the political clout of the unions to keep the federal subsidies flowing—roughly a billion dollars a year. Theirs was a cozy relationship, and Leon Shapiro told me of this strange symbiosis when I joined MEBA. "We are different from most industries, where there is an adversarial relationship between labor and management," he said. "Here the employers are our friends, and we work together on virtually everything."

That tranquility had made it possible for Calhoon to turn his ambitions inland, to pursue labor's historic role of "organizing the unorganized"—but with a twist. This time he was going after white-collar workers: bank clerks and auditors, scientists and engineers, computer programmers and systems analysts—the groups that always had been most resistant to unionism. With athletes and artists now in the union fold, Calhoon believed that professional groups would be open to an approach from a union that had many of its members making six-figure salaries and enjoying superb fringe benefits.

So far, his intuition was looking good. MEBA's organizers had produced some promising yields: several thousand aerospace engineers and scientists in the San Francisco Bay Area; white-collar workers of Seattle First National Bank; and the sheriff's office of Broward County, Florida. And he was opening negotiations with a group of air traffic controllers known as the Professional Air Traffic Controllers Organization, or PATCO.

These developments stirred me. During my newspapering years, I had helped organize Newspaper Guild locals in Boise, Portland, and Eugene, with near-misses at Yakima, Washington, and Vancouver, B.C., and I had been tempted by an offer to become a full-time organizer. Now I realized that the urge to recruit white-collar professionals was still in my blood. Union organizing was an in-the-trenches game, and I wanted to show that I could still play.

But Calhoon had other plans for me. He wanted to establish a strong presence in Congress, and I was his designated point man. Having influence in Congress, he rightly figured, was a prerequisite for his ambitions, and he was smart enough to realize that he knew next to nothing about that peculiar institution. It was the perfect place for me.

What made it even more ideal was the potful of political money that Calhoon had been collecting to carve out his congressional beachhead. I surmised that there was well over a million dollars in the till, with more coming in every week. Eureka! After four years in a penniless political desert, I had found the Treasure of Sierra Madre in lower Manhattan. I couldn't wait to start dispensing the largesse in the name of my new Caesar. What it took, he had.

This concealed cache of political bucks was the legacy of the late Lee Pressman, who had found a loophole around the Taft-Hartley Act's prohibition of the use of the automatic check-off to collect political contributions. Until Taft-Hartley, the political contributions of union members could be deducted automatically from their paychecks along with their union dues. Robert A. Taft, the Ohio Republican riding a postwar backlash against organized labor, had seen the check-off as an instrument of coercion to force contributions from rank-and-file unionists. He eliminated it and forced the unions to seek voluntary political contributions from their members instead.

The prohibition did not include union retirees, however, and by the late 1960s rich little MEBA had about 3,500 of them. Virtually all of them signed up in a Pressman-designed plan that deducted ninety-nine political dollars a year from their pension checks, the under-hundred-dollar sum to avoid reporting the names and addresses of contributors. (Certain that retirees had been coerced into signing this check-off, Jerry Landauer of the *Wall Street Journal* obtained a list of their names. He interviewed most of them but failed to come up with a single complainer, which he admitted in the piece.)

It was from that political pot that I dispensed campaign funds, and it was not small change. More than $40,000 went to Wayne L. Morse in the 1968 race that he lost to Bob Packwood, and contributions up to $5,000 were *de rigueur*. Suddenly my phone was ringing off the hook with calls from "old friends" who had forgotten I existed. The unknown little union's prestige soared overnight, and Jesse Calhoon's name became known on Capitol Hill. Awash with MEBA money, I was seemingly the most popular guy in town. Al Barkan, who ran COPE, the AFL-CIO's political arm, was bemused by my comeback. "With money, you can go from has-been to hero overnight in this town," he observed. "You just did." From a loyal old pal like Barkan, those were sweet words.

What made it all work was Calhoon's willingness to take my word on the congressmen and senators I had selected for support. He questioned some but always acquiesced when I gave my rationale. Fortunately, I batted over .900 on our first election go-round, and the legislators MEBA supported played a significant role in our first big legislative battle in the next Congress.

Calhoon was unique in my experience. He had no discernible ideology or particular prejudices and was without party allegiance. He was as comfortable with Republicans as he was with Democrats. His Southernness resonated with Dixie legislators but was no drawback with Northern liberals, whose language he could speak. Tip O'Neill, the new Democratic leader in the House, had instant rapport with him, and Calhoon was included in Tip's inner circle. Charles (Chuck) Colson, incoming President Nixon's political point man, had the same reaction, and Calhoon became a member of his inner circle. It was an amazing tour de force. His was a Jeb Stuart ride to the top, and I was proud of my role in orchestrating it.

It all seemed too good to last, and it was. Bedazzled by his sudden elevation to minor celebrity status, Calhoon moved to Washington with his family, bought a handsome house in a fashionable suburb, and, with the union's pension fund, purchased a brand new, eight-story office building two blocks from the Capitol. Conditions were perfect for him to make a major splash with the nation's movers and shakers. And he did just that, but into a whiskey glass. Right before my eyes, my cool contender, the dispassionate analyst of men and motives who always seemed to be steps ahead of his more celebrated competition, embarked on a course of senseless self-destruction.

It began at lunch, often the deadliest of times in Washington. Every noon he descended downstairs to LaColline, the stylish restaurant that fronted his building's lobby. There he was greeted at his regular booth with a glass brimming with Chivas Regal scotch, which he quickly drained and then beckoned the waiter for a replacement. It was a dreary routine to watch the cool thinker of the morning become the bragging boozer of the afternoon. Opportunity that he should have capitalized on got drowned in whiskey. Worse, he became prey for clever flatterers who knew how easily he could dispense MEBA's largesse when in his cups.

The Washington-and-whiskey syndrome had claimed thousands of victims before Calhoon, myself included. Yet his disintegration hit me harder than the others I had witnessed, principally because I had seen so much promise in him.

With Calhoon's promise drowned in the filthy brown stuff, it was a downhill game from there on. We won a few minor legislative battles but were routed like the Italians at Caporetto in the fight for the Big One. The Big One was cargo preference, a quota system that would guarantee U.S. flagships a specified percentage of the international oil trade, of which we had zero percent. It was the one issue every maritime faction could unite around. The Carter administration gave us lip-service support, a grudging payoff for Calhoon's enthusiastic fundraising for his fellow Southerner in the late primaries of 1976. Further, we scaled down the required percentage of carriage from the 30 percent we always had campaigned for to a modest 5 percent, an amount that Congress hardly could deny us.

To further ensure our victory, we used the war chest to hire every available "name" lobbyist in town and had enough money left over to finance a splashy advertising campaign. We touched every base there was to touch, not once but at least ten times. If ever there was a picture-book lobbying effort, this was it. Except for one thing—the votes. Big Oil flexed its muscles a couple of times and effortlessly swatted us down on the House floor by a hundred votes or so, destroying with one brutal stroke maritime labor's reputation as a swaggering crew of corsairs who always got what they wanted. No longer would we be cartooned by Herblock in the *Washington Post* as a band of roistering brigands swarming over a ship named the USS *Congress* and making off with chests of booty labeled "taxpayer money."

It was humiliating, but I felt smugly detached from the pain of losing. My own unfailingly accurate sources in the House had told me that we would lose decisively, and I had convinced Calhoon that we should get Tip O'Neill to withdraw it from floor action. Tip privately had urged me to do it—better a withdrawal than a whipping. Paul Hall refused. His lobbyists had told him that we would win by fifty votes or better. Trained by a master headcounter, Missouri Representative Dick Bolling, I had learned never to count a vote as sure unless it was sworn in blood. Lobbyists tend to tell the principals what they want to hear, and the people who pay the bills want to hear that victory is just over the horizon. My bluntness never went over well, either with my colleagues or with principals. It was my main occupational hazard. So I preferred to work by myself, winning or losing as a loner.

Around this time an opportunity came my way, the likes of which lobbyists dream about. In May 1977, I received a phone call from Stewart R. McKinney, a Republican congressman from Greenwich, Connecticut. He and I once had a long conversation in the bar of the Republican Club about my godfather, sculptor Gutzon Borglum, who had made his original models for Mt. Rushmore at his estate in McKinney's district. Now McKinney was on the phone and saying in an urgent, excited voice: "Drop whatever you are doing and get over here right now. One of my guys has found a loophole in your Alaskan pipeline act big enough to float ten supertankers through. If we don't make a move right now, every drop of your precious Prudhoe Bay oil is going to end up in the refineries of Tokyo and Yokohama. And, you may not know it, but your precious Carter administration has elaborate plans to do that when the pipeline starts operating next month."

It couldn't be. In the early 1970s, when legislation to build the trans-Alaska pipeline was being battled over in Congress, the maritime lobby had won a provision that prevented exporting that oil. It was foolproof, we were assured. And besides, the new Carter administration was in maritime's pocket. We had raised a big bundle for them in the campaign on the promise that our key issues would be supported. The new oil of Alaska for domestic consumption was one of those issues, and it already had been projected that the Alaskan trade would employ 25 percent of maritime labor's membership, a multitude of dues payers.

Now I was in McKinney's office, and some kid staffer named Hank, just out of Yale Law School, was telling me that while our heads were buried in the sand, the Carter administration had found a loophole. In return for exporting the Alaskan oil to Japan, the U.S. would receive a comparable supply of Indonesian and Mexican oil. It was a scheme, he said, hatched by the State Department to satisfy our allies with no thought of the domestic implications, and the Carterites—brand new in office—had signed off on it.

It was a Tuesday. On Wednesday, legislation to reauthorize the Export Administration Act was scheduled for the House floor. "This is our main chance," McKinney said, pacing up and down. "Hank is crafting an amendment that will close the loophole for the three-year life of the Export Admin-

istration Act. Then we can make it a permanent ban the next time around."
The administration and Clement J. Zablocki, the bill's floor manager and
chairman of the Foreign Affairs Committee, were going to oppose the amendment. "That doesn't scare me," he said. "Clem is a sweet guy, but hardly a
heavyweight on the floor. As for the administration, those crackers haven't
even found out where the Hill is, let alone know how to lobby Congress.
Besides, we've got a surefire issue: preserving Alaskan oil for domestic use.
Voting against *that* will be tough for any member." McKinney was right. Since
1973, when Middle East oil producers periodically shut their spigots in protest
of U.S. policy toward Israel, gasoline shortages had plagued U.S. consumers.
Long lines of motorists waiting to buy a few gallons of gas had become a familiar sight on television screens.

It was a glorious situation for a loner lobbyist like me. All my fellow maritimers were out of town—at a Propeller Club convention in New Orleans
or something equally useless. I called Calhoon with a rundown, received his
blessing, and went to work. In the House, I always had depended on a core
group of ten to twelve congressmen whom I would talk with about the
prospects of the particular legislation that I was working for or against. They
had both a "sense of the House" and a feel for the way members from their
regions might be leaning. Knowing that I would never quote them, they gave
it to me straight. After adding up everything they had to say, I had a pretty
good idea of how the House was going to act.

My first contact was with a home-state congressman, Tom Foley of Spokane, chairman of the Agriculture committee and an administration loyalist.
Yes, he said, he planned to support the bill without amendments, as a courtesy to his fellow chairman, Clem Zablocki, who was the bill's floor manager.

"Tom," I said, "the Alaskan oil is due on line around July 1. Let us sup-
pose that the Arab countries, for obvious political reasons, decide to shut
down the spigots again. Now imagine CBS News and Walter Cronkite with
the lead story for the coming Fourth of July weekend. The first scene is of
Japanese tankers at Valdez loading up with oil for Yokohama. The second
is long lines of cars on Long Island and in L.A. waiting endlessly for a few
gallons of gas. How is that going to play politically?"

Foley's reaction was so strong—holy cow!—that I knew the McKinney
amendment was a winning hand, but we had fewer than twenty-four hours
to get our message to 400–plus congressmen. We did our damnedest, and we

were reasonably confident when he called up the amendment in the evening hours. The McKinney amendment won in a walk, the *Washington Post* made his surprise ploy its front-page lead story the following morning, and I experienced that incredible feeling one gets when something totally unexpected turns into a triumph. King of the Hill, that's what I felt like. Read all about it in the *Post*. It was undeserved. I had been as asleep as the rest of the maritime lobby. Had it not been for a chance acquaintance with McKinney, I would have been in the dark about the loophole. And where were our lawyers?

Why did McKinney do it? He had no direct interest in the Alaskan oil issue and wasn't even on the Foreign Affairs Committee, which had jurisdiction over exports. Why did he turn himself and his staff inside out over a subject of no importance to him? "I thought it was in the national interest," he told me. "That's what we're sent here for—to serve the national interest, as we see it." Tears come to my eyes as I write of Stewart McKinney. I didn't know him that well, but what I saw was unique in my experience on Capitol Hill. He was as candid a politician as I have ever known, Jack Kennedy included, and he never weaseled. As liberal a Republican as there was, he nevertheless backed Reagan's conservative economic program. When a reporter asked him why, his answer was typical McKinney: "Money for the railroad station in Stamford. I won't get it by being a Republican bad boy." During his sixteen years in Congress, McKinney fought unceasingly for the poor, the homeless, and the disadvantaged. He contracted the pneumonia that helped kill him in 1987 by spending cold nights outdoors as part of a protest on behalf of the homeless. When the House later passed his legislation to help them, they called it the Stewart B. McKinney Act. But Washington being Washington, pretty soon I was ruminating on who we would get to replace McKinney as our point man on the Alaskan oil issue. The next time around, the oil carriage to West and Gulf Coast refineries had grown so much that a swarm of lobbyists materialized to protect and perpetuate the McKinney amendment.

There isn't much more to say about my twenty-five years as a maritime-labor lobbyist. Paul Hall died suddenly in 1980, and others disappeared from the scene as we slogged on, protecting our yearly subsidies and little else. When I hung it up in 1992 without fanfare, it was as if I had never been there. No one even called or took notice. My feelings weren't hurt. It was good for me, made me conscious of my transient insignificance. We all would be better off to know that.

We see what we want to see, and we are blind when it is convenient to be blind. My faint moral misgivings through my twenty-five years as a maritime lobbyist were smothered by the pleasures of living the good life and rationalizing that it was all justified by the final purpose: keeping the American flag flying on all the oceans of the earth and defending our beloved country. It seemed as if there was a patriotic argument to be conjured up in virtually every bill I ever worked on. If patriotism was "the last refuge of a scoundrel," as Samuel Johnson proclaimed, then it also was the when-all-else-fails penultimate argument of the lobbyist.

It wasn't until I retired that I began to see it all with a cold and clear eye. Still, given the identical circumstances, would I do it again? Charles Einstein wrote a short story about a gambler titled "The Only Game in Town." Stranded in a Missouri town, he lost everything he had in a crooked poker game. Back in St. Louis he told his pals about his experience. One of them asked: "Why did you play when you knew that the game was crooked?" "I had to," the gambler replied. "It was the only game in town."

That is the only answer that makes any sense to me.

17

STRIKE! STRIKE! STRIKE!

THE 1981 NATIONWIDE STRIKE OF THE AIR TRAFFIC CONTROLLERS
union still is cited as the domestic landmark of Ronald Reagan's presidency.
His outright firing of the 12,000 federal controllers who struck won him almost
universal acclaim and established him as a decisive tough guy, not merely
the charming former actor who had backed into the presidency through the
incompetence of the Democratic incumbent, Jimmy Carter. Reagan needed
a dragon to slay in order to authenticate his legitimacy, and the Professional
Air Traffic Controllers Organization (PATCO) blundered into his sights.

My involvement with PATCO began because of the soaring ambitions
of MEBA president Jesse M. Calhoon. In the summer of 1968, Helen Delich
Bentley, the transportation editor of the *Baltimore Sun*, came to Calhoon
with something more than just another puff piece. A reporter widely known
for her hats and profane language, Helen had a little-known soft side—Jesse
Calhoon. She had a crush on him that wouldn't quit and was always seeking ways to win his approval. This time, she had the inside track to the affiliation of PATCO with MEBA. She had been covering the congressional
hearings that occurred after PATCO had staged its first nationwide slowdown
of commercial aviation, euphemistically called Operation Air Safety. It had
been a smashing success, aided surreptitiously by the Federal Aviation
Administration, which was using delay figures to justify its requests for massive expenditures for new equipment and more personnel.

Despite their achievement, PATCO's leaders had been having strong second thoughts about the charismatic figure who had brought them into being that January and who had masterminded their slowdown strategy. Helen Bentley had won their confidence with her sympathetic reporting, and they had told her about their doubts. She told them there was an alternative: Jesse Calhoon and MEBA.

The charismatic figure was F. Lee Bailey, who had recently become America's best-known trial lawyer. He also was an accomplished flyer. A former marine fighter pilot who flew his own Learjet around the country, he had become acquainted with air traffic controllers and their long list of grievances. One of the controllers, a street-savvy New Yorker named Mike Rock, had challenged Bailey to do something about their problems, and he had responded—magnificently. Taking Rock with him, he flew his Learjet to key air traffic control centers around the country to promise controllers that he was going to organize them into a "nationwide fighting force." Then, in one lightning stroke—a nationwide meeting of 300 controllers at JFK International Airport in January 1968—he did just that. Professional Air Traffic Controllers Organization was the name selected for the new union, and it immediately began a splashy slowdown in the interests of "air safety." Bailey, now billed as PATCO's executive director, milked the media. From Johnny Carson to *Meet the Press*, he portrayed the controllers as the underpaid and overworked forgotten heroes of American aviation.

While Bailey was a master at publicity and protest, he was inept when it came to wooing the key congressional figures PATCO needed to advance its cause. He further alienated the FAA hierarchy, many of whom were sympathetic to the controllers. Some of the union's street-smart leaders were coming to realize that the ego-driven lawyer was a loose cannon capable of shooting his own troops. The slowdowns and sickouts that he inspired were losing impact, besides running up big fees submitted by Bailey's legal cohorts. In short, Bailey had no second act.

Calhoon and I met with Mike Rock in July 1969 at Washington's Mayflower Hotel to discuss affiliation with MEBA. Rock was ready, but Bailey had to be eased out gently. To most rank-and-file controllers, he was a demigod who had brought them celebrity. Everybody now knew who the controllers were, and it was, by god, because of Bailey. We decided to wait until the PATCO convention at Las Vegas in April 1970, when Bailey could be piped off with a flourish. And it was some send-off. Bailey climaxed a maudlin farewell address by marching out of the ballroom, pausing every few steps to wave farewell to the cheering and chanting controllers as a bagpipe band pumped out "Scotland the Brave."

PATCO affiliated with MEBA at Las Vegas and elected a new president— John Francis Leyden, thirty-six, chief of the New York Center local. A Kennedyesque Irishman whose father was a veteran of the 1916 Easter Rebellion, Leyden had the charm and smarts to sell PATCO on Capitol Hill. He and I spoke the same language, and I could work with him.

It was not going to be an easy sell. Bailey's last blunder had been his acquiescence in a controller sickout during Easter weekend to protest the transfer of three Louisiana controllers for so-called PATCO activity. The sickout had fizzled because the FAA was ready with supervisors and military controllers. Transportation Secretary John Volpe, fed up with these tactics, had struck hard in retaliation. He decertified PATCO as a legal bargaining unit, depriving it of the automatic check-off collection of union dues from paychecks. Further, he fired almost one hundred ringleaders of the sickout. It was a sobering lesson. The Nixon Administration did not play with beanbags.

The average controller was male and had a high school diploma and a couple of years in the military. He had quick aptitude and enough basic skills to make it through the Federal Air Traffic Controller Academy in Oklahoma City. He and his mates lived in a high-stress world all their own and knew little and cared less about the outside world. He was more parochial than a priest, and it showed in his naiveté about government and politics. But until Bailey, no one had known anything about what he did, and it rankled. "You are the key players in America's aviation system," Bailey had told them. "Pilots may have pretty uniforms, but they are really only truck drivers. The real skill is getting the planes up and down and keeping them separated in the air under all manner of conditions. The system cannot function without you, and don't ever forget it."

The controllers weren't about to. Historically undervalued in the FAA schemata, they were privates in a paramilitary organization run by retired generals and colonels. In the 1960s, aviation traffic had doubled, but the FAA had not hired a single new controller or added a piece of new equipment. The six-day work week was mandatory. Stress and fatigue were high, and morale was low. PATCO had been the golden vehicle to change it all, but now Secretary Volpe had made it, in effect, an outlaw organization.

Rebuilding was in order, and Leyden and I spent long hours at it. We found a congressional champion in Republican Wendell Wyatt, who had managed President Nixon's primaries in Oregon. He had a pipeline to the White House and was not afraid to use it. Other Republican leaders, particularly Hugh Scott of Pennsylvania, came aboard, and the anti-PATCO hard noses softened. The fired controllers were rehired, and the union—pledging never again to strike or stage a sickout—was recertified by the FAA. Membership soared from a low of 2,100 to virtually the entire workforce of 15,000.

Thus revived, PATCO proceeded to run a string of legislative victories that still rank as unique in the history of federal employee unions. They included early retirement after twenty years, coupled with a second-career program that offered two years of training at a salary equal to one's highest pay; improved disability retirement for stress or strain; increased appropriations that almost doubled the controller workforce; and sharply increased pay scales at high-density airports. I would like to take credit for a brilliant lobbying effort, but in truth it was pretty easy. The reason was whimsically expressed by a Republican congressman from Pittsburgh named Robert J. Corbett. "I fly home every weekend," he said. "When my big white fanny is up in the air, I want the boys who get it up there and put it down to be well rested and happy."

Yet, many of them refused to be happy. I was shocked by what seemed to be incredible ingratitude at PATCO's 1972 convention in Kansas City, which took place just after passage of the early retirement bill. A meeting with a congressional counsel sent out to explain details of the legislation turned into an inquisition on the "inadequacies" of the new law. "Why didn't you pass the Hartke bill?" they challenged me, referring to a pie-in-the-sky bill that had promised everything and had been impossible to get passed. My explanation was met with blank stares. Bailey had told them they could do anything, and they still believed it. I was starting to have sour thoughts about these lads whom I had romanticized as a brave band fighting the good fight against an unfeeling bureaucracy.

The sour thoughts grew as PATCO continued to stage periodic slowdowns that were barely within the law. I protested to John Leyden that the

goodwill that PATCO had gained could be wiped out through these frivo-
lous slowdowns, a message I was getting loudly and clearly from angry congressmen. John was reasonable and collegial and was well liked by FAA
management. His problem was a small, militant minority within PATCO
that was consumed by the delusion that the nation's aviation system could
not operate without them. Calling themselves the "Choirboys," they dominated union meetings with an agenda of exorbitant demands. Leyden tried
to keep them in the tent by allowing their efforts to be financed by the
union's treasury.

The first augury of disaster occurred in 1978. PATCO's new contract had
a clause that allowed controllers to receive free overseas trips from airlines
to "familiarize" themselves with procedures. Delta Air Lines and Pan American Airways refused to grant so obvious a "perk," and yet another slowdown
followed. It was just what the Air Transport Association (ATA), the industry's lobby, had been looking for. Inconveniencing the flying public for "free
vacations to the Riviera" was a public-relations blunder of the first magni-
tude, and ATA moved fast to exploit it. I knew the ATA people; and Leyden, who had been dubious about the slowdown, asked me to try to negotiate
a way out. ATA wasn't having any. A Boston congressman named Joe Moakley called me: "PATCO is now dead meat. Your guys don't have a friend left
here. Everybody in Congress has been hung up in the air for hours just because
those jerks can't get a free trip to Paris."

He was right. Overnight, public opinion plummeted. Congress, citing widespread violations, withdrew funding for the controllers' retirement program.
For the "Riviera" slowdown, PATCO's leadership was found guilty in U.S.
district court in New York, and the judge threatened Leyden and his vice
president, Robert Poli, with jail. The reaction of PATCO's "crazies," as we
now were calling them, was to call for more militancy; they really believed
they had sole control over the nation's airways. A weird "us versus everybody"
psychosis took over. Calhoon told Leyden: "There is only one thing you can
do with a mad dog, John. Kill it. Do it, and I will back you all the way."

Leyden hesitated. He couldn't quite bring himself to confront the comrades who had promoted his rise to leadership. The delay was deadly. The
Choirboys had decided that Leyden was not militant enough and looked for
someone they could control. They found him in Bob Poli, the PATCO vice
president who had made a fetish of proclaiming his undying loyalty to Ley-

den. At the union's board meeting in January 1981, they ousted Leyden for Poli. The stage was set for disaster.

The Choirboys whirled from one PATCO meeting to another, black-clad and with clenched fists, chanting "Strike! Strike! Strike!" T-shirts and posters proclaiming "I'm one in '81" appeared at every FAA facility. PATCO voted extra dues assessments to build a strike fund. The fervor for confrontation with the federal government built daily as August neared and the contract with the FAA would expire.

The FAA had been preparing for this moment since December 1977, when a PATCO slowdown during the Christmas holiday narrowly had been averted. Knowing that it would happen again, Langhorne Bond, the FAA chief, crafted a contingency plan. Still, Transportation Secretary Drew Lewis was bending over backwards in negotiations to satisfy as many of PATCO's demands as he could. PATCO had been one of only three unions to support Ronald Reagan in his 1980 campaign, and Lewis felt obligated to go the extra mile, offering a sweetened package that included $140 million that could be used for pay raises.

It was an extraordinary concession to PATCO, but it wasn't good enough for the Choirboys. Although Poli had initially agreed to the new contract, his executive board rejected it and called for a strike vote with the stipulation that it had to pass by at least 80 percent. It had been apparent since PATCO's New Orleans convention weeks earlier that the strike vote would succeed. Absent the temporizing influence of Leyden and other moderates, the Choirboys had dominated the proceedings with their incessant "Strike! Strike! Strike!" Jesse Calhoon took it all in from the wings. "These crazies are mad, totally insane," he muttered, pulling hard on his Cuban cigar. "They are going to destroy this union. Worse, it could be a disaster for the entire labor movement."

Then Calhoon was introduced as the next speaker. An ear-splitting roar rocked the auditorium. Since 1970, he had enjoyed a near-demigod status with controllers. His provocative, sometimes incendiary speeches had been taped and widely distributed; some controllers boasted that they had listened to them thirty or forty times. PATCO wives held their children out to receive his benediction as he made his way to the podium, surrounded by chanting and cheering controllers. The thunderous sound went on endlessly. Calhoon forgot his sense of foreboding. The roaring adulation was just too much. The speech he made could have been drafted by the Choirboys themselves, and he ended by pledging MEBA's resources to back "PATCO's brave battle for its just rights."

The last hope for any restraining influence was gone. The strike vote received the required 80 percent approval, and the stage was set. Paradoxically, Calhoon still was confident that the collision could be averted. He based it on the fear that Poli had shown when the judge in New York had threatened Leyden and him with jail. "He will hear the rattle of the jailhouse door and find an excuse to call it off," Calhoon predicted.

That wishful thought evaporated when Calhoon and I had lunch with Poli two days before the scheduled strike on August 3. He was like a man possessed. "Can you imagine it?" he almost burbled. "Phil Donahue is calling me. They want me on *Meet the Press* and *Face the Nation*, the *Today Show* and *Good Morning, America*. Can you believe it? I'm going to be famous." He was totally in the grip of the celebrity craze that is one of the sorrier hallmarks of our times. That he might be jeopardizing the careers and livelihoods of thousands of his colleagues was forgotten.

Poli airily, almost contemptuously, dismissed our warnings that the FAA might be able to keep the planes flying. "The skies will be silent," he said. "I guarantee it. We are absolutely united. There will be no defections. And no one, not even President Reagan, can stand up to us when we are united. This country runs on commercial aviation, and we have the power to control it. When the planes stop flying, the country will stop, and they will have to give us what we want. I guarantee it." His words were so chilling that I realized—for the first time in my life—that I was going to be silently rooting for the other side. PATCO now represented little that could be considered legitimate trade unionism.

Leyden and I flew to Chicago on Sunday, August 2, the day before the scheduled strike. He had become executive director of the AFL-CIO's public employee department, and we were bound for the AFL-CIO's regular executive board meeting at the Hilton. Leyden told me there had been no contact between PATCO and the AFL-CIO leadership—not a phone call, not a conversation—even though the issue had been on the front page for days. I found this incomprehensible. The most significant strike in years, a patently illegal action against the federal government, was about to occur, and no one—from AFL-CIO President Lane Kirkland on down—had called Calhoon or Poli to find out what was going on. Not even Leyden, PATCO's president for ten years, had been consulted. If any one thing illustrated to me the indifference of labor's leadership to what was happening on the streets, it was this failure to recognize that a disaster was about to happen. I thought that if crusty old George Meany were still running things, he would have knocked some heads together and averted the whole mess. PATCO was equally guilty of failing to consult with the other aviation unions—the Air Line Pilots Association, the Association of Flight Attendants, and the International Association of Machinists, which represented the ground crews.

The strike began with great fanfare on August 3. For all practical purposes, it was over in twenty-four hours because the planes kept flying and nothing was going to stop them; military controllers and FAA supervisors were poised and ready to fill the void. At Chicago's Hilton Hotel, media crews were interviewing various union presidents about what the rest of labor would do. It was embarrassing to watch. Bill Wimpisinger, the self-proclaimed super-militant president of the Machinists, fulminated against Reagan but, when asked if his aviation mechanics would strike in sympathy with PATCO, the answer was a whispered no. J. J. O'Donnell, the airline pilots' chief, had to admit that his pilots would keep on flying regardless of what he urged them to do. Lane Kirkland and a handful of union presidents made a brief, picture-taking appearance on the PATCO picket line at O'Hare Airport and then chartered busses for their return to Washington. That was the AFL-CIO's total contribution to what turned out to be the most significant strike of the last quarter of the twentieth century.

A day later, President Reagan dropped the big bomb: all the striking controllers would be fired outright unless they returned to work within twenty-four hours. Despite the evidence that the strike had failed, Poli and the Choirboys—accepting advice from no one—were adamant. They were staying out. Most controllers did, in a remarkable but sad display of solidarity. Poli had run his lemmings into the sea, and they were not swimming back.

Reagan basked in the applause of practically everyone, and the strike soon faded from Page One as the PATCO pickets continued their lonely trudging outside the nation's airports. It was a bitter ending. I felt bad for many of the members that I liked very much, but the outright defiance of the law and the president was hard to stomach. Others, as pro-union as I, agreed.

At one of the first meetings we had with PATCO's leaders prior to their 1970 affiliation with MEBA, Jesse Calhoon made one point bluntly clear: "You cannot strike the federal government and get away with it. No one is bigger than the feds, and don't ever forget it." He continued: "If you still are entertaining any ideas of striking or sicking out under the umbrella of MEBA and the AFL-CIO, we don't want you. We are not looking for out-law or mad-dog unions to give labor a worse black eye than it already has. It isn't worth it."

The subsequent merger was effected on that basis; and sometime later, when PATCO regained the federal certification it had lost in a pre-MEBA sickout, its officers signed affidavits pledging not to strike. Unfortunately, in the MEBA merger, PATCO was given complete autonomy. When Poli *et al.* dishonored the pledges in 1981, Calhoon had no authority to stop them. It had been a mistake not to insist on a no-strike clause in the PATCO constitution.

Ego run riot. I had been exposed to egregious hubris before but nothing I had seen in politics or the arts and literature compared to the supreme cock-sureness of Bob Poli and his minions. No one could tell them anything. They were invincible and were going to show everyone by humbling the presi-dent of the United States. It was madness, of course. One had to experience it to believe it was really happening.

Why did organized labor let it happen? One explanation is that as the great old lions such as George Meany died off, the people who succeeded them, like Lane Kirkland, were sleek bureaucrats and technicians. Strong leaders historically have been notoriously lax about grooming successors. I remembered my first participation in national labor councils and conven-tions forty-some years earlier. The men and women at those gatherings had come right out of the factories and mills, the back shop and the foundry. Faces were craggy and hands gnarled. Their voices were rough and laced with the sometimes profane language of the streets. Many liked to drink and tell stories of the organizing wars, sit-down strikes, and battles with scabs and other union-busters. Everyone knew "Solidarity Forever," "Union Maid," "Joe Hill," and the other old labor hymns that dated back to the Home-stead strike.

By the time of the PATCO strike, most representatives of American work-ing people were smooth-faced technicians, with degrees from colleges such as Hofstra and Hollins. They were generally sincere and well-motivated people, filled with knowledge of legislative arcanities and cyberspace, but most did not speak with the voices of working people. The national workforce had undergone a revolutionary change. Muscular occupations such as steelmaking, railroading, and manufacturing were natural arenas for traditional trade unionism. With the downsizing and computerization of those industries and the increase in public-sector, service-industry, and high-tech workers, labor's face changed. The old bulls from the hoary past will not reappear even though John Sweeney, who ousted Kirkland, promised a return to labor's old fundamentals.

We can see the face of the future in the leaders of the union that replaced PATCO as the controllers' bargaining agent—the National Air Traffic Controllers Association (NATCA), affiliated with MEBA and the AFL-CIO. Learning from PATCO's excesses, they are an understated group, quietly advancing the controllers' cause without fanfare and staying out of the limelight. The lessons of the PATCO misadventure have not been lost.

18

BATTLE OF THE "BLACK HATS"

WHEN LLOYD DUXBURY AND NED BREATHITT ASKED ME TO BECOME the railroads' lobbyist in the upcoming congressional battle over coal slurry pipelines, I had finally given up on the fiction that lobbying was merely an interregnum in a career that would be dedicated to improving the human condition. There was not a smidgen of social significance in coal slurry.

It was the spring of 1977, and I had just come off my most successful lobbying performance ever—the passage of four major bills that would greatly benefit my forest-products, maritime, port, and county government clients. The bills had passed Congress on the final day of the 94th Congress, September 28, 1976, and I had been on a high ever since. I also finally admitted that I had come to love the lobbying game. I liked the hard scrabbling for votes, the head counting, the mobilizing of pressures on undecided legislators, the long hours in the Senate reception room and outside the House, "showing the flag" to members, even the endless committee hearings and strategy sessions.

And I liked dealing with members. What a rich range of personalities: outrageous characters such as Phil Burton, whose final legacy was the redistricting of California's congressional districts in his own Democratic demographic image; tough, old machine politicians such as Johnny Dent of Pennsylvania; charmingly cynical young realists like John Breaux of Louisiana; the players who saw a laugh in every situation, such as Bill Clay of Missouri; warm-hearted people like Dante Fascell of Florida; the "Irish

Dukes," headed by their chieftain Michael J. Kirwan of Ohio; and the total political pragmatists such as Bob Packwood of Oregon. Congress has been called many names, some of them true, but one thing it surely is—a microcosm of the nation's remarkable diversity. That one fact made it both a joy and a never-ending challenge to do business there.

I also loved the setting: the Capitol in all its glistening majesty, the imperial Senate and House office buildings, the nearby bars of the Democratic and Republican clubs, and the restaurants where I knew everybody. It was an incredible luxury to walk three or four blocks to work from my Capitol Hill townhouse and to come home in minutes from the legislative war-front to sleep in my own bed. I had spent fourteen years on the campaign trail in thirty-seven states, bunking in fleabag hotels from Bangor to Boise. Being one of the "boys on the bus" no longer held any charms for me. I liked battling in my own backyard and sleeping in my own bed.

The money was good. I was surprised to find myself making a substantial income, even though my retainers were modest compared to the big-timers such as Bob Strauss and J. D. Williams. My wife said that I undercharged my clients, and she was right. I still couldn't believe that one could get paid so much for doing so little, and it inhibited my billing. There is an abundance of amorality in politics and lobbying, and I was as amoral as anybody. When winning was at stake, you did whatever it took and thought about the niceties later. You knew your opponent would do or was doing the same. My only ethic was the need to believe in what and who I was lobbying for. Some lobbyists wore "this gun for hire" labels and could easily be on either side of an issue, depending on who showed them the money. I couldn't. When I joined a lobby, I wanted to be a permanent player on the team.

So I responded with unfeigned enthusiasm when Duxbury and Breathitt invited me to become a member of the railroad lobby. Since boyhood I had been a passionate rail buff. The rail exhibition at Grand Central ranked with baseball's Opening Day as among the most memorable events of my youth, and one summer I had been a "punk" on a Bangor and Aroostook road crew in Maine. At the time, I was maritime labor's representative on the railway unions' executive council. I was a natural for the new role and was thrilled that it had been offered to me.

The Burlington Northern's Duxbury and the Southern Railway's Breathitt were new to lobbying but savvy to the ways of politics. Duxbury had been the longtime speaker of the Minnesota legislature and Breathitt governor of Kentucky, and they were emblematic of the railroads' belated recognition that the Washington lobbying game had to be played by political professionals. The trucking industry, employing political pros, had been clobbering the railroads in the legislative arena for years. Now the railroads had awakened, and my recruitment was part of that arousal.

My sole problem with accepting the offer was my years of friendship with many of the building trades unions' lobbyists, all of them now campaigning hard for the coal slurry legislation. I went directly to Bob Georgine, president of the AFL-CIO's Building Trades Department. He could not have been more magnanimous. "Go ahead and take their money," he advised me. "We've got the votes, and we're going to win it big. You might as well get some of that money they're going to throw around."

There was reason for Georgine's confidence. I quickly learned that coal slurry's advocates held most of the high ground in the House and Senate. Ever-popular Morris K. "Mo" Udall, the Arizona Democrat who chaired the Interior committee considering the bill, was slurry's principal proponent, strongly backed by House wheelhorses Speaker Jim Wright, John Dingell, Phil Burton, and an army of others. On the Senate side, where a slurry bill had easily passed in 1974, J. Bennett Johnston of Louisiana and Chairman Scoop Jackson (my wife Erna's boss) were out in front. And the incoming Carter administration had also indicated its support for slurry. "It looks like 'Murderers' Row' against us," I said to Breathitt.

The financial stakes were big. Coal represented 38 percent of the railroads' nationwide haulage of bulk materials, and the rails had a near-monopoly of this trade, which was so essential to many of the nation's electric utilities. These utilities and their supplier coal companies were the chief instigators of coal slurry legislation, reflecting their unhappiness at being "captive shippers held in hostage" and "at the mercy of whatever the railway barons decide to charge to move our coal." This kind of harsh rhetoric indicated the growing enmity between the two groups. To the president of the Potomac Electric Power Company (PEPCO), the slurry movement had become a "crusade to shed our captive chains."

Of all the coal-carrying railroads, no one had more verbal "coals of calumny" heaped on it than the one I knew best, the Burlington Northern (BN). It had built an expensive line into the coal-rich Powder River Basin of northeastern Wyoming and was delivering 150–car unit trains of the low-sulphur stuff to the Southwest, South, and Midwest. Utilities such as San Antonio Municipal Light were complaining that the BN had lured them into Powder River coal with introductory low transportation rates and then more than doubled them once the power companies were hooked. Mo Udall's voice would quiver with rage as he railed at the "sins" of the BN.

Slurry was a proven technology—coal was crushed and mixed with water at the mine-mouth, then conveyed through a large pipeline to its destination. One line had been successfully operated in the 1940s from Cleveland to a power plant at Cadiz, Ohio. The Chesapeake and Ohio Railroad finally had put it out of business by drastically lowering coal transportation rates. Now there was only one coal slurry line in the nation—Black Mesa, a 273–mile line that ran from the Navajo Indian Reservation coalfields in north-eastern Arizona to a huge power plant on the Mojave Desert. Paradoxically, it was owned and operated by the Southern Pacific Railroad, because railroad tracks were impractical over this rugged terrain. Black Mesa had functioned successfully for some years, yet its builder had said that if he had it to build again, he wouldn't have done it. Nevertheless, there was a dominant attitude on Capitol Hill that the railroads were Luddites, fighting against the inevitability of technological progress and competition in the American spirit of free enterprise. God forbid being against either.

Five major pipelines had been on the drawing boards for years, but they would cross and parallel railroad lands. The railroads, understandably not wanting to share or relinquish the profitable coal-hauling business, had refused rights-of-way to the pipelines. The slurry bill would give the Department of the Interior the authority to grant pipeline developers federal powers of eminent domain, that is, the power to take private lands in the public interest at fair market value.

Other lobbyists and some congressional staffers advised me against taking on such an obvious loser. "We're loaded for bear on this one," Tommy Boggs, a preeminent gun-for-hire, told me. "We're going to run the railroads right off the track." A senior lobbyist, an old New Dealer, advised, "Only take it if you need the money." I didn't. The logic was that coal slurry had been overwhelmingly approved by the Senate on a voice vote in 1974 and would have sailed through the House had it not been too late in that election-year session to get it to the floor. The railroad lobby was able to block the bill procedurally—the only reason slurry was not already a *fait accompli*.

I like to "walk around" an issue before I take it on—talk to a network of people on Capitol Hill who I have known over the years, visit the Library of Congress to read the periodical material on the subject, talk to reporters who have been covering the issue, that sort of thing. It is still a surprise to me that few of my fellow lobbyists follow this procedure. The more I "walked around" this one, the more I became convinced that the prevailing wisdom was wrong, that the issue was winnable. My basis for this growing confidence was my knowledge of the railroad labor lobby. As maritime labor's representative to that lobby, I had a good working relationship with the group and was a close friend of its top gun, the brilliant and dogged J. R. (Jim) Snyder of the United Transportation Union. I asked Jim if rail labor was going to make an all-out fight on slurry. "It is our biggest issue in years," he said. "At least 16,000 jobs of ours are involved—and probably many more. We are going to commit all our troops to this battle."

That was the key. Rail labor had one of the most effective lobbies in Washington when it decided to concentrate on a piece of legislation. Its state political directors in all the 48 continental states doubled as lobbyists to their state congressional delegations. The railway unions' long history of giving generous sums to candidates they supported made for a depth of political relationships that the building trades unions, the coal companies, and the utilities—with all their high-priced guns—could not match.

Beyond Duxbury, Breathitt, and Scott Anderson (the "child prodigy" of Quentin Burdick's 1960 election), I did not have much confidence in the rail management lobby that I had joined. A year or so before, representing the Port of Portland in Oregon, I had been part of the barge transportation lobby that had defeated rail management on an increased diesel-fuel tax on barges and construction of new locks on the Mississippi River. The rails had made a spirited but ineffectual fight. Rail management was in the process of evolving from an imperial mindset formed in the halcyon years when it was the only transportation game in town, an attitude that encrusted its very ethos. The truckers had taken spectacular advantage of this arrogance. Playing politics to the hilt, the American Trucking Associations and its Teamsters Union ally had won some remarkable victories.

A prime example was the 1956 Interstate Highway Act, which had been written with the truckers lobby involved in every section and clause. I was in Washington all that spring setting up three Senate campaigns and had an insider's view. The point man for Senate Democrats on campaign contributions was Neil J. Curry, finance chairman of the Democratic Senatorial Campaign Committee (DSCC). Curry also happened to be president of the American Trucking Associations (ATA). If that wasn't enough, the DSCC's executive director was Neal Roach, on leave from his job as public relations director of Curry's ATA. It is no surprise that railroads had little input in this situation. True, the interstate highway system was badly needed, but whether it should have been at the expense of the nation's rail system is questionable.

The highway bill passed the Senate on a balmy April evening. Afterward, I shared a taxi to the Mayflower Hotel with Senator Kerr Scott of North Carolina. "I have some grave doubts about what we did tonight," he said. "We may have imbalanced our transportation system in favor of the auto and the truck." When he had been governor, he was known as "Good Roads" Scott because he built farm-to-market roads. "But I voted aye tonight with considerable misgiving because it was at the expense of the nation's rail system," he continued, "which, after all, did make the country what it is today. It remains to be seen how it will turn out."

Now it was 1977, and it had turned out badly for the railroads. But adversity forces change. The Association of American Railroads had a vibrant new president in forty-five-year-old William Henry Dempsey, and he was rebuilding the rails' team. The coal slurry bill was going to be the first big test.

Slurry appeared to be on a fast congressional track; but the railroads were not without friends. Some in Congress, seeking to stall the vote, had successfully moved for an in-depth study of the issue by the newly created research arm of Congress, the Office of Technology Assessment (OTA), whose study was scheduled for delivery in early 1978. Its proponents had argued that slurry was a complex issue involving economic and environmental questions to which no scientific answers existed. Surely, it was not unreasonable to use Congress' newest creation, the OTA, which had been designed for this very purpose. Mo Udall, a thoughtful man, may have philosophically agreed with this approach, but he was driven by a congressional imperative best expressed by Warren G. Magnuson: "When you have the votes, vote," he said. "When you don't, talk." Mo had the votes and wasn't going to hang around wait-ing for OTA's study.

Michigan's Philip Ruppe, a Republican member of Udall's Interior Com-mittee, moved to checkmate the Arizonan by offering a resolution stipulat-ing that the Interior committee take no action until the OTA study was out. It was to be voted on in early June, the week after I joined the rail lobby. If it was rejected, the slurry fight was liable to be over before we had the chance to get warmed up.

Mo put the Ruppe resolution before the two subcommittees claiming juris-diction over slurry—Public Lands and Mines and Mining. And to stack the deck against us, he had added the delegates of the Virgin Islands, Guam, and American Samoa, who always voted with him. It was here that my string of luck held up. Two of Udall's "sure" votes were Democrats James Weaver of Oregon and Antonio B. Won Pat of Guam, and they "owed" me. Don't ask me how or why; it was part of the arcane currency of Capitol Hill. A marker was a marker, to be redeemed when the holder needed it. I saw both of them, and, despite much grumbling over having to vote against their beloved chairman, they agreed to vote with Ruppe—and to tell no one, par-ticularly Mo.

The markup was held in an ornate hearing room in the Rayburn Build-ing. Weaver and Won Pat were seated at the end of an elevated horseshoe around which the committee sat. Minutes before the chairman rapped for order they came down from the bench to where I was sitting in the audi-ence in a sea of rail lobbyists, my new comrades. Beckoning me over, Weaver said in a stage-whisper: "Now, you want Tony and me to vote with Ruppe on this one—right?" Then he winked, and they went back to their seats. "Honest," I muttered to Breathitt. "That wasn't my idea." He grinned. "No matter. You just earned your retainer for the year." The vote was 13 to 12 in favor of Ruppe's resolution. We had upset Mo Udall in his own commit-tee and put slurry on the sidelines for at least six months. This would give us the time we needed to get our coalition organized.

OTA started the action on January 19, 1978, by delivering its 190–page study, exactly eighteen months after it had undertaken the project. It clearly favored the railroads' position. On point after point, the study shot down the more extravagant claims of the slurry proponents: only in certain situations could slurry pipelines haul coal more cheaply than railroads; development of coal resources would not be increased nationally through the use of slurry pipelines; there was enough water available to service the planned pipelines, but its use could restrict future agricultural development; legislating rights of federal eminent domain to the pipeline companies would result in significant regulatory advantages over the railroads; and, without such federal and state eminent domain powers, pipelines could still be competitive with the railroads in certain areas.

Mo Udall didn't waste any time. Bypassing the subcommittees, he called the full Interior and Insular Affairs Committee into markup on February 8. With a preponderance of westerners on the panel, the issue of state water rights dominated the discussion. Teno Roncalio, a Wyoming Democrat, was leading our charge with a series of amendments to protect those rights. He lost most of them by narrow margins, but he got the one he wanted: a pipeline could not be licensed unless the U.S. Geological Survey conducted a comprehensive study of the project.

The bill was voted out of committee on George Washington's Birthday by a lopsided 30 to 13 margin. Our 13 nay votes were indicative of how nonideological the slurry issue was. Pure Democratic liberals such as Jim Florio of New Jersey, Bruce Vento of Minnesota, and Jim Weaver of Oregon had lined up against H.R. 1609 with rock-hard Republicans Bob Bauman of Maryland, Eldon Rudd of Arizona, and Steve Symms of Idaho. Two more committees had a shot at the bill—the Public Works and Transportation Committee and Energy and Commerce. Speaker Tip O'Neill determined that the bill would be withheld from the floor to allow Public Works to "develop a position on the legislation."

The Public Works Committee was alien turf to the railroads, but we played every hand we had. When the committee voted on May 16, we were pleased with the closeness of the vote: 23 to 20. If we had changed two more, we would have scored a major upset and perhaps averted a floor fight. David Bonior of Michigan had turned out to be a tough battler on our side, and we enlisted him to lean on his friend John Dingell as H.R. 1609 moved to its last hurdle, Energy and Commerce, where we had no doubt about winning. Fred B. Rooney of Pennsylvania, chairman of the Surface Transportation Subcommittee, was one of our most vociferous supporters, along with Harley Staggers of West Virginia, the full committee chairman. The vote was 19 to 9.

Spring training was over. The real season was beginning, and we were ready. The coalition that we had stitched together was as diverse and balanced a group as I had been involved with in twenty-five years. In addition to all segments of the rail industry, our active allies included the United Mine Workers, the International Association of Machinists, all major farm organizations, and the Environmental Policy Center. Other environmental bodies such as the Sierra Club and the Wilderness Society supported us in principle but eschewed active lobbying. At the first meeting, Ned Breathitt proposed me for coalition chairman. I was delighted to have the gavel. We had found a great place for our twice-weekly meetings—an old residential hotel named the Bellevue, two blocks from the Senate side of the Capitol. It had a big meeting room in the rear of the lobby, where food and drink from its excellent kitchen and bar could be delivered.

As we headed nearer to a floor vote, I was feeling better about the request I had made to Bill Dempsey when I signed aboard with the railroads. "Let's steer clear of the hired guns," I suggested. "It has been my experience that they are not worth a damn when a piece of legislation is publicly spotlighted as this issue surely will be. They can be effective when a bill doesn't attract attention and also in the committee backroom when an amendment is needed. But on an out-front bill like slurry, they aren't going to do much good." He had listened. We only had one hired gun in the coalition, brought in by one of the railroads. He was a nice fellow but didn't contribute much. On a spotlighted issue, legislators are far more inclined to listen to home folks than "hit men" hired to work a particular bill. The home folks will always be around; the "hit men" disappear when the retainer stops. We also had a couple of unexpected windfalls. One of them involved W. Pat Jennings, former Virginia Democratic congressman and chief clerk of the House, now working for the Coal Slurry Transport Association as its chief lobbyist. As chief clerk, Jennings had alienated several members of the House. "I'm against *anything* he is for, even motherhood," one member told me.

With the July 4 congressional recess coming up, I had planned to accompany my wife Erna to her family reunion in Norway. I asked Mo Udall, a longtime personal friend, if he was planning to ask the Rules Committee for a rule to bring H.R. 1609 to the floor right after the recess. "I have no plans now," he said. "You should be able to go." The day before we were due to depart I got a call from a staff member of the Rules Committee. "You better not go," he said. "Slurry is going to be scheduled for a vote right after the recess."

We cancelled Norway, and I accepted an earlier offer—from my slurry opponents in the building trades unions and from which I could get back in time—to make a five-day swing around the country in the Westinghouse Corporation's DC-9 to view nuclear power plants in Illinois, Washington State, and California. "We want to keep an eye on you," Dan Mundy, the building trades' chief lobbyist, explained. It was a great trip, and we climaxed it with a riotous final night at the MGM Grand Hotel in Las Vegas. Before the party, I had a drink with one of the building trades' lobbyists in his hotel suite. He was expansive. "We've got slurry won," he said. "In fact, I'm going to show you our scorecard. Read it and weep." He handed me a House work-sheet. I was amazed. These lists were ultra-confidential and, as such, guarded. I focused on the undecided and "soft" votes listed on his worksheet, then slipped back to my room to scribble down the names. The next day we returned to Washington and learned that we had about ten days before H.R. 1609 hit the House floor. We decided to concentrate on the undecideds and soft votes on the building-trades list and enlisted our congressional allies— notably Jim Oberstar of Minnesota, Gene Snyder of Kentucky, and Guy Molinari of New York—to use their talents for persuasion in the House cloakroom.

The final tally was 246 to 161, an 85–vote margin. Only 45 Republicans and 116 Democrats had voted for it, compared to 90 and 156 against. The shock at the railroads' easy victory was evidenced by the *Washington Post*'s three-column, front-page headline: "Railroad Lobby Scores Surprisingly Lopsided Victory in Coal Slurry Vote." Nothing in a long time had pleased me as much.

The big victory had healthy reverberations. It paved the way for passage in 1980 of the Staggers Act, now regarded as the Magna Carta of the railroad industry because it removed the anti-competitive shackles of the Interstate Commerce Commission. Since then, the railroads have held their own against the truckers and have begun to gain market share—and rates went down. The coal companies and electric utilities did not come away from the conflict empty-handed. They had hammered the railroads so hard on the issue of "price-gouging captive shippers" that the industry bent over backwards to avoid giving them ammunition. The result was a number of long-term contracts at attractive coal-transportation rates.

The coal-slurry group spent a year or so rethinking the issue and made an all-out final effort in 1982–1983. They fielded a new team of lobbyists and charged anew. Heading for one of the interminable hearings, I ran into Tom Foley, who was then House Agriculture Committee chairman. "Where are you going?" he asked. "A coal slurry hearing," I said. Foley shook his head in amazement. "Is that turkey still alive?" he queried. "They should subtitle it 'The Lobbyists' Relief Act' and leave the year or maybe the century blank. It's had a longer life than Methuselah."

Despite slurry's new team, it was "déjà vu all over again." This time the vote was closer, 235 to 182, and I bought drinks for the coalition at the National Democratic Club, where we officially buried coal slurry.

19

THE WICKED WINE
OF THE DEMOCRATIC PROCESS

IS THERE ANYTHING NEW ON MONEY AND LOBBYING, ANYTHING TO be said that hasn't already been said a thousand times over? Senator John McCain aired it all in his early run for the presidency in 2000. Washington is being run, he said, by an "Iron Triangle" of lobbyists, money, and legislators, with the filthy lucre the connecting link. Why, then, a chapter on money? Simply because it can't be ignored. It is central to virtually every aspect of lobbying and politics. And I have some thoughts, derived from my experience, that hardly fit the orthodoxy of reform and political correctness.

First, let me make my *mea culpa.* I have trafficked in every kind of dollar awash in our political system: legitimate and all the rest—corporate and labor union treasury checks, Las Vegas skim and Mexican "laundry." Illegal contributions-in-kind were a specialty of mine, the kind of stuff that couldn't be traced. And, of course, the old reliable folding stuff—cash, gelt, mazuma, shekels.

My one ethic was that none of it stuck to my fingers. I shielded myself from temptation by always sending a registered letter from the candidate to the giver at his home address, naming the amount and time and place of the transaction. This practice also removed the suspicion candidates have that they are being ripped off when cash is given to a middleman. Padding expenses was one thing; stealing from candidates is another.

An old friend, the late Jesse Unruh, enhanced his political celebrity with the wry observation: "Money is the mother's milk of politics." True, but I like the "wicked wine" analogy a little better. If Utopians took over and political money were outlawed, slick operators would still find ways to infuse it into the process. This skepticism is largely based on my 1974 experience, the post-Watergate reform year with liberal Democrats firmly in control of both houses of Congress. Federal taxpayer financing of presidential campaigns was a big-ticket item, and, as a member of the AFL-CIO lobby, I was pushing hard for its passage. We succeeded—a great triumph for influence-free government. No longer would the Big Money Boys be calling the shots from the White House.

Included in this reform package was an unnoticed amendment sponsored by a pro-labor Democrat from New Jersey, Frank Thompson, and a moderate Idaho Republican, Orval Hansen. What Thompson-Hansen did was to make it legal for labor unions, corporations, and business trade associations to use union and corporation money to finance the raising of money for partisan political use. Up to this point, organized labor, with 16 million members to solicit, had dominated mass fundraising. All of the eighty-two international unions affiliated with the AFL-CIO had long-flourishing political action committees, or PACs. Corporate-business efforts were principally confined to large contributions from top brass, and you could count the number of business PACs on your fingers.

Passage of Thompson-Hansen set off a stampede similar to the Great Oklahoma Land Rush. Corporations, business trade associations, and law firms formed PACs to seek the political dollar. Almost overnight, Washington was awash in new political money. Elected officials are human beings; they lined up at the new troughs as if it was Bank Night in Canarsie. And the cost of campaigns skyrocketed.

As an example, Al Ullman of Oregon, who became chairman of the House Ways and Means Committee, spent less than $10,000 in each and every campaign from 1954 to 1974. In 1980, when he was defeated in the Reagan rush, his campaign cost $796,000. That is how the price of politics shot up. Ullman's case was not unusual. Congressional districts where a good campaign could be made for around $50,000 now demanded a million dollars or more. Fundraising suddenly became a necessity and an all-consuming proposition, and lobbying changed with it.

The best fundraiser became the best lobbyist, which suited Big Business, not Big Labor. So, why did the AFL-CIO lobby the Thompson-Hansen amendment into law, thereby creating the mechanism that spawned corporate special-interest PACs? Self-preservation, plain and simple. The National Right to Work Committee, an anti-labor lobby, had been legally challenging organized labor's right to spend money collected from union dues to pay for its political action committees. This, the RTW Committee contended in various court cases, was a clear violation of the 1947 Taft-Hartley Act, which prohibited unions from spending union dues in partisan political campaigns. One court in Georgia and another in Texas had upheld the RTW case, and, as Al Barkan, the AFL-CIO's top political honcho, put it to me: "Some ugly handwriting was already on the wall."

The new PACs proliferated. With expensive media consultants suddenly becoming the new vogue and television entrenched as the main medium of politics, costs increased manyfold. Entrenched incumbents, such as Ullman, now felt the need to wage full-scale media campaigns. Some, who heretofore had never taken a nickel in contributions, began shaking every money tree in the new PAC forest.

My exemplar of what went wrong was a man I considered to be the modern personification of Thomas Jefferson's citizen-legislator—Dr. Thomas E. Morgan, Democrat of Pennsylvania. First elected in 1944, for decades "Doc" doubled as his district's congressman and its leading general practitioner. Tuesday to Thursday, he legislated in Washington, D.C.; Friday to Monday, he took care of his patients in Washington, Pennsylvania. He seldom spent more than a few hundred dollars to get re-elected and never solicited campaign contributions. Everyone in his south-of-Pittsburgh district knew him; he didn't need to remind them at election time. He was just what Jefferson had in mind.

Then came the new PACs. Doc had a nice fellow on his staff, and he and the PAC money-givers discovered each other. They staged a "birthday party" for Doc at $500 a head. Then an "anniversary party," same price. Hardly a month went by without some kind of a party for Doc, belatedly basking in all the attention and money that he didn't need. Now, mind you, it was all legal, and Doc did nothing wrong. No one bought his vote. Yet, somehow, I found it sad.

There are still some who will argue that Thompson-Hansen and the 1974 reforms worked, that they brought campaign finance out of the shadows and into the sunlight of full disclosure so that there was no longer any doubt about who was contributing to whom. True and conceded. It is further argued that the creation of so many PACs greatly expanded participation in the democratic process, the goal of the American system. And with the $1,000 limit on individual contributions and $5,000 on PAC contributions, no one person or PAC could dominate. Possibly.

Yet, we all know that Washington is laced with smart lawyers who make careers of figuring ways around such obstacles. Soft money and independent expenditures are obvious loopholes, but there are others, too. Plenty of them. Short of a Draconian thunderclap that would ban all money except federal financing (Theodore Roosevelt's idea), I don't see anything—McCain-Feingold or whatever—curing the disease.

And how do you regulate the oldest loophole of all—cash? In all the campaigns I worked, cash made up around one-third of contributions. That cash was historically a principal coin of the political realm was spotlighted when Idaho's famous senator, William Edgar Borah, died in 1940. In his safety deposit box at the Idaho First National Bank in Boise, investigators found $215,000 in cash, a huge sum at that time. Unspent campaign contributions, they decided, and finally gave the money to his widow. On a number of occasions, I slipped a cash-filled envelope into a legislator's pocket and mumbled that it was for his campaign, knowing that it would never get there. There is, I once heard Senator Russell B. Long observe, "a fine line between bribery and campaign contributions, but I've never determined where it was."

Some years ago, I was asked to put together a media campaign for John C. Watts of Kentucky, the ranking Democrat on the tax-writing House Ways and Means Committee. I did, and then told Watts that $52,000 was needed to reserve his radio-TV time and billboards. He nodded and padded off to an anteroom of his commodious Rayburn House Office Building office and opened a huge, old-fashioned safe. I sat in the main office, sipping the fine bourbon his secretary had poured for me. Some time went by, and finally Watts called to me for help. He was nearly blind, but hated to admit it. I entered his inner sanctorum—and was almost blinded myself! A mountain of green sat in that ancient safe, and Watts had spilled some of it on the floor. It was high-denomination stuff, piles of $50s, $100s, and $500s. I had seen bundles of cash before, but never anything like this, an emerald cornucopia that made me salivate. Many of the piles still had lobbyists' cards attached. Calling in his secretary to observe the counting, I left shortly with the $52,000. When I told Clements about it, he chuckled and his cheeks dimpled in appreciation. "John's a businessman, my boy. John's a businessman!"

Lyndon Johnson loved cash and hated checks. "Cash is clean and leaves no fingerprints," he informed me when we first met in 1957. "Stay away from checks. Always ask for cash. Checks can trip you up when you least expect it."

The late Tip O'Neill had a story about John F. Kennedy that he loved to tell. "In the 1960 campaign," said Tip, "I was a nobody, consigned to a minor-league circuit of tank towns where I beat the drums for money with the Democratic pols. On my first swing from Massachusetts across New York, Ohio, and Indiana, I did pretty good and arrived in Chicago on the eve of the first Kennedy-Nixon debate with a bundle. Jack was in a suite at the Morrison getting ready, so I went there and checked in with my pal Kenny O'Donnell, told him what I had. He said for me to wait while he checked with JFK. Then he came back and said Jack wanted to see me. He was lying on a bed, nursing a beer, reading briefs for the debate.

"Without even saying hello, he asked, 'What you got, Tip?' I told him, so much in checks and the rest in cash. I asked him what he wanted me to do with it. Kennedy waved his arm. 'Give the checks to Kenny,' he said, 'and leave the cash here.'"

Tip chuckled in appreciation. "When I told my roommate [Massachusetts Democratic congressman] Eddie Boland about it, Eddie said: 'It doesn't matter whether they're running for alderman or president of the United States. It's always: Give him the checks. I'll take the cash.'"

Converting illegal checks—corporate and union treasury ones were the most common—was not all that easy. President Nixon's people had to go all the way to Mexico to do it. I found that a train trip to Philadelphia was easier. Ben Franklin's town contained two upstanding citizens who happened to be staunch Democrats, always willing to help their party. Among their holdings was a bank where such checks could be discreetly converted into cash, a transaction to be made selectively and with great care. It made for a very good day—a train ride, lunch at the Philadelphia Club with the two gents listening to their marvelous stories, and a return trip to Washington clutching a full attaché case.

The politicians of my experience had varying attitudes about money.

Some prodded staff to shake the money tree twenty-four hours a day. Others were content to be apprised and even were willing to make a phone call or two to big contributors and schmooze them at fundraisers. Then there were what I call the "don't-tell-me-about-it" politicians—a rarified, above-it-all group. They recognized that it took money to win and that not all contributions were made by disinterested citizens seeking good government as their only reward, but they shied away from knowing about such grubby transactions, leaving them to underlings. Hence, "don't tell me about it"—a phrase that I was to hear many times during my time in the lobbying-political trenches.

The late Al Barkan had a telling story. In 1948, when he was political director of the Textile Workers Union, Al took a $10,000 check to his old University of Chicago labor economics professor who was making an apparently hopeless race against U.S. Majority Leader C. Wayland "Curly" Brooks. The professor, Paul H. Douglas, his campaign in debt, almost broke down with tears of gratitude. Then Al added, "Professor, this is money from our union treasury, illegal under the Taft-Hartley Act. But here in Chicago you shouldn't have any trouble exchanging it with the Cook County Democrats, and we left the payee blank for that reason."

Douglas's reaction was one of anguish. "Al, I can't touch that kind of money, desperate as I am for it. Doing so would be to repudiate everything I have stood for all my life. I'm sorry, but you will have to take it back." Barkan, disgusted by his failure, left and walked back to his hotel. A block away, he was overtaken by a puffing Douglas campaign aide. "Damn you, Barkan," he panted, why did you expose the professor to the dirty details? He's a goo-goo!"—contemptuous political argot for good government. "Give me that check," he ordered. "I'll take care of it with Jake Arvey and the prof won't know the difference."

Early in my Washington years, Douglas and I became neighbors and friends. Once, over a couple of drinks, I asked him if he knew what had happened to the Textile Workers' illegal check. He smiled and shook his massive head. Then I told him. Douglas chuckled. "Charley Callahan shouldn't have done that," he said. "But, you know, I'm kind of glad now that he did!" The white-maned Illinoisan was a man of total rectitude, and in his eighteen years in the U.S. Senate he fought tirelessly for campaign reforms. Yet, the Barkan story demonstrates how even the purest can be compromised. The same thing happened with other "goo-goos" as well—whether or not to their eventual knowledge, I don't know. (I know of one who did return a large sum, post-election, when he learned its source.)

Cash, I learned early, had a near-narcotic effect on some, including me. Its peculiar power? The following was my most vivid experience. Of the twenty-two Republican Senate seats to be contested in 1958, none appeared easier to win than that of George W. "Molly" Malone in Nevada. Early polling data showed any respectable Democrat beating him handily. The trouble was the state's only congressman, Walter S. Baring, a decidedly not-respectable Democrat who, the polls showed, would run away with the nomination if he entered the race. Originally elected as an orthodox Democrat, Baring had turned to the far right, influenced by Nevada anti-government fanatics.

My boss, Earle C. Clements, was determined to head him off. One morning, he said to me: "My boy, we've got to find $10,000 in cash. Don't ask me any questions. Just help me raise it from every source we have." The money was raised, and Clements put it in an attaché case. It was the prettiest wad of cash I'd ever seen. He called Baring and invited him to a private lunch in his ornate Senate office. He said to me, "You might as well join us. This may teach you something about human nature and, besides, I might need a witness."

Baring came in, wearing a rumpled blue double-breasted suit. He sat down at the table, declined a drink, and said, "Let's eat." Vernon, a courtly gray-haired black waiter who served senators at private functions, went for the food as Clements and I had a drink. Baring took no note of my presence and, when the food came, not much of Clements's either. We were with a true glutton.

It was time for Clements's pitch. "Walter," he began in a voice dripping with honey, "you are one of the most valuable western members of the House, a vital presence on the Interior and Labor committees with a value there beyond compare." Baring nodded, a self-satisfied smirk emerging from his jowls. Clements picked up the attaché case and put it on the table. He opened it, rows of crisp green bills dazzling the eye. I began to salivate and, from the rapacious glare in his eyes, I sensed that Baring was undergoing a similar reaction.

Clements returned to his pitch. "Walter, you are so valuable where you are that some of your friends have raised this money to encourage you to run for re-election. They entrusted it to me while you decide. I can assure you that it will be yours the moment after you make your announcement. It will be here for you in my safe." As he spoke, Clements's big farmer's hands played lovingly with the piles of freshly minted bills. Leaving, Baring mumbled to Clements that he could be counted on. A day or so later, a press release was delivered from his office that announced his candidacy for re-election. Afterward, Clements said to me: "That was ugly but necessary. His kind does not belong in the Senate. Bribing him to keep him out was a public service in my book, even though your good-government people would be horrified by what I did."

That November, Howard W. Cannon, a moderate Democrat, was handily elected and served for twenty-four years. Baring was re-elected for a few more terms, ultimately losing a primary to an aggressive young challenger.

I end this tour through the Stygian darkness, the murky and dank forests of money in the lobbying trade, on a somewhat hopeful note. George Bernard Shaw once famously observed that Richard Wagner's music was "better than it sounds." Shaw's aphorism may be applied here. Granted, it seems that the Mitch McConnells always win because nothing ever happens on campaign finance reform. (He, you recall, is the Kentucky Republican senator who has fiercely fought any change in the present system.) Yet, underneath the surface, the currents are running strongly against McConnell and those who would preserve the status quo, secure in their claim that the electorate at large "doesn't care a tinker's damn about campaign reform."

The public does care—big time. Following John McCain's campaign for reform, the issue now registers high in surveys of the electorate's concerns. Historically, it always has been a concern, but because campaign financing has opaque and amorphous aspects, it never quite became a cutting issue. "They all do it," shrugged the public, an accurately cynical summation. McCain's charge against campaign financing gave them a focus for their concern. Another factor, never much discussed, is the Washington presence of so many competing interests, equally armed with PAC money, that often cancel or compromise each other out. With competing groups trying to buy legislative support on a controversial issue, it is a basic instinct of legislators to seek compromises that may partially satisfy both sides.

The old-time pros, such as Warren G. Magnuson, made an art form out of crafting such compromises. Years ago, when legislation was deliberated behind closed doors, I was one of an army of lobbyists clustered outside the doors of the Senate Finance Committee. That body was considering a controversial tax package that the House had passed. Finally, word came to us that the committee had recessed, and the waiting lobbyists repositioned themselves to buttonhole senators friendly to their concern to find out what was happening. Everett Dirksen was the first to emerge, accompanied by the committee's newest member, Hiram L. Fong of Hawaii. Dragging on his ever-present cigarette, a roguish grin crinkling his rumpled face, Dirksen surveyed the faces in the waiting crowd, all of whom he knew. Then he rubbed his manicured hands together, exuding pleasure at what he was seeing. "Hiram," he cried to Fong in his nicotine-scarred baritone, "look at this! We've got ourselves a real money bill. Everyone is here."

What he meant, and Dirksen could be remarkably candid, was that campaign contributions from the assembled army of lobbyists soon would be flowing their way. And that is how it works. There isn't a scintilla of subtlety to it, none whatsoever. Let a "real money bill" land in a key committee, and the contributions flow like the Mississippi on a rampage.

Does it work? Almost always. There is no mystery about it. What is different these days is the aggressive way that money is pursued, by both sides. Ev Dirksen might rub his hands and wisecrack, but that was generally as far as it went. There was no big pressure to contribute. Trent Lott, Mississippi Republican and former Senate majority leader, is typical of today's trend. Some years ago, he called a group of lobbyists into his office to give them the name and address of a Republican organization promoting its Senate candidates—Americans for Job Security. Unlimited sums of money could be made to this committee and spent for purely partisan purposes, he said, and nobody would be the wiser. A loophole had been found in the Internal Revenue tax code, Section 527, that allowed organizations to set up separate "political committees" and thus avoid reporting contributions to the Federal Elections Commission. This king-sized gap in the disclosure rules embodied in the 1974 "reforms" was legal.

It was the Sierra Club that originally found this egregious loophole back in 1996, spending almost $4 million in pro-environment ads against Republicans, and it was the AFL-CIO that used Section 527 to spend $35 million attacking GOP House members that same year. What President Bill Clinton did with so-called soft money has been told so many times that it does not bear repeating. Yet, despite Republican outrage, he merely riffed on what Ronald Reagan, George Bush, and Richard Nixon had done before him: "Everybody does it."

The enduring genius of the American two-party system is competition, which prevents one party or the other from dominating for too long. That nothing too outrageous has happened in this period when money has become the be-all and end-all is a tribute to that balance. Remember Shaw on Wagner: His music is better than it sounds? So it is with money in the political arena. All legislators will tell you that they can't be bought. Former Senator John Breaux of Louisiana, the most refreshingly candid politician I know, puts a qualifying twist on his protestation. "I can't be bought," Breaux likes to say, "but I can be rented." And even that one, Breaux admits, isn't exactly original. He borrowed it from Dudley LeBlanc, a Louisiana state senator who was the promoter of Hadacol, that postwar cure-all out of the canebrakes.

20

REFLECTIONS

IT IS VIRTUALLY OBLIGATORY THAT MORE THAN A HALF-CENTURY involvement with politics and government has to produce some profundities about what's wrong and, of course, a plan to fix it. Short of the impossible-to-do "get the money out of the game," I have scant advice to offer. Most remedies that I have seen are boilerplate Political Science 101—mostly unpassable, undoable, or loaded with loopholes. And having seen "cures" ultimately worse than the diseases they were designed to eradicate, I have become a go-slow skeptic. What I do have some hope for is the spotlight that the media has put on the role of money in lobbying and campaigns. Unfortunately, its reporting on lobbying has not reached the level of its political coverage, which now routinely covers the influence of political money on government. Political writing advanced a few light years when the media turned to in-depth reporting on the accuracy of television spots, who was making them, and what they cost. The voters get a far more accurate picture now than they did when campaign coverage was merely glorified sports writing.

The media routinely needs to highlight the activities of lobbyists in the same way it has publicized political consultants. With more exposure, the playing field becomes more level.

For a period in the late 1970s and 1980s, I was filled with rage, liable to erupt in profane fury at dinner parties or in meetings. What precipitated my outbursts? Anger at what was suddenly happening in money-mad Washington. The proliferation of PACs seemingly had turned every legislator and his staff people into Calcutta street beggars swarming our sacred shrines. Everybody had his hand out, and the cheapness of it all made me furious.

I shouldn't have been. As part-custodian of a million-dollar labor union political fund, I was being increasingly wooed by congressmen and their staffs, an ideal situation for a special-interest lobbyist like me. When I walked into a Capitol Hill fundraiser or meeting, the money-seekers sought me out and volunteered to bring me drinks. It was downright embarrassing. I came to believe that I had dollar signs emblazoned on my forehead, like Hester Prynne's Scarlet A. Fundraising calls by the score came in daily. I grew sick of honeyed female voices seeking our bounty, and congressmen crying—literally—that their campaign was at Armageddon and would fail if we did not contribute.

My reaction to my such celebrity status among the money-seekers was curious, to say the least. I *disliked* it. My pride as a lobbyist was my intimate knowledge of the politics of the issues I advocated, my reputation for candor, and a word that was known to be good. Now I was turning into little more than a political cash cow, to be milked regularly.

"It's a totally new ballgame up here," an enterprising lobbyist from Oklahoma named J. D. Williams told me. "The political dollar has become king of the hill." The House majority leader's son, a sweet-faced idealist named Tommy Boggs, emerged as a master dealer of the political dollar to attain his lobbying ends. A famously funny, profane, and oh-so-shrewd Texan named Bob Strauss came out of nowhere to become a "Washington wise man," primarily because of his smarts with the political dollar.

Jesse Calhoon, the perceptive president of a maritime union that I represented, said to me early in 1977: "Our party used to be the party of FDR, Truman, Rayburn, and JFK. Now the lobbyists have taken over Washington like a swarm of locusts destroying a cornfield."

The last quarter-century or more has witnessed the accuracy of Calhoon's comments. Yet, there are significant signs that the Era of Money, with its egregious excesses, may be ending. Public revulsion has been at an all-time high, and Congress has tried to provide some partial palliatives, prodded by public demands that something be done. And the states are acting. Maine already has an ingenious public-financing program for state legislative candidates, which has been so successful that other states are considering it or have moved to adopt it.

Forgive me, as a disenchanted lobbyist, for dwelling long on money's role as I have seen it. It is the paramount problem in government today, costing the nation the services of many outstanding people who refuse to submit to the cynical cheapness of fundraising. Nothing is more corrosive of democracy; that is an obvious given. No single issue is more important to the health of our republic.

So, I ask myself, if I had it all to do over again, would I become a lobbyist? Right now, I honestly don't know. On the negative side, I gave up journalism and politics—both trades that I loved and had some talent for—for a trade tarnished in the public eye, a trade that hardly dared speak its name. Being a newspaperman, I learned when I was twenty, carried with it an automatic respect that I cherished; people were solicitous of someone who was going to put their names in the paper. And political campaign managers were exotic, even romantic like a ship's captain or an oilfield boomer.

Giving up that aura to become a tacky lobbyist? My timing was lousy. I left politics just before the backroom operator was coming out of the closet and becoming, in some cases, a bigger name than the candidate he promoted. Journalism, once the most raffish of professions, underwent a similar transformation after two obscure *Washington Post* reporters, Bob Woodward and Carl Bernstein, uncovered the Nixon scandal named Watergate. Their subsequent lionization established a new star system for journalists. The political talk show on television became the rage, and many obscure media mavens turned into overnight celebrities.

I have to conclude that I did the right thing—for me. Politics had burned me out, and I was ready for something less demanding. That was lobbying, and it was played in an arena that I knew well and loved, the U.S. Capitol. The money was good; and I was my own boss, made my own hours, and slept in my own bed at night. I learned that lobbying is a necessary function of democracy. Without advocacy and opposing forces fighting issues in the legislative arena, the democratic concept would lose its body. I was surprised and pleased as I began to realize that lobbyists were key players in the governmental process. Without us, legislators might function in a vacuum. Maybe what we did sometimes wasn't pretty, but it was necessary.

In the past, I gradually learned that there is joy in anonymity and that it didn't mean a damn if you weren't a household name in Peoria. As a faceless, backroom campaign operator, getting my name mentioned in the media was a no-no. I actually eschewed publicity, a big switch for me. Now that I am retired, I treasure another newfound gift—solitude. It is pure pleasure to go through the entire day without the phone ringing to interrupt my thoughts, which I am trying to plunk down on this old Royal manual typewriter. But what I am most grateful for, overwhelmingly grateful, is time. Along with health, it is probably the greatest gift of all. When I was younger, time seemed limitless, and I envisioned plenty of it to do everything ever dreamed of. Now, I realize how finite it is and treasure every minute that I have to reflect and report on my life and times on Capitol Hill. It has been a compensation beyond compare, and I have done my damnedest to tell the lobbying story as straight as I know how.

When I began this book, it started as my attempt to say "I Was Here." As I slogged on, it began to dawn on me that the subject was far bigger. Lobbying affected the lives of all Americans, and it was a subject that the vast majority had only the sketchiest knowledge about. We lobbyists were in the shadows, where most of us wanted to be. The media people knew we were around but covered us superficially or not at all. Literature on lobbying was virtually nonexistent, and we reveled in silently influencing legislation that determined who got what. We never questioned—at least I never did—the fairness of it all. My clients saw themselves as righteous and deserving underdogs, when in reality they were simply little pirates trying to be big ones.

Probably the most hopeful development in my forty years of lobbying is that lobbyists are now out of the shadows and in the spotlight. We need much more of this sunshine. Media exposure is the most effective way to curb our excesses. Regulation by governmental fiat either doesn't work or, by becoming excessive, can be detrimental to the democratic process. A merciless media spotlight is the one instrument that has a proven track record of controlling outrageous greed and slippery shenanigans by the dark of the moon.

This book has been my attempt to provide a shaft of light from the viewpoint of one who has been in the lobbying pits and, ex post facto, found some of it hard to justify. My faith in the American Political Way—despite its corruptions, contradictions, and confusions—is unshakable. We have overcome many challenges over two centuries and have always emerged a stronger and more democratic nation as a result.

A WORD ABOUT SOURCES

I FELL IN LOVE WITH THE PACIFIC NORTHWEST LONG BEFORE I arrived there, in 1936 at age fourteen, singing "Lilacs in the Rain." My dad, Herbert R. Miller—born in Iowa but raised in Portland, Seattle, and Tacoma—had reversed Horace Greeley's maxim, "Go West, Young Man, Go West!" In 1913, after passing the bar in Washington State but without a law degree, he moved to New York City. Overnight, he became a dedicated Gothamite. Yet, his passion for the land of his upbringing only intensified, which he passed on to me.

Long before I reached the Pacific Northwest, I was steeped in its lore and dreamed its dreams. I studied maps, newspapers, books—all the Pacific Northwestiana I could find in New York City. I devoured Bernard DeVoto's account of the *Journals of Lewis and Clark,* the saga of Chief Joseph of the Nez Perce, the diaries and journals of the pioneers who trekked the Oregon Trail from 1840 to 1859, when Oregon achieved statehood, and stories of Abigail Scott Duniway and women's suffrage and the Weyerhaeusers and other lumber barons. I found my spirit in "Battling Sixteen," a short story in a Street and Smith pulp magazine about a punk city kid who went to Oregon to work in the harvests and became a powerful Ivy League football star. As a teenager, I spent two summers in the region's wheat fields and orchards and wore number sixteen at Parkrose High School in Portland and later for a short while at the University of Oregon.

When I eventually found my niche in newspaper city rooms, I was blessed to be broken in by an extraordinary series of editors: Bill Tugman of the Eugene *Register-Guard*; A. L. "Bud" Alford of the Lewiston *Morning Tribune*; Thomas Lamphier Jr., of the Boise *Idaho Statesman*; Don Sterling of the Portland *Oregon Journal*; John A. Armstrong of the Portland *Oregonian*; Dick Johnston, founding editor of *Sports Illustrated*; and, above all, Ed Stone of the Seattle *Post-Intelligencer*. What a post-graduate education in journalism—and life!

By my late twenties I had a deepening knowledge of the territory and its people, particularly the politicians and the media. I continued to read extensively the many authors who chronicled the Pacific Northwest. I offer the following sampling of rich and varied works: Ken Kesey, whose magnum opus, *Sometimes a Great Notion*, was the saga of an iconoclastic lumberman fighting the system in Oregon; the writings of Stewart H. Holbrook, concentrating on the forest products and railroad industries; my friend Richard L. Neuberger (*The Promised Land*); Nancy Wilson Ross, the first of the feminist writers, who also wrote great travel books about the region (e.g., *Farthest Reach*); Robert Ormond Case, chronicler of the Columbia's earlier days; Jack Olsen, master of macabre but true tales of eccentric locals; and the irrepressible Betty McDonald (*The Egg and I*) and other hilarious tales of country living in the Puget Sound area.

Let me also mention three whose writings embody the best of all who have preceded them: Timothy Egan of Seattle, long-time regional correspondent for the *New York Times* (*The Good Rain*); Jonathan Raban, an Englishman transplanted to Seattle whose writing conveys the idea that the bountiful resources are not always all they are cracked up to be (*The Bad Land*); and Ivan Doig, now based in Seattle. His trilogy of a Scottish family's migration to Montana Territory in the 1880s (*Dancing at the Rascal Fair* especially) is a national classic.

I've been an avid reader all my life and an eager student of human nature. In the 1960s, I developed the habit of maintaining a daily journal. It began as a means to discipline myself to ensure that I was using my considerable freedom in a productive way. I noted everything important to me, including the number of cigarettes I bummed that day. I kept these records for over forty years.

For many years, I considered writing my memoirs. When I finally started the process, I wrote what became the chapters of this book as stand-alone accounts of the events they describe. I remember most of these events in my book—the people, the places—as if they happened yesterday.

I have been known my entire life for having a talent for remembering names, dates, places, and obscure details of events from years past. My memory is good, but not perfect, so I was careful in this book to confirm the specifics at the time I wrote the chapters. I relied on available sources—my diaries, personal correspondence, and public records. My wife, Erna Wahl Miller, painstakingly read every word of my drafts with an astute eye. My first wife, Rosalie Daggy Miller, read them also and challenged me to be precise. In addition to family, I regularly sent completed chapters to a wide group of friends and associates for comments.

Since I began this process, I have had many conversations with friends and acquaintances to confirm my understanding of events. I am indebted to Jerry Hoeck, Shelby Scates, Perry Swisher, John Melcher, and my friends from Oregon (the late Ray and Pat Doerner, Bob Duncan, Mark Hatfield, Bob Packwood, Doug Robertson, and Wendell Wyatt) for their perceptive comments. I also benefited from the wit and wisdom of my Friday lunch gang, a group of old and new pols and profs who have met at the Irish Times on Capitol Hill for the last thirty-two years. Many of the quotes in this book are from my memory, but they are as vivid to me now as when they occurred.

—JSM

INDEX

Francis, Dave, 179
Frankfurter, Felix, 205
Franklin, Jerry, 192
Fraud. *See* Corruption
Freeman, Orville, 65, 153, 182
Friendly, Alfred, 73
Fund-raising, 86, 109–10, 123, 128, 237

Garmatz, Eddie, 201
Garrison Diversion Project, 111
Gay, Connie B., 160
Georgine, Bob, 227
Get-out-the-vote (GOTV), 66–67, 70, 72
Giacomo, John, 65
Giesler, Jerry, 49, 55
Gill, Mike, 112
Gill, Tom, 103, 105
Ginsburg, Bob, 41
Gleason, Mike, 197
Gleason, Thomas J. "Teddy," 204–5
Glinn, Burt, 130
Gluck, Joe, 23
Goldberg, Arthur J., 133, 167–68
Golden, Harry, 162
Goldmark, John, 38
Goldstein, Shelley, 21
Goldwater, Barry, 64, 112
Graham, Philip, 75
Grand Coulee Dam, 17, 180
Gray, Frank, x
Greater Houston Ministerial Association, 151
Greeley, Arthur, 185
Green, Bill, 195
Green, Edith, 31, 131
Green, Theodore Francis, 115
Greenfield, George, 51
Green River Rural Electric Cooperative, 174

Gregory, Bill, 42
Griffin, Robert, 131–33, 136, 167, 171, 174
Grinstein, Jerry, 201
Gruening, Ernest, 82, 97
Guy, William L., 114, 116

Haak, Howie, 49
Haberman, George, 65
Haggerty, Jim, 27
Hall, Jack, 103
Hall, Len, 27
Hall, Paul, 200–201, 203–4, 205, 210, 213
Hamilton, Al, 116
Hannegan, Bob, 84
Hansen, Julia Butler, 197–99
Hansen, Orval, 237
Hardin, John R., 174
Harris, Guy, 174, 176
Harris, Louis, 9–10, 56, 89, 90–91
Hart, Philip A., ix, 82, 83, 169
Hartke, Vance, 82
Hatfield, Mark, 189
Hawaii: Democratic Party in, 97–98, 100, 102–3; land sales in, 104–5; organized labor in, 101–4; Republican Party in, 97, 102; Senate race in, 97, 99–103, 105–6; statehood, 97–98, 102, 103; tourism in, 104–5
Heen, Bill, 101
Hells Canyon, Ore., 16, 17–18, 28
Henderson-Union Rural Electric Cooperative, 174
Herbert, Frank, 26–27
Herman, Babe, 49
Higgins, Eddie, 115
High tech industry, 191
Ho, Chinn, 104–5
Hobby, Oveta Culp, 162

Hoblitzell, John, 77, 80
Hoeck, Gerald A., 8, 10, 11, 33–35, 142
Hoff, Irvin A., 34, 41, 46, 52, 56, 139
Hoffa, James, 172
Hoffman, Frank Nordhoff "Nordy," 34,
    41–42, 51, 142–45, 170, 173
Holden, Bill, 51
Honolulu *Star-Bulletin*, 103–4
Hoover, Herbert, 37
Horwitz, Solis, 75
H.R. 163, 200–203
H.R. 1609, 232–34
Humphrey, Hubert, 65, 72, 114, 135–36,
    137–39, 172, 188, 202
Hydroelectric power, 6, 17, 36, 38, 164

Ice Harbor Dam, 37
Idaho, 185; Democratic Party in, 51–52;
    Senate race in, 48–59
Idaho Power Company, 17
Idaho Statesman, 54
Illinois, 142
Indiana, 82
Inland Empire Waterways Association, 37
International Association of Machinists,
    222
International Longshore and Warehouse
    Union (ILWU), 101–2, 103
International Longshoremen's Associa-
    tion (ILA), 204
International Mine, Mill, and Smelter
    Workers, 51
Interstate Highway Act (1956), 229–30
"Irish Dukes," 195–96, 225–26
Isolationism, 53–54
Ives, Irving, 172

Jackson, Henry M. "Scoop," ix, xiv,
    15, 46, 97, 112, 149, 164, 184, 189,
    227; JFK campaign, 150–52; vice-

presidential run, 139, 142, 145–47;
    senate campaign of, 7–9, 11, 33, 50
Jake's Crawfish House, 18
Japan: oil to, 211; timber to, 181–82
Japanese Americans, 97–98, 101–2
Jenner, Bill, 77
Jennings, W. Pat, 233
Jews, 15, 23, 151
Johnson, Lyndon Baines (LBJ), x, xi, xv,
    88, 98, 123, 163, 170, 240; conflict
    with, 4, 73, 75, 144, 200; and DSCC,
    60–64, 67, 75–78, 99, 107–8, 119,
    120; presidential run by, 122, 138,
    139–40, 142, 143; vice-presidential
    nomination of, 146–47, 148, 150
Johnston, J. Bennett, 227
Johnston, Felton "Skeeter," 76
Johnston, Victor A., 62, 84, 106, 112–13,
    115, 117
Jones, Darrell, 194, 197
Jones, John, 19
Jones, Wesley "Yakima," 37
Journalism, ix, 55

Kahn, Joe, 201
Kahn, Steve, 14
Kaiser, Edgar J., 170
Kaiser Steel Company, 170–71
Kansas, 150–51
Keck, Howard, 86
Keenan, Joseph D., 133, 174
Kefauver, Estes, x, 65–66
Kelly, George "Highpockets," 49
Kelly, Jack, 152
Kennedy, Jacqueline, 148, 154
Kennedy, Joe, 133, 134, 144, 154, 161
Kennedy, John, x, 157–58, 195; criticism
    of, 133, 137, 149–51; election of,
    152–55; foreign-aid policy, 161–63;
    labor reform, 168–69, 172–74; presi-

dential campaign of, 123–25, 130–40, 141–55, 167, 240; religion of, 136, 138, 142, 150–51; senate campaigning by, 66–69, 98–100, 104, 114; and women, 134

Kennedy, Robert, 145, 148–49; conflict with, 4, 132, 134–35, 137–39, 140, 141, 152; and labor reform, 64, 125, 131–32, 172, 174

Kentucky: Democratic party in, 88–89; governors race, 88–96; public power, 174–76, 178–80

Kentucky Public Service Commission, 175

Kentucky Public Utilities Commission, 179

Kentucky Utilities, 175

Kerr, Andy, 190

Kerr, Robert S., 121

Kilpatrick, Carroll, 73

Kirkland, Lane, 221–23

Kirwan, Michael J., 194–99, 226

Koch, Ed, 128

Knight, Bill, 29

Knight, Goodwin J., 9–10

Knowland, William F., 10, 37, 71, 120

Kohler, Walter, 60, 64, 67

KPTV (Ore.), 21

KREM (Wash.), 43

Ku Klux Klan, 15

Lambert, Bill, 178

Landauer, Jerry, 208

Landrum, Phil, 131–33, 136, 167, 171, 174

Land-use, xi, 16–17, 160. See also Forests; Timber

Langer, William, 107–11

Langlie, Arthur B., 34–35, 38, 39, 41–47

Lanier, P. W. "Bill," Jr., 119

Lasker, Mary, 39–40, 128

Law, Vernon, 48–49

Lawrence, David, 146

Lazzeri, Tony, 49

League for CVA, 6

LeBlanc, Dudley, 245

Lederer, William, 100, 105

Lee, Harry, 91

Leigen, Sid, xi

Leiken, Sidney, 183

Lemieux, Wally, 69

Levee, Michael, 85

Lewis, Drew, 220

Lewis, John L., 205

Leyden, John Francis, 217–22

Life Magazine, 71, 74, 178

Lincoln, Evelyn, 67–68, 98–99, 133

Linde, Hans, 25

Lindsay, John V., 129

Lippmann, Walter, 74

Little Steel. *See* Steel

Lobbying, 155, 156–59, 161–63, 166, 225–26; corruption in, 163–64, 165, 236–37, 246–50. *See also* Marine Engineers Beneficial Association; Railroads; Steel industry; Timber

Long, Oren, 101

Long, Russell B., 239

Lott, Trent, 244

Loveless, Herschel, 146

Lower Snake River, 37

Luce, Henry R., 50, 162

Lumber. *See* Timber

Lund, Ru, 19

Lutherans, 45

Maas, Peter, 130

MacGowan, Howard, 44–45

Magnuson, Warren G. "Maggie," ix, xvi, 139, 146, 154, 243; Senate campaign of, 7, 33–47; in Senate, 61, 164, 201–2, 230–31; and women, 41–42

Maguire, John, 188
Mahoney, Florence, 39–40, 56
Mailer, Norman, 144
Maine, 82–83, 86
Malone, George "Molly," 77, 78, 80, 242
Maloney, Tom, 191
Mansfield, Michael J., 61, 76
Marine Engineers Beneficial Association
   (MEBA), 200–203, 205–7; fund-
   raising by, 208–9; and PATCO, 207,
   215–19, 223–24
Maritime labor, 200–201, 203–4, 210–14.
   See also Marine Engineers Beneficial
   Association
Martin, Dr. Bob, 90, 93
Martin, Dean Boyd A., 151
Martin, Dolores, 98–99
Martin, Joe, 25
Matsunaga, Spark, 103
May, Bill, 92
McCall, Tom, 31
McCarthy, Eugene, ix, 74, 82, 83, 184
McCarthy, Joseph, 48, 60, 65, 112
McClellan, 64, 169, 172
McCloskey, Matt, 152
McConkey, Oscar, 134
McCracken, Joseph W., 181, 184, 186
McCraken, Tracy, 138
McDonald, David J., 85, 124, 143, 147,
   167, 171, 200, 206
McDonald, Joe, 79
McFarland, Ernest W., 82, 84
McGee, Gale W., 82
McGinley, Don, 173
McGovern, George, 112, 130, 152, 153,
   174, 184
McKay, Douglas, 16, 17, 25, 36, 40, 47
McKinney, Stewart R., 211–13
McNary, Charles, 16, 20
McNary Dam, 38

McPherson, Harry, 75, 122
Meany, George, 162, 201, 206, 222, 223
Medical research, 39–40, 128
Mesta, Perle, 141, 144
Metcalf, Lee, 130, 135
Meyer, André, 128
Meyner, Robert, 146
Michener, James A., 100, 103, 105
Michigan, 82
Miller, Cattie Lou, 94–95
Miller, Erna, xiv, 178
Miller, Herbert Rinehart, 4
Miller, James Rufus, 174–76, 178–80
Miller, Jonathan, xi, 4
Miller, Joseph Spencer: early life of, x, 4–
   6; early political career of, 6; family
   of, x, 4–5, 178; media accounts of, 4,
   73–74, 155; newspaper career of, ix,
   x–xi, xv, 5–6, 11–12, 48, 54, 55, 100,
   207, 248; as sports scout, 48–50; and
   women, 57–58, 129–30, 176–78
Miller, Nancy, 87
Miller, Rosalie, 8–9, 87, 154, 178
Miller, Sue, 87
Mills, Jack, 112
Milwaukee, Wisc., 62
Milwaukee *Journal*, 62, 69
Milwaukee *Sentinel*, 137
Mining, 185
Minnesota, 82
Mitchell, Hugh B., 6–7
Moakley, Joe, 219
Molinari, Guy, 234
Money, xi, 92; campaign contributions,
   22, 56, 64, 66, 85–86, 113, 236, 239–
   41, 244; finance reform, 238–39, 241,
   243, 247–49; and lobbying, 236–37,
   246–49. *See also* Corruption; Fund-
   raising
Monongahela National Forest, 188

Moody, Bill, 201, 202

Moody, Joe, 164

Moore, Johnny, 49

Morgan, Howard, 16, 18, 21–22, 28, 30

Morgan, Thomas E., 238

Morin, Relman "Pat," 114

Morrison, Frank, 82–84

Morrow County *Journal*, 23

Morse, Wayne L., ix, 15, 21, 40, 47, 182, 194–96, 208

Morton, Thurston B., 61, 88, 95

Moses, George Higgins, 107

Moss, Frank, 82, 84, 86–87

Mundt, Karl, 152, 153

Mundy, Dan, 234

Murray, Esther Higgins, 66, 72

Murray, Philip, 205

Muskie, Edmund S., ix, 79, 82–83, 86, 144, 184

Myers, Debs, 162–63

Nash, Philleo, 62–63, 65

National Air Traffic Controllers Association (NATCA), 224

National Association of Manufacturers, 169, 171

National Cancer Institute, 39

National Coal Policy Association, 164

National Committee for an Effective Congress, 22, 159

National Environmental Policy Act (NEPA), 188

National Forest Management Act (NFMA), 188–89

National Forest Products Association (NFPA), 187, 189

National Institutes of Health, 39, 128

National Maritime Union, 133

National Right to Work Committee, 238

National Timber Supply Act, 186

Native Americans, 37, 119–20

Nebraska, 82, 83–84

Neeley, Matt, 61

Nelson, Gaylord A., 72, 145, 184, 189

Neuberger, Maurine Brown, 12, 14, 19, 21, 25, 31–32

Neuberger, Richard L., ix, 121, 195; and conservation, 17, 22; death of, 31–32; journalism career of, 12, 14; religion of, 15, 23, 31; Senate campaign of, 12–31, 36, 83

Nevada, 78–80, 82

New Forestry, 192

Newspaper Guild, 6

New York City, N.Y., 127–29

Nixon, Richard M., 7, 26, 61, 71, 123, 202, 217; presidential campaign of, 148–49, 152–53, 240

Non-Partisan League (NPL), 108–9

North Dakota, 137; agriculture in, 108–10; Democratic Party in, 107, 111, 114, 119–20; Native Americans in, 119–20; organized labor in, 110; Republican Party in, 108, 112–15, 119; Senate race in, 107–20, 140

North Dakota Farmers Union, 110

Northern spotted owl, 188, 189–93

Norwegians, 35

Nuclear power, 164

Nuveen, John B., 161

Oberstar, Jim, 234

O'Brian, Jack, 174

O'Brian, Larry, 125, 148, 163

O'Donnell, J.J., 222

O'Donnell, Kenny, 125, 240

Office of Price Stabilization (OPS), 7, 11, 50

Office of Technology Assessment (OTA), 230–31

Prostitution, 176–78
Protestants, 150–52
Prouty, Winston, 126
Proxmire, Ellen, 64, 71
Proxmire, William Edward, ix, 121;
    Senate campaign of, 60–72, 73
Pulliam, Eugene, 84

Quill, Mike, 133
Quinn, William F., 102–3, 105, 106

Racism, 97–98, 101
Radio, 10, 19–20, 22, 27, 113
Railroads, 225, 227–35
Randolph, Jennings, 81, 89, 135, 136,
    188
Raskin, Hyman B., 158
Rauh, Joe, 147
Rawlings, Calvin, 84
Rayburn, Sam, 148
Reagan, Ronald, 215, 220–22
Reardon, Ted, 124
Reclamation projects, 15
Reedy, George, 75, 76, 122, 150
Renton, Wash., 45
Republican Party, 71–72, 108, 122, 244;
    national conventions, 41. *See also*
    names of Republicans; names of states
Republican Senatorial Campaign Com-
    mittee (RSCC), 62, 84, 106, 112
Reston, James, 74, 77
Reuss, Henry, 60
Reuther, Walter, 147
Revercomb, Chapman, 77, 80
Riley, Rod, 65
Rinehart, Jonathan, 100, 104–5
Ringler, Paul, 65, 69
Rinke, Ken, 18
Roach, Neal, 230
Roberts, Oral, 45

Rock, Mike, 216
Rollette Reservation, 120
Roncalio, Teno, 138–39, 232
Rooney, Fred B., 232
Roosevelt, Franklin D., 14
Rosellini, Albert D., 34, 142, 154
Rosenblatt, Maurice, 56, 156–59, 160,
    164, 197
Rowe, Jim, 75, 122
Rudd, Eldon, 232
Ruppe, Philip, 231
Rusen, Paul, 136
Rusk, Dean, 163
Russell, Lew, 36
Russell, Mark, 126
Russell, Richard, 97

Sackett, Russ, 178
Salter, John L., 7–8, 11, 47, 50, 161–62;
    and Kennedy campaign, 132, 134–35,
    139, 142, 147
Sammons, Eddie, 40
Saund, Dalip S., 163
Sawyer, Grant, 79
Saylor, John P., 186–87
Scammons, Richard, 70
Schiff, Dorothy, 128
Schotland, Roy, 22, 28
Schrunk, Terry, 131–32
Schulman, Lee, 36
Schultz, Charley, 64
Scott, Hugh, 218
Scott, Kerr, 230
Scotto, Anthony, 204–5
Seafarers Union, 200–201
Seattle, Wash., 15, 135
Seattle Nurses Guild, 34
Seattle *Post-Intelligencer*, ix, 6, 48
Senate Rackets Committee, 131
Seventeenth Amendment, 30